ADVANCE PRAISE FOR *HOLY HELL*

"Robert Spencer is to be applauded for reporting, in clear prose, what the main stream media in the West has failed to do, for fear of being labelled 'racist' or 'Islamophobic,' namely men of Pakistani-origin are up to four times more likely to be reported to the police for child sex grooming offences than the general population in, for example, of England and Wales. Not only has he pointed out this basic statistic, Spencer has also quite fearlessly followed where the argument leads: Islam. The grooming gangs of Britain have been inspired by the anti-women customs of Pakistan, or Syria, or any other Islamic country, where the misogyny is prevalent. The misogyny in turn, depends on the way Islam treats Women, as second-class citizens who are the property of men, and where in the West they are 'easy meat.' The West, and Western society, in general, and the Police, Politicians, and Intellectuals, in particular, have totally failed in their duties to its women. Robert Spencer, with his customary thoroughness and meticulous research, has rendered us all a great service, and one hopes, it will awaken some kind of conscience in the politicians, and finally, that it will lead to some kind of justice for the victims, many in their teens, of sex-grooming gangs."

—Ibn Warraq, Author of *Why I Am Not a Muslim*

ALSO BY ROBERT SPENCER

Antisemitism: History and Myth

Muhammad: A Critical Biography

Empire of God: How the Byzantines Saved Civilization

The Sumter Gambit: How the Left Is Trying to Foment a Civil War

The Critical Qur'an: Explained from Key Islamic Commentaries and Contemporary Historical Research

Did Muhammad Exist?: An Inquiry into Islam's Obscure Origins—Revised and Expanded Edition

Obama and Trump: Who Was Better for America?

Rating America's Presidents: An America-First Look at Who Is Best, Who Is Overrated, and Who Was An Absolution Disaster

The Palestinian Delusion: The Catastrophic History of the Middle East Peace Process

The History of Jihad: From Muhammad to ISIS

Confessions of an Islamophobe

HOLY HELL

HOLY HELL

ISLAM'S ABUSE OF WOMEN AND THE INFIDELS WHO ENABLE IT

ROBERT SPENCER

Published by Bombardier Books
An Imprint of Post Hill Press
ISBN: 979-8-89565-300-5
ISBN (eBook): 979-8-89565-301-2

Holy Hell:
Islam's Abuse of Women and the Infidels Who Enable It

Cover Design by Jim Villaflores

This book, as well as any other Bombardier Books publications, may be purchased in bulk quantities at a special discounted rate. Contact orders@bombardierbooks.com for more information.

All people, locations, events, and situations are portrayed to the best of the author's memory. While all of the events described are true, many names and identifying details have been changed to protect the privacy of the people involved.

Post Hill Press
New York • Nashville
posthillpress.com

Published in the United States of America
1 2 3 4 5 6 7 8 9 10

Dedicated to all the women who have been abused, abandoned, and forgotten in the mad rush to "diversity."

TABLE OF CONTENTS

INTRODUCTION

THE WEST'S RAPE CRISIS

The Western world is facing a rape crisis.

In 2015, there were 62.02 rapes per every 100,000 people in England and Wales. By 2022, that rate had grown to 117.3, second in the entire world only to the tiny Caribbean nation of Grenada.[1] Sweden was sixth in the world in 2022 with 85.6 rapes per 100,000 people, up from 56.29 in 2015.[2] During the same seven-year span, the rape rate in France nearly tripled, going from 20.09 per 100,000 people in 2015 to 58.94 in 2022.[3] In Germany, there was a relatively low 8.56 rapes per 100,000 people in 2015, but by 2022, that rate had almost doubled to 15.06.[4] By comparison, the rape rate in the United States remained fairly static, going from 38.85 in 2015 to 41.82 in 2022.[5]

---

1 "crime-violent-offenses," United Nations Office on Drugs and Crime, https://dataunodc.un.org/crime-violent-offences. Accessed April 17, 2025.

2 Ibid.

3 Ibid.

4 Ibid.

5 Ibid.

Meanwhile, in 2016, Muslims comprised 6.1 percent of the population of Germany, 6.3 percent of the United Kingdom, 8.1 percent of Sweden, and 8.8 percent of France.[6] Since then, millions of Muslim migrants have settled in those countries and others in Europe. According to the British census, "the proportion of the overall population who identified as 'Muslim' increased from 4.9% (2.7 million) in 2011 to 6.5% (3.9 million) in 2021."[7] Eight hundred thousand Muslims entered Germany in 2015 alone.[8] Because of the low birth rates among the native populations and the high birth rates among the migrants, many predicted that there would be Muslim majorities in many Western European countries by the end of the twenty-first century.

Did the massive influx of Muslims into Europe account for the sharp rise in rape rates? The reflex action of Western political and law enforcement authorities, as well as the Western media, is to regard such questions as offensive and "Islamophobic," and hence unworthy even to be asked, much less answered. Yet this is not simply an instance of the *post hoc, ergo propter hoc* fallacy: the rise in rape rates followed a rise in the number of Muslims in Europe, therefore Muslims are responsible for the rise in the number of rapes. However unwelcome the fact may

---

6 "Europe's Growing Muslim Population," Pew Research Center, November 29, 2017, https://www.pewresearch.org/religion/2017/11/29/europes-growing-muslim-population/. Accessed April 17, 2025.

7 Prabhu Chawla, "Europe facing identity challenge," *New Indian Express*, July 15, 2024, https://www.newindianexpress.com/opinions/columns/pc/2024/Jul/15/europe-facing-identity-challenge. Accessed April 17, 2025.

8 The Associated Press, Reuters, and F. Brinley Bruton, "Germany to Spend $6.6 Billion on 800,000 Refugees and Migrants," NBC News, September 7, 2015, https://www.nbcnews.com/storyline/europes-border-crisis/billions-migrants-germany-spend-6-6b-800-000-newcomers-n422811. Accessed April 17, 2025.

be, there is a good reason to think that Europe's rape problem is a component of its problem with Islam.

This may appear to be counterintuitive at first glance, for rape rates in Muslim countries are generally extremely low. In Pakistan, the rape rate in 2022 was 2.22 per 100,000 people.[9] In Indonesia, the world's most populous Muslim country, it was 0.52 in the same year.[10] In Iraq, it was 2.53 in 2021.[11] So how can it possibly be argued that Muslims are responsible for the rise in the number of rapes in Europe, when they don't commit the same crime in any significant numbers in their home countries?

The answer is twofold. One is that many rapes go unreported in Muslim countries because the behavior involved simply isn't considered a crime. As we shall see, Islamic law, based on words attributed to the Islamic prophet Muhammad himself, forbids a woman to refuse sexual intercourse to her husband under any circumstances. With such a rule in place, how can a rape ever even be said to have occurred? It never could in the context of a marriage; it could only take place when a man forces himself upon a woman who is not his wife.

The second reason is as shocking as it is unmistakable: the Islamic religion forbids the rape of Muslim women, but it does not forbid the rape of non-Muslim women. In fact, the Qur'an specifically allows for this as a legitimate sexual outlet for Muslim men. And such activity doesn't make its way into crime statistics, as it is not considered to be a crime at all.

In light of these two factors, it's no surprise whatsoever that rape rates in Muslim countries would be low to nonexistent,

---

9 "crime-violent-offenses," United Nations Office on Drugs and Crime.
10 Ibid.
11 Ibid.

but that mass Muslim migration into Europe would account for the continent's new rape crisis.

This is not solely a European problem, either. As Muslim populations continue to rise all over the West, if Islam does indeed justify the rape of non-Muslim women, we can expect that there will be a great deal more such crimes than we have seen up until now. Yet any public discussion of this problem thus far has been stifled completely with claims that such concerns are "Islamophobic" and "racist."

The supposedly enlightened, non-bigoted stance is to find other explanations, however implausible, for the spike in rape rates in the West, and steadfastly to ignore, or deny outright, that there is or could be any connection between the growth of Islam and rising rape rates.

Societies with a healthy sense of self-preservation, however, and those may not include some of the great nations of Western Europe in these dark days, cannot afford to take refuge in fantasies and self-delusion. If there is a connection between Islam and the rape of infidel women, Western authorities would be doing an extraordinary disservice to their own people if they ignored or discounted it.

This book, therefore, explores the issue of Islam and rape, and is offered with love in particular to the citizens of the countries where the rape rates have risen most sharply. May it be an impetus for them to find their way back to sane, rational, and humane policies to deal with this growing problem.

CHAPTER ONE

ISLAM FORBIDS RAPE, BUT...

ISLAM FORBIDS RAPE

Could it possibly be that Islam, which is taken for granted as being one of the great religions of the world, actually condones the rape of infidel women?

For many, the question itself is inconceivable, and to be dismissed out of hand. There is the widespread assumption, particularly in the West, that anything that bears the name of "religion" exhorts its adherents to be kind, charitable, and magnanimous to all, and to observe generally recognized moral standards.

In the case of rape and Islam, also, there is plenty of evidence that it is just as much of a crime in Islam as it is in other contexts. "The punishment for rape in Islam," says the popular fatwa site Islam Question & Answer, "is the same as the punishment for zina, which is stoning if the perpetrator is married, and one hundred lashes and banishment for one year if he is not married."[12]

As if that weren't clear enough, the site adds that "the Arabic word *ightisab* refers to taking something wrongfully by force. It is now used exclusively to refer to transgression against the honour of women by force (rape)." It explicitly rules out the idea that a rapist could or should marry his victim:

> Rape is an abhorrent crime that is forbidden in all religions and in the minds of all wise people and those who are possessed of sound human nature. All earthly systems and laws regard this action as abhorrent and impose the strictest penalties on it, except a few states which waive the punishment if the rapist marries his victim! This is indicative of a distorted mind let alone a lack of religious commitment on the part of those who challenge Allah in making laws. We do not know of any love or compassion that could exist between the aggressor and his victim, especially since the pain of rape cannot be erased with the passage of time – as it is said. Hence many victims of rape have attempted to commit suicide and many of them have succeeded. The failure of these marriages is proven and they are accompanied by nothing but humiliation and suffering for the woman.[13]

---

12 "Punishment for Rape in Islam," Islam Question & Answer, August 21, 2005, https://islamqa.info/en/answers/72338/punishment-for-rape-in-islam. Accessed March 4, 2025.

13 Ibid.

Islam Question & Answer adds that "Islam has a clear stance which states that rape is haram and imposes a deterrent punishment on the one who commits it. Islam closes the door to the criminal who wants to commit this crime. Western studies have shown that most rapists are already criminals who commit their crimes under the influence of alcohol and drugs, and they take advantage of the fact that their victims are walking alone in isolated places, or staying in the house alone."[14]

BUT IMMODEST WOMEN MAY BE TO BLAME

Intriguingly, however, Islam Question & Answer's explanation of why rape is a crime quickly turns from this to considerations about female modesty that veer close to blaming the victim: "These studies also show that what the criminals watch in the media and the semi-naked styles of dress in which women go out, also lead to the commission of this reprehensible crime. The laws of Islam came to protect women's honour and modesty. Islam forbids women to wear clothes that are not modest and to travel without a mahram [close male relative]; it forbids a woman to shake hands with a non-mahram man."[15]

Islam Question & Answer also suggests that rape can in some circumstances be a result of a couple's lack of self-control: "Islam encourages young men and women to marry early, and many other rulings which close the door to rape. Hence it comes as no surprise when we hear or read that most of these crimes occur in permissive societies which are looked up to by some Muslims as examples of civilization and refinement!"[16] This

---

[14] Ibid.
[15] Ibid.
[16] Ibid.

became the occasion for a little America-bashing: "In America – for example – International Amnesty stated in a 2004 report entitled 'Stop Violence Against Women' that every 90 seconds a woman was raped during that year. What kind of life are these people living? What refinement and civilization do they want the Muslim women to take part in?"[17]

Pakistani Sharia judge Fida Mohammed Khan was adamant about the evil of rape, saying: "The zina [sexual crime] ordinance protects the honour of women and their families. For us, women are the jewel of creation; the respect we show them, particularly as mothers, is without equal anywhere. Islam believes fornication and adultery undermines their dignity and, to protect the moral and ethical values of the community as a whole, considers it just and proper to punish those who have offended. Rape is an even more serious offence."[18]

The chief justice of Pakistan's Sharia court, Mehboob Ahmed, followed Islam Question & Answer in favorably comparing his country's view of women, and of rape, with that of the West: "I really don't know why this particular law gets people so worked up. With the greatest respect, I think women in western societies are not respected as much as they are in ours. Male chauvinism in the West has seen to it that the law is flexible enough for them to molest women with impunity. But we cannot allow such attitudes to dominate to the detriment of our women; it is precisely the zina ordinance that gives them security and freedom."[19]

---

17 Ibid.

18 Valérie Ceccherini, "Rape and the Prophet," Sage Journals, 1999, 19, https://journals.sagepub.com/doi/pdf/10.1080/03064229908536496. Accessed March 4, 2025.

19 Ibid.

During one of his popular speeches defending Islam and purporting to answer questions from Muslims, the internationally renowned Indian Muslim preacher Zakir Naik was asked: "May Allah bless you! I have a query. May Allah forgive me if I'm saying something wrong. Allah is the most merciful and most gracious. If I rape a girl and kill her, but it is not proved in the court, resulting in my acquittal and freedom. After a long time, I truly repent for my actions before Allah as we know he can forgive all transgressions. However, if he forgives me too then where is the justice for the victim?"[20]

In response, Naik first sounded a pious note: "It is Allah who has created death and life to test which of you is good indeed. So this life is a test for thereafter. We are being evaluated. Allah examines different people in different ways. He tests some people by giving them luxury or others through poverty."[21]

Then he said to the questioner: "You are correct. If an individual has committed acts of rape and murder but genuinely repents and seeks forgiveness, five essential criteria must be met. Firstly, one must acknowledge that their actions were wrong. Secondly, it is imperative to cease such behaviour immediately. Thirdly, there must be a commitment to never engage in these actions again. The fourth step involves seeking forgiveness from Allah. If all these conditions are satisfied, then, inshallah,

---

20 OpIndia Staff, "'Getting raped is a test from Allah': Old video of Zakir Naik engaging in victim blaming goes viral, says 'violation of Sharia', 'provocative dress' can lead to rape," OpIndia, January 6, 2025, https://www.opindia.com/2025/01/getting-raped-is-a-test-from-allah-old-video-of-zakir-naik-engaging-in-victim-blaming-goes-viral-says-violation-of-sharia-provocative-dress-can-lead-to-rape/. Accessed March 14, 2025.

21 Ibid.

forgiveness may be granted, even for grave sins such as rape and murder as he is the most gracious, the most merciful."[22]

Naik then began blaming rape on the immodestly dressed victims: "Coming to the second part, I would say no because both (the perpetrator [and the victim]) are undergoing a test in this world. Let me explain to you that Allah has provided specific guidelines for women, advising them to dress modestly and to cover their bodies, with certain exceptions such as the face. If, hypothetically, a woman chooses not to adhere to these rules and instead dresses in a manner deemed immoral, which may provoke inappropriate reactions leading to an act of rape, then who should be blamed? It is the girl's responsibility."[23]

Naik followed this by an attempt to backtrack: "That doesn't mean that the boy has the right to rape but besides him, the girl is also expected to observe the principles outlined in the Quran. She is accountable if she chooses to wear an outfit that could lead to such an act. On the other hand, if she is dressed decently and is still subjected to rape, the incident serves as a test for her. The critical consideration is whether she was following Allah's recommendations concerning her attire. If she was not, she is responsible for attracting the rapist."[24]

PAKISTAN'S CAVEATS

Yet Pakistani law on rape contains some significant caveats. The *International Journal of the Sociology of Law* noted as far back as 1990 that "the Offense of Zina (Enforcement of Hudood) Ordinance, VII of 1979 provides for Islamic standards of proof

22 Ibid.
23 Ibid.
24 Ibid.

and punishment for the crimes of adultery, fornication, rape, and prosecution. Punishments include stoning to death, amputation of limbs, whipping, imprisonment, and fines."[25]

However, Islam's rules of evidence for such crimes make convictions difficult: "A confession by the rapist or testimony from four Muslim adult male witnesses constitutes proof for the more severe punishments, but these standards are so strict that no rapist has yet been punished this severely. Less stringent standards of proof apply to the less severe punishments, which also apply to fornication and adultery." This applies, however, only to men, for a woman's very accusation can be taken as self-incriminating: "In addition, women coming to court in a rape case risk conviction for fornication or adultery. Thus, the laws protect men against false accusations of rape, while female rape victims are vulnerable to accusation of a sexual crime."

The Islamic rules of evidence have devastating consequences in Pakistan. Journalist Valérie Ceccherini reported in 1999 that "a woman is raped every three hours in Pakistan. Sixty-five per cent of them are under age and one in four is the victim of a group rape. And according to Hina Jilani, a lawyer working for women's rights, that is not the worst of it: 'If a woman is raped but has no evidence to prove it, the very fact that she had admitted to the sexual act may lead to her own prosecution for adultery or fornication — zina.'"[26]

---

25 R Mehdi, "Offence of Rape in the Islamic Law of Pakistan," *International Journal of the Sociology of Law* 18, no: 1 (February 1990), 19–29: abstract. https://www.ojp.gov/ncjrs/virtual-library/abstracts/offence-rape-islamic-law-pakistan. Accessed March 4, 2025.

26 Ceccherini, "Rape and the Prophet."

THOSE WHOM YOUR RIGHT HANDS POSSESS

Even worse, several passages of the Qur'an make it not at all clear that the prohibition of rape applies to non-Muslim women at all. The Qur'an tells Muslims to "marry the women who seem good to you, two or three or four, and if you fear that you cannot do justice, then one, or those that your right hands possess. In this way it is more likely that you will not do injustice." (4:3) A bit later, the Qur'an enumerates the women whom a Muslim man is forbidden to marry: "Forbidden to you are your mothers, and your daughters, and your sisters, and your father's sisters, and your mother's sisters…" and so on (4:23). This long list concludes with this: "And all married women except those whom your right hands possess." (4:24)

The renowned medieval Qur'anic scholar, Ibn Kathir, whose commentary on the Qur'an is still widely popular among Muslims today, explains this passage by noting that Muslim males "are prohibited from marrying women who are already married," but that there is one key exception to this rule: Muslims may marry, or simply have sexual relations, with "those whom you acquire through war, for you are allowed such women after making sure they are not pregnant."[27] Islamic law doesn't allow a man to marry a married woman, but this poses no problem when it comes to captive women, for, as one manual of Islamic law stipulates, "when a child or a woman is taken captive, they become slaves by the fact of capture, and the woman's previous marriage is immediately annulled."[28]

---

27 Ibn Kathir, *Tafsir Ibn Kathir* (abridged) (Riyadh: Darussalam, 2000), II, 422.

28 Ahmad ibn Naqib al-Misri, *Reliance of the Traveller ('Umdat al-Salik): A Classic Manual of Islamic Sacred Law*, trans. Nuh Ha Mim Keller (Amana Publications, 1999), o9.1–2.

Ibn Kathir quotes a tradition of Muhammad in which the prophet of Islam allows his men to have sexual relations with captive women; nothing whatsoever is said about obtaining the women's consent. "Imam Ahmad recorded that Abu Sa'id Al-Khudri said, 'We captured some women from the area of Awtas who were already married, and we disliked having sexual relations with them because they already had husbands. So, we asked the Prophet about this matter, and this Ayah [verse] was revealed…Consequently, we had sexual relations with these women.'"[29] Ibn Kathir adds that other respected Islamic authorities agree on this, including "At-Tirmidhi, An-Nasa'i, Ibn Jarir and Muslim in his Sahih."[30]

The hadith collection Sahih Muslim, which Muslims consider along with Sahih Bukhari to be the most reliable source of traditions about Muhammad, contains a version of this story that differs only slightly from the one that Ibn Kathir records. Muhammad's men hesitate before engaging in sex with the women they have captured, but once again neither the women's marital status nor their consent is the issue. Instead, they are unsure that they should go ahead "because of their husbands being polytheists."[31] Muhammad, however, tells them that it is all right to go ahead.

Sahih Muslim also contains another variant of this tradition, in which the men hesitate because they hope to exchange the captive women for ransom:

> Abu Sirma said to Abu Sa'id al Khadri (Allah he pleased with him): O Abu Sa'id, did you

29 Ibn Kathir, *Tafsir Ibn Kathir*, 422.

30 Ibid.

31 Muslim ibn al-Hajjaj, *Sahih Muslim*, trans. Abdul Hamid Siddiqi (New Delhi: Kitab Bhavan), revised edition 2000, no. 3432.

> hear Allah's Messenger mentioning al-azl [*coitus interruptus*]? He said: Yes, and added: We went out with Allah's Messenger on the expedition to the Bi'l-Mustaliq and took captive some excellent Arab women; and we desired them, for we were suffering from the absence of our wives, (but at the same time) we also desired ransom for them. So we decided to have sexual intercourse with them but by observing azl (Withdrawing the male sexual organ before emission of semen to avoid-conception). But we said: We are doing an act whereas Allah's Messenger is amongst us; why not ask him? So we asked Allah's Messenger, and he said: It does not matter if you do not do it, for every soul that is to be born up to the Day of Resurrection will be born.[32]

Once again, no one involved seems troubled in the slightest degree by the question of whether or not these women consent to sexual intercourse. They are captives. They are slaves. Consent is simply not a factor.

NOT IN MARRIAGE, EITHER

In fact, consent wasn't a factor in Islamic marriage, either. A hadith depicts Muhammad saying: "If a husband calls his wife to his bed [i.e. to have sexual relation] and she refuses and causes him to sleep in anger, the angels will curse her till morning."[33]

---

32 Ibid., no. 3371.

33 Sahih Bukhari, vol, 4, bk. 54, no. 460, https://sunnah.com/bukhari:3237. Accessed March 20, 2025.

And: "By the One in Whose Hand is the soul of Muhammad! No woman can fulfill her duty towards Allah until she fulfills her duty towards her husband. If he asks her (for intimacy) even if she is on her camel saddle, she should not refuse."[34]

If wives had no right to refuse sexual relations, what chance did slave women have?

[34] Ibn Majah, vol. 3, bk. 9, no. 1853, https://sunnah.com/ibnmajah:1853. Accessed March 20, 2025.

CHAPTER TWO
THE SPOILS OF WAR

SPOILS OF WAR

A twentieth-century commentary on the Qur'an, the *Tafsir Anwarul Bayan*, reflects the same understanding of the passage, and defends the practice as a just punishment for the unbelievers' refusal to accept Islam: "During Jihad (religion war), many men and women become war captives. The Amirul Mu'minin [leader of the believers, or caliph—an office now vacant] has the choice of distributing them amongst the Mujahidin [warriors of jihad], in which event they will become the property of these Mujahidin. This enslavement is the penalty for disbelief (kufr)."[35]

The same Qur'an commentary specifies that the rules about taking infidel women captive and enslaving them do not apply only to the Muslims of Muhammad's time, but for all time: "None of the injunctions pertaining to slavery have been

[35] Mufti Muhammad Aashiq Muhajir Madani, *Illuminating Discourses on the Noble Qur'an* (*Tafsir Anwarul Bayan*), trans. Mufti Afzal Hussain Elias and Maulana Muhammad Arshad Fakhri (Karachi: Darul Ishaat, 2005), I, 501.

abrogated in the Shari'ah. The reason that the Muslims of today do not have slaves is because they do not engage in Jihad (religion war). Their wars are fought by the instruction of the disbelievers (kuffar) and are halted by the same felons. The Muslim [sic] have been shackled by such treaties of the disbelievers (kuffar) whereby they cannot enslave anyone in the event of a war. Muslims have been denied a great boon whereby every home could have had a slave. May Allah grant the Muslims the ability to escape the tentacles of the enemy, remain steadfast upon the Din (religion) and engage in Jihad (religion war) according to the injunctions of Shari'ah. Amen!"[36]

The Qur'an returns to the theme of the captives of the right hand later, stating: "O prophet, indeed, we have made lawful to you your wives to whom you have paid their dowries, and those whom your right hand possesses of those whom Allah has given you as spoils of war," and on through the list of women with whom sexual relations are permitted (33:50). From this passage we learn that "those whom your right hands possess" are "the spoils of war," just as a Pakistani Christian had stated about how the Muslims in his country viewed non-Muslim women.

Another Qur'anic passage makes it absolutely clear that Muslim men may use those whom their right hands possess in a sexual manner: "The believers are successful indeed, who are humble in their prayers, and who shun vain conversation, and who give alms, and who guard their private parts, except from their wives or those that their right hands possess, for then they are not blameworthy." (23:1–6)

Another influential commentary on the Qur'an, the *Tafsir al-Jalalayn*, explains this verse in a straightforward manner: One

---

36 Ibid., 502.

must guard one's private parts "except from their wives or those they own as slaves, in which case they are not blameworthy in approaching them."[37] A twentieth-century Islamic scholar of international renown, Syed Abul Ala Maududi, agrees, saying that in this Qur'an verse, "it is made clear that one need not guard one's private parts from two kinds of women – one's wives and slave-girls."[38]

One other Qur'an passage reiterates the major points of all this: "Indeed, the torment of their Lord is before which no one can feel secure and those who preserve their chastity except with their wives and those whom their right hands possess, for thus they are not blameworthy." (70:28–30)

CONCUBINES FROM THE BYZANTINES

The Qur'an states: "They tried previously to cause sedition and raised difficulties for you until the truth came and the decree of Allah was made clear, though they disliked it. Among them is he who says, Give me permission and do not tempt me. Surely it is into temptation that they have fallen. Indeed, Gehenna truly is all around the unbelievers."

In his explanation of the context of various Qur'an passages, the eleventh-century Islamic scholar Ali ibn Ahmad al-Wahidi relates this verse to a story about Muhammad. "This was revealed," al-Wahidi says, "about Jadd ibn Qays the hypocrite" when Muhammad was "preparing for the Battle of Tabuk," an expedition against the Roman Empire that he is said to have

37 Jalalu'd-Din al-Mahalli and Jalal'd-Din as-Suyuti, *Tafsir al-Jalalayn*, trans. Aisha Bewley (London: Dar Al Taqwa Ltd., 2007), 730.

38 Sayyid Abul A'la Mawdudi, *Towards Understanding the Qur'an* (*Tafhim al-Qur'an*), trans. Zafar Ishaq Ansari (Leicester, England: The Islamic Foundation, 1995), VI, 81.

undertaken a year and a half before his death.[39] As al-Wahidi tells the story, Muhammad tried to entice Jadd to come along by telling him that he would be able to come home with slaves, including sex slaves: "O Abu Wahb, would you not like to have scores of Byzantine women and men as concubines and servants?" Abu Wahb, or "father of Wahb," was Jadd ibn Qays.

Jadd is depicted as replying: "O Messenger of Allah, my people know that I am very fond of women and, if I see the women of the Byzantines, I fear I will not be able to hold back. So do not tempt me by them, and allow me not to join and, instead, I will assist you with my wealth."[40] At this, says al-Wahidi, Muhammad "turned away from him and said: 'I allow you,' and so Allah, exalted is He, revealed this verse."[41]

Jadd's response that he would "not be able to hold back" is odd, since Muhammad was trying to convince Jadd to come along on the basis of the fact that he would not have to hold back; he would be able to enjoy the Byzantine women to his heart's content. His refusal to do so results in the Qur'anic condemnation.

JIHADIS PREFER BLONDES

In light of the behavior of so many twenty-first-century Muslim migrants in Britain and in many areas of Europe, it is noteworthy that in other versions of this story, Muhammad tries to tempt his men into going along on the expedition to attack the Romans precisely on the basis of the fact that their women are blondes.

39 Ali ibn Ahmad al-Wahidi, *Asbab al-Nuzul,* trans. Mokrane Guezzou, (Amman: Royal Aal al-Bayt Institute for Islamic Thought, 2019), 122.
40 Ibid.
41 Ibid.

The scholar of the Arabs Ahmad M. H. Shboul notes that among the Arabs of the time of the origins of Islam, "the Byzantines as a people were considered as fine examples of physical beauty, and youthful slaves and slave-girls of Byzantine origin were highly valued… The Arab's appreciation of the Byzantine female has a long history indeed. For the Islamic period, the earliest literary evidence we have is a hadith (saying of the Prophet). Muhammad is said to have addressed a newly converted [to Islam] Arab: 'Would you like the girls of Banu al-Asfar?'"[42] The very name "Banu al-Asfar" in reference to the Romans referred to their being blonde: the phrase means "Children of the Yellow Ones." In his version of the story of Jadd ibn Qays, Ibn Kathir has him saying: "I fear that if I see the women of the yellow ones, I would not be patient."[43]

Shboul explains that "not only were Byzantine slave girls sought after for caliphal and other palaces (where some became mothers of future caliphs), but they also became the epitome of physical beauty, home economy, and refined accomplishments. The typical Byzantine maiden who captures the imagination of *litterateurs* and poets, had blond hair, blue or green eyes, a pure and healthy visage, lovely breasts, a delicate waist, and a body that is like camphor or a flood of dazzling light."[44]

Many of the women of Britain, Western Europe, and Scandinavia today could be described in much the same way.

---

42 Ahmad M. H. Shboul, "Byzantium and the Arabs: The Image of the Byzantines as Mirrored in Arabic Literature," in *Arab-Byzantine Relations in Early Islamic Times*, ed. Michael Bonner (Burlington: Ashgate Publishing, 2004), 240, in Sam Shamoun, "The 'Prophet' of Temptation and Lust," Answering Islam, https://www.answering-islam.org/authors/shamoun/blonde_fetish.html. Accessed March 20, 2025.

43 Ibn Kathir, *Tafsir Ibn Kathir*, 4, 43.

44 Shboul, 248, in Shamoun, "The 'Prophet.'"

HOW CONTEMPORARY ISLAMIC AUTHORITIES EXPLAIN ALL THIS

Islam Question & Answer contains this question: "In Ar-Raheeo Al Makhtum (The Sealed Nectar)," a popular biography of Muhammad, "the author says in the section called 'The Prophet Household' that the Prophet (S.A.W.) had four concubines. 1. Why is it that having concubines is not haram? 2. Can other muslims have concubines?"[45]

The answer begins: "With regard to your question about it being permissible for a master to be intimate with his slave woman, the answer is that that is because Allaah has permitted it."[46] The author of the fatwa then quotes the Qur'an passage (23:6) about guarding one's private parts except from his wives and those whom his right hand possesses. He offers one caveat, that the slave woman must not have been sold to someone else: "That is subject to the condition that he has acquired her in a proper manner, and that this slave woman has not been given by her master in marriage to another man to whom she is still married. The reason why this is permitted is that this slave woman belongs to him, either because he has paid money to buy her or he has fought for the sake of Allaah (and acquired her among the war booty)."[47]

The fact that the slave woman must have been taken as the spoils of war was all-important. The site quotes a Shaykh al-Shanqeeti saying: "The reason for which people may be taken as slaves is if they are kaafirs [unbelievers] who are waging war

45 "What is the Ruling on Intimacy with Slave Women?" Islam Question & Answer, March 18, 2004, https://islamqa.info/en/answers/13737/what-is-the-ruling-on-intimacy-with-slave-women. Accessed March 4, 2025.

46 Ibid.

47 Ibid.

against Allaah and His Messenger. If Allaah grants victory to the mujaahid [jihadist] Muslims, who are offering their souls, their wealth and all their resources and everything that Allaah has given them so that the word of Allaah might prevail over the kuffaar [unbelievers], then these kuffaar may become slaves, unless the imam chooses to let them go or to ransom them if that serves the interests of the Muslims."[48]

So Islam forbids rape, but it is clear from the Qur'an, the words of Muhammad according to Islamic tradition, and Islamic scholars that using captive women sexually is not considered rape. Infidel women can be taken as spoils of war, and what happens to them after that is entirely at the discretion of their Muslim captors.

RAPE AS A WEAPON OF WAR

In one sense, Islam is not unique in this. Numerous cultures throughout history, and in our own age, accept rape as a justified weapon of war. A December 2004 Amnesty International report found rape being used to humiliate and demoralize enemy forces in conflicts in Colombia and Nepal as well as in Afghanistan, Chechnya, Iraq, and Sudan. The BBC noted that "the use of rape as a weapon of war goes back much further," pointing to "the systematic rape of women in Bosnia, to an estimated 200,000 women raped during the battle for Bangladeshi independence in 1971, to Japanese rapes during the 1937 occupation of Nanking."[49]

---

[48] Ibid.

[49] Laura Smith-Spark, "How did rape become a weapon of war?" BBC News, December 8, 2004, https://archive.globalpolicy.org/component/content/article/163-general/28294.html. Accessed April 16, 2025.

To those examples could be added the notorious behavior of the Soviet troops invading National Socialist Germany in April 1945. Soviet commanders turned a blind eye to their soldiers' engaging in the wholesale rape of German women, often thinking that the Germans deserved what they got after their unprovoked invasion of the Soviet Union that began in June 1941. Rape was a weapon of revenge and humiliation.

Amnesty International's Gita Sahgal insisted that these rapes were not principally a matter of taking "spoils of war," and said that instead, "rape is often used in ethnic conflicts as a way for attackers to perpetuate their social control and redraw ethnic boundaries." Sahgal explained: "Women are seen as the reproducers and carers of the community. Therefore if one group wants to control another they often do it by impregnating women of the other community because they see it as a way of destroying the opposing community."[50]

Islam is unique even in comparison to the acceptance of rape as a weapon of warfare in other cultures, for it combines all of these motivations. Infidel women are taken as the spoils of war, but the goal is ultimately the expansion of the Islamic community and the diminishment of the infidel community. And so rape of infidel women is also useful as a means to humiliate the defeated infidel force, as well as a means of social control and to aid in the redrawing of ethnic boundaries. On top of all that is the divine sanction given to it all. Rape of infidel women in a jihad war is not just something the commanders permit, as a means to humiliate the infidels. It is a holy act.

50 Ibid.

IS THERE A WAR BETWEEN MUSLIMS AND NON-MUSLIMS?

Many would insist, however, that none of this illuminates the question of whether Islam condones the rape of infidel women, for in our own day, such rapes do not take place in the context of a war, as no war currently exists between the Islamic world and non-Muslims. However, this is to take a Western and modern view of what constitutes warfare.

Islamic law regarding the obligation to jihad establishes a situation in which, at least in modern times, a state of perpetual war exists between the Islamic world and non-Muslims. Classic Sunni law stipulates that jihad is *fard kifaya*, that is, a general obligation upon the entire Muslim community. If some of the Muslims are discharging the responsibility of waging jihad, others need not do so. A manual of Islamic law explains that "jihad is a communal obligation.... When enough people perform it to successfully accomplish it, it is no longer obligatory upon others."[51]

However, there is a significant caveat. If infidels attack a Muslim land, the obligation to jihad becomes *fard ayn*, that is, required from each individual in the entire Muslim community worldwide. Once infidels attack, jihad is "obligatory for everyone" when "the enemy has surrounded the Muslims...on every side, having entered our territory, even if the land consists of ruins, wilderness, or mountains, for non-Muslim forces entering Muslim lands is a weighty matter that cannot be ignored, but must be met with effort and struggle to repel them by every

---

[51] Naqib al-Misri, *Reliance of the Traveller,* o9.1–2.

possible means."[52] In such cases, "every able bodied man who has reached puberty and is sane" must wage jihad.[53]

Nowadays, numerous Islamic authorities have pointed to the American incursions in Iraq and Afghanistan, as well as to the very existence of the state of Israel, to declare that the infidels are at war with Islam, and thus jihad is obligatory upon every Muslim. In this scenario, a Muslim who travels to Britain or France or Germany and rapes a woman may consider that he is entirely justified in doing so, in light of the Qur'an's permission to use the "captives of the right hand" in this way. They are, after all, the spoils of war.

The Qur'an itself also provides justification for the idea that perpetual war exists between Muslims and non-Muslims when it says: "And fight them until persecution is no more, and religion is all for Allah." (8:39). If Muslims are to fight non-Muslims until there is no more persecution, then the fighting has an end point. If, on the other hand, Muslims must fight on until "religion is all for Allah," then they must continue fighting even against those who are minding their own business, but whose religion is not "for Allah." This establishes endless warfare between Muslims who take this command to heart and the non-Muslim world, and allows for non-Muslim women to be violated as the spoils of war in virtually any circumstance.

Non-Muslim women also bring all this upon themselves by not obeying Islam's modesty laws, as Islam Question & Answer argued. The Qur'an says: "O prophet, tell your wives and your daughters and the women of the believers to draw their veils close around them. That will be better, so that they may be recognized and not molested. Allah is always forgiving,

---

52 Ibid.

53 Ibid.

merciful." (33:59) The implication of this is clear: women who cover themselves are not to be molested, but those who do not are fair game, as the veil is protection against molestation.

There is no shortage of contemporary authorities who have advocated for this practice, which is understandable, given its widely recognized Qur'anic foundation. In February 2004, a Muslim in Britain asked the South African Mufti Ebrahim Desai on his own fatwa site, Islam Q & A Online, a series of questions on this topic. The questioner began by explaining: "Recently I saw a question on the status of women taken as prisoners during Jihad."[54] His questions included one that had in mind the well-being of the captive woman, as well as the apparent transgression of the Islamic marriage vow that would be involved in having sex with slave women: "Don't you think sex without marriage is a disgrace to that particular woman? Please give a detailed reply to this point as to why sex is allowed without marriage."[55]

The questioner also asked: "To what sort of women does this rule apply. I mean can they be ordinary citizens (mothers/sisters/wives of men) of any city Muslims capture or they must have taken part in the battle against Muslims so that this rule may apply to them."[56]

The mufti began his answer by exonerating Islam of any role in originating slavery, although this had nothing to do with anything the questioner had asked about: "Firstly, it should be borne in mind that slavery was not something that was introduced by Islam; on the contrary, it was something that had its

---

54 "Recently I saw a question on the status of women taken as prisoners during Jihad." Islam Q & A Online with Mufti Ebrahim Desai, February 24, 2004, https://www.webcitation.org/mainframe.php. Accessed March 6, 2025.

55 Ibid.

56 Ibid.

roots planted long before the advent of Islam. It would not be an exaggeration to state that slavery is probably as old as war itself, because it is one of the consequences of war."[57]

THE RIGHT OF OWNERSHIP

After a lengthy justification of the practice of enslaving prisoners of war, Desai said: "In the 'Jihads' (Islamic wars) that took place, women were also, at times, taken as prisoners of war by the Muslim warriors. These women captives used to be distributed as part of the booty among the soldiers, after their return to Islamic territory. Each soldier was then entitled to have relations ONLY with the slave girl over whom he was given the RIGHT OF OWNERSHIP and NOT with those slave girls that were not in his possession. This RIGHT OF OWNERSHIP was given to him by the 'Ameerul-Mu'mineen' (Head of the Islamic state.) Due to this right of ownership, it became lawful for the owner of a slave girl to have intercourse with her."[58]

"It may, superficially, appear distasteful," Desai continued, "to copulate with a woman who is not a man's legal wife, but once Shariah makes something lawful, we have to accept it as lawful, whether it appeals to our taste, or not; and whether we know its underlying wisdom or not."[59] He nonetheless went on to explain that wisdom, saying that "the LEGAL possession that a Muslim receives over a slave woman from the 'Ameerul-Mu'mineen' (the Islamic Head of State) gives him legal credence to have coition with the slave woman in his possession, just as

57 Ibid.
58 Ibid.
59 Ibid.

the marriage ceremony gives him legal credence to have coition with his wife. In other words, this LEGAL POSSESSION is, in effect, a SUBSTITUTE of the MARRIAGE CEREMONY."[60] Since "a slave girl can be possessed and even bought and sold, thus, this right of possession, substituting as a marriage ceremony, entitles the owner to copulate with her."[61]

As a result, "permission to have intercourse with a slave woman was not something barbaric or uncivilised; on the contrary, it was almost as good as a marriage ceremony."[62] What if she was already married? The mufti has a ready answer: "if a slave woman was married previously in enemy territory to a non-Muslim, and is then captured alone, i.e. without her husband, it is not permissible for any Muslim to have relations with her until her previous marriage is nullified, and that is done by bringing her to an Islamic country and making her the legal possession of a Muslim."[63]

Desai explains that it is not only not necessary to marry a slave woman, or even possible to do so. This is because Islamic law requires that the groom give his bride a dowry; as a slave doesn't own anything, but everything she has is the property of her owner, it is not possible to give her anything that would become her own. And so no dowry, and hence no marriage, is even possible.

Mufti Desai argued that "it would be difficult to implement" this system today, "because of the stringent conditions attached to it. Firstly, the prisoners have to be captured in 'Jihaad' in the true sense of the word. Then again, If true 'Jihaad'

60 Ibid.
61 Ibid.
62 Ibid.
63 Ibid.

did break out somewhere, there are still a number of other laws and conditions to abide by which are far too stringent for any Islamic country in the world to abide by in this time and age when people's personal gains and whims and desire are being given preference to [*sic*] over Islamic Law."[64]

This would appear to rule out the abuse of infidel women in this way today, but that actually depends on the point of view of individual Muslims as to whether jihad is being waged against unbelievers today. The mufti did maintain that if jihad is being waged, taking slave women as spoils of war was an integral part of that struggle: "According to Islamic Law, captive female prisoners are also part and parcel of the booty...The Ameerul-Mu'mineen (Head of the Islamic State) remains the guardian of the female prisoners until he allocates them to the soldiers. Only after a soldier has been allotted a slave girl, and made the owner of her, will she become his lawful possession."[65]

Another online fatwa site, IslamQA.com, gave the same view: "Islam allows a man to have intercourse with his slave woman, whether he has a wife or wives or he is not married."[66] This teaching "is indicated by the Qur'aan and Sunnah, and this was done by the Prophets. Ibraaheem (peace be upon him) took Haajar as a concubine and she bore him Ismaa'eel (may peace be upon them all). Our Prophet (peace and blessings of Allaah be upon him) also did that, as did the Sahaabah, the righteous and the scholars. The scholars are unanimously agreed on that and it is not permissible for anyone to regard it

64 Ibid.

65 Ibid.

66 "Ruling on having intercourse with a slave woman when one has a wife," IslamQA.com, June 12, 2011, https://www.webcitation.org/query?url=http://www.islamqa.com/en/ref/10382&date=2011-06-13. Accessed March 6, 2025.

as haraam or to forbid it. Whoever regards that as haraam is a sinner who is going against the consensus of the scholars."[67]

The site states that "the scholars are unanimously agreed that it is permissible," and quotes one such scholar, Ibn Qudaamah, saying: "There is no dispute (among the scholars) that it is permissible to take concubines and to have intercourse with one's slave woman, because Allaah says..." Then the site quotes Qur'an 70:28-30: "Indeed, the torment of their Lord is before which no one can feel secure and those who preserve their chastity except with their wives and those whom their right hands possess, for thus they are not blameworthy." (70:28–30)

As a result, the fatwa says, "the wife has no right to object to her husband owning female slaves or to his having intercourse with them."[68] Another fatwa on the IslamQA site answers the question of whether a married Muslim man commits adultery by having sex with his slave: "Allaah has permitted intimacy with a slave woman if the man owns her. This is not regarded as adultery as suggested in the question."[69]

---

67 Ibid.

68 Ibid.

69 "Intercourse with a slave woman is not regarded as zina (adultery)," IslamQA.com, December 26, 2002, https://islamqa.info/en/answers/20802/intercourse-with-a-slave-woman-is-not-regarded-as-zina-adultery. Accessed March 6, 2025.

CHAPTER THREE

'SEX SLAVES ARE NOT FORBIDDEN BY ISLAM'

AN ERA OF JIHAD

In May 2011, an Egyptian sheikh, Abu-Ishaq al-Huwayni, began a justification of the sexual enslavement of infidel women by situating it within Islam's doctrine of jihad. Al-Huwayni began by noting that the modern era was one of war between Muslims and non-Muslims, and that Muslims should regard this as a positive development: "We are in the era of jihad. The era of jihad has come over us, and jihad in the path of Allah is a pleasure. It is a real pleasure. The companions (of the Prophet) used to compete to (perform jihad)."[70] Al-Huwayni stated, in accord with the Qur'an's guarantee to

[70] "Egyptian Shaykh: Jihad Is Solution to Muslims' Financial Problems," *Translating Jihad*, May 31, 2011, in Billy Hallowell, "Egyptian Cleric: Poverty Can be Solved by Selling Humans 'Like Groceries,'" Blaze Media, June 1, 2011, https://www.theblaze.com/news/2011/06/01/egyptian-muslim-cleric-poverty-can-be-solved-by-selling-humans-like-groceries. Accessed March 6, 2025.

the righteous of prosperity in this world as well as the next (24:55), that the Muslim community was not doing so well because of its failure to obey Allah's commands to wage jihad: "The poverty that we're in—is it not due to our abandonment of jihad? But if we could conduct one, two, or three jihadist operations every year, many people throughout the earth would become Muslims."[71]

If Muslims returned to waging jihad, they would be able to take captives, and profit from doing so. *Da'wa* is the call to unbelievers to accept Islam, which in Islamic theology should precede jihad, with jihad being waged against those who decline the invitation to convert to Islam:

> And whoever rejected this *da'wa*, or stood in our way, we would fight against him and take him prisoner, and confiscate his wealth, his children, and his women—all of this means money. Every *mujahid* who returned from jihad, his pockets would be full. He would return with three or four slaves, three or four women, and three or four children. Multiply each head by 300 *dirhams*, or 300 *dinar*, and you have a good amount of profit. If he were to go to the West and work on a commercial deal, he would not make that much money. Whenever things became difficult (financially), he could take the head (i.e. the prisoner) and sell it, and ease his (financial) crisis. He would sell it like groceries.[72]

---

71 Ibid.
72 Ibid.

After his remarks sparked a controversy, al-Huwayni appeared on an Islamic television channel, al-Hikma TV, on May 22, 2011, in order to clarify his remarks. The chief cause of the controversy, however, was not that al-Huwayni had spoken about buying and owning slaves, but that he had given some of his hearers the impression that he was saying that Muslims could be enslaved. He thus hastened to assure his television audience that he had meant to speak only of the enslavement of non-Muslims. First, he outlined Islamic doctrine regarding waging war against infidels, including the right of the victorious jihad warriors to seize the spoils of war from their vanquished enemies:

> It is clear that offensive jihad, which I was talking about in that interview, that its purpose is to call people to Islam, and it is not permissible for anyone to hide the divine guidance from the people, under any name. They rejected Islam and the jizya, that's it. The Prophet (PBUH) said: "If they refuse, then seek Allah's aid and fight them." If fighting occurs, there is going to be a winner and a loser. If the army of the Muslims is victorious, it will take spoils. Taking spoils is a fixed ruling in the Qur'an. Allah permitted it at the day of the Battle of Badr, as it is (recorded) in Surat al-Anfal. Allah Almighty said: "And know that out of all the booty that ye may acquire (in war), a fifth share is assigned to Allah, and to the Messenger, and to near relatives, orphans, the needy, and the wayfarer, if ye do believe in Allah and in the revelation We sent down to Our servant on

> the Day of Testing, the Day of the meeting of the two forces. For Allah hath power over all things" [Qur'an 8:41].[73]

Al-Huwayni emphasized that his position was firmly rooted in Islamic tradition, based on the teachings of the two collections of hadiths, traditions of Muhammad's words and deeds, that Muslims considered most reliable, Sahih Bukhari and Sahih Muslim. The taking of the spoils of war, he said, was a special privilege that Allah gave to the followers of Muhammad, although he had not given any similar privilege to any of the followers of earlier prophets:

> This (position) on spoils is clear. There is also the saying in the two Sahihs [Sahih Bukhari and Sahih Muslim] from Abi-Hurayra, the first of which is, "One among the prophets (PBUH) raided…" In the other hadith from Yusha bin Nun, the Prophet (PBUH) said, "When Allah saw our weakness, he made it permissible for us," meaning spoils. The Prophet (PBUH) said, "Spoils were not permitted for any masters besides you." Allah Almighty forbade (the taking of) spoils for all nations before us. He permitted it on the day of the Battle of Badr, as agreed to by all scholars. Not a single Muslim scholar has a problem with this.[74]

---

73 Shaykh Abu-Ishaq al-Huwayni, "When I want a sex slave, I just go to the market and choose the woman I like and purchase her," al-Hikma TV, May 22, 2011, https://wikiislam.net/wiki/Qur%27an,_Hadith_and_Scholars:Rape_of_Slaves,_Prisoners,_and_Wives. Accessed March 6, 2025.

74 Ibid.

Al-Huwayni emphasized that these spoils of war included not just the belongings of defeated enemy warriors, but prisoners as well, provided that they were not Muslims:

> "Spoils" refers to what? It refers to people and wealth. The people are those who are taken prisoner. I want to say that it is not at all permissible to take prisoners from among Muslims, even if they are heretics, because the rule for Muslims is that they are free, and not prisoners. Jihad, as I stated in the beginning, is between Muslims and non-Muslims, from among the infidels. But if two Muslims fought each other, like from Iraq and Iran for example; if Iraq invaded Iran to occupy it, it would not be permissible for an Iraqi man to take a Shi'ite woman captive, because she is Muslim, even though she's a heretic. Likewise if Iran invaded Iraq, it would not be permissible for one of their men to take a Muslim woman captive, because she is free.[75]

Non-Muslims, however, could not expect the same protections:

> Therefore jihad is only between Muslims and infidels. That between Muslims and Muslims is called oppression, or fighting: "If two parties among the believers fall into a quarrel…" [Qur'an 49:9]. They are called "believers," and this name is not taken from them, even though

[75] Ibid.

> they are fighting. "If one of them transgresses beyond bounds against the other, then fight ye (all) against the one that transgresses…" Here they are called transgressors, but the name of believers is still not taken away from them. In the verse directly following this one, Allah Almighty says: "The believers are but a single brotherhood…" They were brothers, even though a party of them transgressed against the other, and some of them fought each other. But the name of believers was not taken from them.

Al-Huwayni concluded that this meant that Muslim warriors could legitimately seize non-Muslim women as sex slaves:

> Do you understand what I'm saying? Spoils, slaves, and prisoners are only to be taken in war between Muslims and infidels. Muslims in the past conquered, invaded, and took over countries. This is agreed to by all scholars — there is no disagreement on this from any of them, from the smallest to the largest, on the issue of taking spoils and prisoners. The prisoners and spoils are distributed among the fighters, which includes men, women, children, wealth, and so on.[76]

Al-Huwayni invoked Qur'an passages on "those whom your right hands possess" to justify this teaching:

> When a slave market is erected, which is a market in which are sold slaves and sex-slaves,

[76] Ibid.

> which are called in the Qur'an by the name milk al-yamin, "that which your right hands possess" [Qur'an 4:24]. This is a verse from the Qur'an which is still in force, and has not been abrogated. The milk al-yamin are the sex-slaves. You go to the market, look at the sex-slave, and buy her. She becomes like your wife, (but) she doesn't need a (marriage) contract or a divorce like a free woman, nor does she need a wali [guardian or protector]. All scholars agree on this point — there is no disagreement from any of them.

These slaves could still enter paradise if they converted to Islam. Their slavery would thus lead to their salvation:

> These are called slaves. The Prophet (PBUH) talked about them in the hadith narrated by al-Bukhari in his Book of Jihad: "Allah is delighted at a people who enter the Garden in chains." Also as narrated by Abu-Dawud: "They are led to the Garden in chains." Naturally, many people might not understand someone being jerked along in chains in order to enter the Garden. This is because all people, even the worst of the unbelievers, say the garden is for them and no others. They run to the Garden without anybody pulling them in chains.
>
> The meaning of the hadith is this: these slaves were in a religion other than Islam. However, when they were conquered, and defeated, and

> taken prisoner, they came to live in the land of Islam. Then when they witnessed the justice, compassion, and mercy of Islam, they became Muslims. These did not convert to Islam except in the chains of war. If they had not been chained, bound, and had their freedom taken from them, they would not have converted to Islam. Therefore this hadith is referring to these slaves.[77]

The possibility that a slave could turn to Allah and ultimately enter paradise, as well as Qur'anic commands to free individual slaves under certain prescribed circumstances, amounted for al-Huwayni to the idea that Islam actually forbids slavery:

> I am very shocked and surprised at those who say that we permit slavery. We don't call people to become slaves. In fact, there are vows to free the necks (i.e. slaves). The same Islam which permits us to take slaves, also urges us to free their necks....[78]

However, just as forcing a slave to engage in sexual intercourse was not rape, so also the sex slavery as allowed in the Qur'an and sanctified by the example of Muhammad was perfectly acceptable as far as al-Huwayni was concerned, and he didn't appear to see any contradiction between approving of this practice and insisting that Islam did not permit slavery. He continued:

---

77 Ibid.

78 Ibid.

> When I want a sex slave, I just go to the market and choose the woman I like and purchase her. I choose the man I like, one with strong muscles, or if I want a boy to work in the house, and so forth. I choose one, and pay him a wage. I employ him in a variety of different tasks, then I sell him afterwards. Now, the country that I entered and took captive its men and women — does it not also have money, gold, and silver? Is that not money? When I say that jihad — offensive jihad — with the well-known conditions that I already mentioned from the hadith of the Prophet (PBUH), from the hadith of Burayda in Sahih Muslim, the coffers of the Muslims were full. Would someone who is pious and intelligent — would he say that this is a type of poverty? Or that it is a type of wealth? No — this will fill the coffers of the Muslims with riches and wealth, but as we said, with the recognized conditions.[79]

"A YOUNG MAN WHO LIKED WOMEN A LOT"

Another voice justifying the seizure and enslavement of infidel women was a female Kuwaiti politician, Salwa al-Mutairi, who in a May 2011 video unhesitatingly recommended the practice:

> Peace, mercy, and blessings of Allah be upon you. My name is Salwa al-Mutairi. I received a message that was a little strange. A merchant

79 Ibid.

told me that he would like to have a sex slave. He said he would not be negligent with her, and that Islam permitted this sort of thing. He was speaking the truth. The topic that he brought up is an old topic. I have been working on it for two years now.

I was working with this man, a young man, who (liked) women a lot. I was sympathetic to his situation, and also dedicated to my work. I was given the opportunity to visit Mecca, and when I did so, I brought up (this man's) situation to the muftis in Mecca. I told them that I had a question, since they were men who specialized in what was *halal*, and what was good, and who loved women. I said, "What is the law of sex slaves?"

The mufti said, "With the law of sex slaves, there must be a Muslim nation at war with a Christian nation, or a nation which is not of the religion, not of the religion of Islam. And there must be prisoners of war."

"Is this forbidden by Islam?" I asked.

"Absolutely not. Sex slaves are not forbidden by Islam. On the contrary, sex slaves are under a different law than the free woman. The free woman must be completely covered except for her face and hands. But the sex slave can be naked from the waist up. She differs a lot from the free woman. While the free woman requires a marriage contract, the sex slave does not—she only needs to be purchased by her husband, and that's it. Therefore the sex slave is different than the free woman."

Of course, I also asked religious experts in Kuwait (about this issue), and they told me about the problem with the passionate man, or even the man who is committed to his religion. For every good man in our religion, the only solution for him—when forbidden women come around, if he's tempted to sin, then the solution to this issue is for him to purchase sex slaves. I hope that Kuwait will enact the law for this category, this category of people—the sex slaves....

I hope that a law will be enacted for this category, and they will open the door for this, just as they have opened the door for servants (to come into the country). They should open the door for sex slaves, by enacting a sound law, so that our children don't waste away in the abyss of adultery and moral depravity. Allah-willing, this will work out. I believe, look, the (sex slaves could come from) a country like Chechnya, where there is a war between an (Islamic) state and another state. Certainly there are prisoners. These prisoners could be purchased. They could be purchased and sold to the merchants in Kuwait. This is better than (the merchants) committing that which is forbidden. There is nothing wrong with this.

Harun al-Rashid [the Abbasid caliph from 786 to 809] had many more sex slaves than this. When he died he had 2,000 sex slaves. But he only had one wife. This was not forbidden. Our *shari'a* permits such a thing as this. Praise be to Allah, here in Kuwait there are many merchants who are committed (to Islam). I hope the best for Kuwait, Allah-willing.[80]

A Muslim state must [first] attack a Christian state—sorry, I mean any non-Muslim state—and they [the women, the future sex-slaves] must be captives of the raid. Is this forbidden? Not at all; according to Islam, sex slaves are not at all forbidden. Quite the contrary, the rules regulating sex-slaves differ from those for free women [i.e., Muslim women]: the latter's body must be covered entirely, except for her face and hands, whereas the sex-slave is kept naked from the bellybutton on up—she is different from the free woman; the free woman has to be married properly to her husband, but the sex-slave—he just buys her and that's that.[81]

---

80 Dave, "Islamic Sex Slaves!!!" Skeptical Science, June 26, 2011, https://www.skeptical-science.com/religion/islamic-sex-slaves/. Accessed March 6, 2025.

81 Raymond Ibrahim, "Muslim Woman Seeks to Revive Institution of Sex-Slavery," Middle East Forum, June 6, 2011, https://www.meforum.org/muslim-woman-seeks-to-revive-institution-of-sex. Accessed March 6, 2025.

The popular Saudi preacher Muhammed al-Arifi echoed all this in a fatwa that granted jihad warriors in Syria permission to engage in "intercourse marriage" with captive women.[82] He warned them, however, that this "intercourse marriage" should be of a brief duration, "in order to give each fighter a turn." He said that women who complied with this would gain a place in paradise, as the practice "boosts the determination of the Mujahideen in Syria." These women did, however, have to be at least fourteen years old, divorced, or widowed.

Another Saudi Islamic scholar, Sheikh Saleh Al-Fawzan, agreed. In a February 2018 lecture, he noted:

> The Muslims captured women in the [630] Battle of Awtas.... They took from the [infidels] money and women as booty. The Companions of the Prophet Muhammad became confused. It was customary for the owners of women captured at war to take them as concubines. They have the right to take them as concubines and have sex with them, by virtue of possessing them. The possession of a captured woman outweighs her marriage contract. It allows the master to have sex with the woman he owns. This is called concubinage.
>
> But the Prophet's Companions were confused, because Allah has made married women haram, and these women had infidel husbands. So Allah sent down the verse 'married women

82 Steve Emerson, "Fatwa Permits Rape of Syrian Women," Newsmax, January 10, 2013, https://www.newsmax.com/Emerson/fatwa-rape-Syrian-women/2013/01/10/id/470865/. Accessed March 6, 2025.

> except those you possess.' When a woman is taken captive, her marriage contract to her [infidel] husband is annulled. If she is taken captive, she becomes property of the Muslims, and the infidel's marriage contract with her is annulled. She becomes the property of the Muslim, and he can take her as a concubine."[83]

These teachings were issued as other Muslims were applying them in large numbers, not in Muslim countries, but in Britain and on continental Europe.

---

83 "Senior Saudi Islamic Scholar Sheikh Saleh Al-Fawzan In 2018: According To Islamic Law, Muslims Have The Right To Take Captive Women As Concubines And Have Sex With Them Even If They Are Married To An Infidel – Archival," Middle East Media Research Institute (MEMRI), February 22, 2018, https://www.memri.org/tv/snr-saudi-islamic-scholar-sheikh-saleh-fawzan-right-captive-women-concubines-married-infidel-archive. Accessed March 20, 2025.

CHAPTER FOUR

'A PERVERTED, OPPRESSIVE IDEOLOGY'?

THE ISLAMIC STATE TAKES SLAVES

It was during the Islamic State's caliphate in Iraq and Syria, which was formally established in June 2014 and largely destroyed by 2017, that the contemporary world came to know of the practice of Islamic sex slavery. The Islamic State became notorious for seizing non-Muslim girls and women, particularly Yazidis and Christians, and making them into sex slaves. Just as in the case of Britain's Muslim rape gangs, however, the Islamic aspect of this activity was routinely ignored, and dismissed out of hand whenever it was mentioned.

The August 2014 statement of UK Shadow Home Secretary Yvette Cooper was typical. She declared that Islamic State "extremists are beheading people and parading their heads on spikes, subjugating women and girls, killing Muslims, Christians and anyone who gets in their way. This is no liberation movement—only a perverted, oppressive ideology that bears no relation to Islam."[84]

This was the unanimous view of non-Muslim politicians in the West at that time. Barack Obama declared magisterially that the Islamic State "speaks for no religion. Their victims are overwhelmingly Muslim, and no faith teaches people to massacre innocents."[85] British Prime Minister David Cameron explained: "What we are witnessing is actually a battle between Islam on the one hand and extremists who want to abuse Islam on the other. These extremists, often funded by fanatics living far away from the battlefields, pervert the Islamic faith as a way of justifying their warped and barbaric ideology – and they do so not just in Iraq and Syria but right across the world, from Boko Haram and al-Shabaab to the Taliban and al-Qaeda."[86]

Secretary of State John Kerry pointed out proudly that he didn't use the common terms that the media and most public figures used to refer to the Islamic State: ISIS, that is, the Islamic State of Iraq and Sham (the Arabic word for Syria and its environs, or the Levant), or ISIL, the Islamic State of Iraq and Levant. Neither of these acronyms was correct, as the

---

84 Natasha Culzac, "James Foley beheading was an 'utter betrayal of Britain', says Philip Hammond," *Independent*, August 24, 2014, https://www.independent.co.uk/news/uk/home-news/killing-of-james-foley-an-utter-betrayal-of-britain-foreign-secretary-philip-hammond-9687959.html. Accessed March 9, 2025.

85 "Transcript: President Obama's remarks on the execution of journalist James Foley by Islamic State," *Washington Post*, August 20, 2014, https://www.washingtonpost.com/politics/transcript-president-obamas-remarks-on-the-execution-of-journalist-james-foley-by-islamic-state/2014/08/20/f5a63802-2884-11e4-8593-da634b334390_story.html. Accessed March 9, 2025.

86 David Cameron, "David Cameron: Isil poses a direct and deadly threat to Britain," *Telegraph*, August 16, 2014, https://www.telegraph.co.uk/news/worldnews/middleeast/iraq/11038121/David-Cameron-Isil-poses-a-direct-and-deadly-threat-to-Britain.html. Accessed March 9, 2025.

Islamic State had by that time dropped the second half of its name and was calling itself simply the Islamic State, but calling it that was precisely what politicians wanted to avoid doing.

And so Kerry offered them a way out, recommending that instead of saying "ISIS" or "ISIL," people could use the Arabic acronym instead: "I've been on a lot of campaigns to get everybody to say "Daesh" because it's a pejorative in Arabic — the initials — and I haven't won that campaign at all."[87] Daesh was derived from ad-Dawla al-Islamiyya fil Iraq wa'ash Sham, or "the Islamic State of Iraq and Sham" in Arabic.

Kerry resorted to this to avoid calling the group "Islamic," or at least doing so in a language that most of his listeners could understand: "But it's just — you kind of resort to the use of those letters because it refers to a state — it's the Islamic State — and it's not a state. There's nothing legitimate about it. There's nothing Islamic about it. It's a complete misnomer. It's their title and we shouldn't use it and I feel that very strongly. But it has gained — it's the recognized term and if you want people to know what you're talking about, unfortunately, sometimes you are forced to. It would be great if we could get away from that, and the key is the media to begin really to call it something else. The terrorist group Daesh — that would be the best moniker, I think. Or the most evil — the world's most evil terrorist group."[88]

Yet while the elected leaders of Britain and the United State and their loyal courtiers were absolutely certain that the Islamic State had nothing whatsoever to do with Islam, the group itself

---

87 Bridget Johnson, "Kerry: To Avoid 'Islamic' or 'State,' Call ISIS 'World's Most Evil Terrorist Group,'" PJ Media, October 11, 2016, https://pjmedia.com/bridget-johnson/2016/10/11/kerry-to-avoid-islamic-or-state-call-isis-worlds-most-evil-terrorist-group-n94609. Accessed March 9, 2025.

88 Ibid.

was never convinced. It published numerous detailed Islamic justifications of its actions, including of its practice of, as Yvette Cooper put it, "subjugating women and girls." In October 2014, it published an issue of its glossy, slickly produced magazine, *Dabiq*, in which it echoed the Islamic authorities quoted above and stated adamantly: "Enslaving the families of the kuffar [non-believers] and taking their women as concubines is a firmly established aspect of the Sharia."[89]

"A WOMAN FROM AMONG AHL AL-HARB WHO HAS BEEN CAPTURED BY MUSLIMS"

In a video that began circulating widely in November 2014, Islamic State jihadis, in a celebratory mood, await their chance to buy slaves at auction. One of them explains happily: "Today is the slave market day. Today is the day where this verse applies, '[Guard your private parts] Except with their wives and the (captives) whom their right hands possess, for (then) they are not to be blamed.'"[90]

The following month, the Islamic State produced a pamphlet that explained in detail the proper treatment of sex slaves in Islam. It also provided information for doubters on why the practice was completely accepted from an Islamic standpoint.

---

89 Zachary Davies Boren, "Yazidi sex slave escapes Isis to tell her story: 'They took us away like cattle,'" *Independent*, December 22, 2014, https://www.independent.co.uk/news/world/middle-east/yazidi-sex-slave-escapes-isis-to-tell-her-story-they-took-us-away-like-cattle-9939770.html. Accessed March 9, 2025.

90 Rose Troup Buchanan, "Isis fighters barter over Yazidi girls on 'slave market day' - the shocking video," *Independent*, November 3, 2014, https://www.independent.co.uk/news/world/middle-east/isis-fighters-barter-over-yazidi-girls-on-slave-market-day-the-shocking-video-9836589.html. Accessed March 9, 2025.

First, it made clear exactly what was being discussed: "Al-Sabi is a woman from among *ahl al-harb* [the people of war] who has been captured by Muslims."[91] She would, therefore, be the spoils of war; in fact, it was entirely because of her status as the spoils of war that she could be treated this way: "What makes *al-sabi* permissible [i.e., what makes it permissible to take such a woman captive] is [her] unbelief. Unbelieving [women] who were captured and brought into the abode of Islam are permissible to us, after the imam distributes them [among us]."[92]

Like al-Huwayni, and apparently to refute the claim that they were "extremists" who were twisting the true teachings of Islam, or representatives of a tiny sect or perspective that the vast majority of Muslims rejected, the Islamic State invoked the unanimity of Islamic tradition on this point: "There is no dispute among the scholars that it is permissible to capture unbelieving women [who are characterized by] original unbelief [*kufr asli*], such as the *kitabiyat* [women from among the People of the Book, i.e. Jews and Christians] and polytheists."[93] The only disagreement was over whether women who had left Islam could be treated this way: "[The scholars] are disputed over [the issue of] capturing apostate women. The consensus leans towards forbidding it, though some people of knowledge

---

91 "Islamic State (ISIS) Releases Pamphlet On Female Slaves," Middle East Media Research Institute, December 3, 2014, https://www.memri.org/jttm/islamic-state-isis-releases-pamphlet-female-slaves. Accessed March 9, 2025. Robert Spencer, "Islamic State releases pamphlet justifying sex slavery of infidel women, Jihad Watch, December 8, 2024, https://jihadwatch.org/2014/12/islamic-state-releases-pamphlet-justifying-sex-slavery-of-infidel-women. Accessed March 9, 2025.

92 Ibid.

93 Ibid.

think it permissible. We [ISIS] lean towards accepting the consensus…"[94]

In agreement with numerous other Islamic authorities, the Islamic State then declared: "It is permissible to have sexual intercourse with the female captive. Allah the almighty said: '[Successful are the believers] who guard their chastity, except from their wives or (the captives and slaves) that their right hands possess, for then they are free from blame [Koran 23:5-6]'…"[95]

The slave woman in question had no rights that the owner was bound to respect: "It is permissible to buy, sell, or give as a gift female captives and slaves, for they are merely property, which can be disposed of [as long as that doesn't cause [the Muslim ummah] any harm or damage."[96] All this applied even to girls who were prepubescent if they were physically capable of sexual relations: "It is permissible to have intercourse with the female slave who hasn't reached puberty if she is fit for intercourse; however if she is not fit for intercourse, then it is enough to enjoy her without intercourse."[97] It was permissible, in line with the tradition in which Muhammad allows for this, to practice coitus interruptus with a slave woman, and the Islamic State specifies that her consent is not required: "*Al-'azl* is refraining from ejaculating on a woman's pudendum [i.e. coitus interruptus]…. A man is allowed [to use] *al-'azl* during intercourse with his female slave with or without her consent."[98]

The slave woman could be beaten as long as her bones were not broken, or the owner was a sadist or simply torturing

94 Ibid.
95 Ibid.
96 Ibid.
97 Ibid.
98 Ibid.

his slave: "It is permissible to beat the female slave as a [form of] *darb ta'deeb* [disciplinary beating], [but] it is forbidden to [use] *darb al-takseer* [literally, breaking beating], [*darb*] *al-tashaffi* [beating for the purpose of achieving gratification], or [*darb*] al-*ta'dheeb* [torture beating]. Further, it is forbidden to hit the face."[99] Marriage with slaves who were Muslim or members of one of the groups the Qur'an designates as "people of the book," that is, Jews, Christians, and Zoroastrians, was forbidden: "It is impermissible for a free [man] to marry Muslim or *kitabiyat* [people of the book] female slaves, except for those [men] who feared to [commit] a sin, that is, the sin of fornication…"[100]

It would have been interesting and enlightening to read a detailed Islamic refutation of all this, demonstrating that the taking of sex slaves was not permitted, but none was forthcoming. This was not surprising. The October 2014 issue of *Dabiq* insisted, according to *The New York Times*, that in seizing non-Muslim women and using them as sex slaves, "it was reviving a custom justified under Shariah."[101] *Dabiq* even announced that in accord with the Qur'an's command, "one fifth of the slaves were transferred to the Islamic State's authority to be divided as *khums*."[102]

Khums was a fifth of the spoils of war that had to be turned over to the Islamic leaders, in accord with the Qur'anic injunction: That is, the cut of the spoils of war due to Islamic leaders,

99 Ibid.

100 Ibid.

101 Kirk Semple, "Yazidi Girls Seized by ISIS Speak Out After Escape," *New York Times*, November 14, 2014, https://www.nytimes.com/2014/11/15/world/middleeast/yazidi-girls-seized-by-isis-speak-out-after-escape.html. Accessed March 9, 2025.

102 Ibid.

in line with the Qur'an: "And know that whatever you take as spoils of war, indeed, a fifth of it is for Allah, and for the messenger and for the relatives and orphans and the needy and the traveler, if you believe in Allah and what we revealed to our slave on the day of *furqan*, the day when the two armies met. And Allah is able to do all things." (8:41)

"THE MEN WILL HAVE THE RIGHT TO SEXUAL CONGRESS WITH THEM"

Shabir Ally appeared to be on the opposite end of the Islamic theological spectrum from the Islamic State. He was a respected imam in Canada who frequently engaged in debates with non-Muslims and was unusual among Muslim debaters for being generally courteous to his opponents. Possessed of a quiet, gentle mien, Ally nevertheless published a video in September 2016, "The Historical Roots of Female Slavery," in which he justified both marital rape and the sexual enslavement of infidel women.[103]

Nearly four years after it first appeared, the video began to get renewed attention, as a group of ex-Muslims called attention to it to draw attention to Islam's misogyny. The video certainly gave them a great deal of ammunition. Ally said to the host of the show *Let the Quran Speak*, who was his own daughter: "The woman's main responsibility in a marriage is to fulfil the sexual needs of her husband. And for that reason the husband has the

[103] "The Historical Roots of Female Slavery | Dr. Shabir Ally," Let the Quran Speak, YouTube, September 16, 2016, https://www.youtube.com/watch?v=WjHB7DZke_c. Accessed March 18, 2025.

right and claim to this (referring to sexual intercourse). And she cannot refuse."[104]

Ally expanded on this idea by saying: "Some speak of the possibility that the man can force himself onto his wife. And she cannot refuse because that is his 'right.'"[105] Ally conceded that this was not an "ideal situation" but nonetheless emphasized that women indeed could not refuse: "When her husband calls her for that particular action, she should be ready and willing to engage."[106] As if his point weren't clear enough already, he added: "The women are with them like slaves."[107]

Ally also discussed sex slavery, saying forthrightly: "A Muslim man can have up to four wives at once, in addition to the four wives, he can have an unlimited number of concubines which basically refers to women with slave status."[108] Slave women likewise could not refuse sex: "A woman owned by her master has to freely give herself to the master. The master has the right to have sexual relations with her as though she were one of his wives. The understanding is that by virtue of the fact that she's owned, she does not have the right to consent or to withhold herself from her master. The master has the full right over her and her consent does not play anything in this relationship."[109]

This was not a theological view that had been reformed or rejected. Ally emphasized that it was still applicable today:

---

104 OpIndia Staff, "'No role of consent in marriage and slavery': Video of Canadian Islamic cleric Shabir Ally justifying marital rape, sex slavery in Islam goes viral," OpIndia, August 30, 2020, https://www.opindia.com/2020/08/canada-islamic-scholar-shabir-ally-justify-marital-rape-sex-slavery-video-interview/. Accessed March 18, 2025.

105 Ibid.

106 Ibid.

107 Ibid.

108 Ibid.

109 Ibid.

"Theoretically, it is still applicable and they state so in clear terms. If there is a war between Muslims and non-Muslims today and the Muslims capture the non-Muslim women, then they will be made slaves. And the men will have the right to sexual congress with them."[110]

[110] Ibid.

CHAPTER FIVE

WHAT DID MUHAMMAD DO?

MUHAMMAD'S EXAMPLE

Islamic tradition records Muhammad acting in accord with these teachings. Ninth-century Islamic traditions depict Muhammad carrying out a surprise raid against the oasis of Khaybar, where the Jews he had previously exiled from Medina had settled. The spoils of war were considerable: according to a hadith, "the Messenger of Allah divided it into eighteen portions. The army contained one thousand and five hundred people. There were three hundred horsemen among them. He gave double share to the horsemen, and a single to the footmen."[111] A variant tradition contends that "Khaybar was divided by the Messenger of Allah into three sections: two for Muslims, and one as a contribution for his family. If anything remained after

[111] Sunan Abi Dawud, bk. 20, no. 3015, https://sunnah.com/abudawud:3015. Accessed March 20, 2025.

making the contribution of his family, he divided it among the poor Emigrants."[112]

Captured women of Khaybar were among the spoils. A jihad warrior, Dihya ibn Khalifa al-Kalb, came to Muhammad and said: "O Allah's Prophet! Give me a slave girl from the captives."[113] Muhammad replied generously: "Go and take any slave girl."[114] Dihya chose one of the most striking of the captive women, Safiya bint Huyayy, whom Muhammad's ninth-century biographer Ibn Sa'd says "was a handsome girl."[115] One of the jihadis marveled to Muhammad: "We have not seen the like of her among the captives of war."[116]

Safiya was also an aristocrat among the Jews of Khaybar; her father Huyayy bin Akhtab and her husband Kinana ibn Rabi had been leaders of the community until the Muslim invaders killed them both. In light of her beauty and high status, some of the Muslims believed that only Muhammad should have Safiya as a slave. One Muslim said to Muhammad: "O Allah's Messenger! You gave Safiyya bint Huyai to Dihya and she is the chief-mistress of [the ladies] of the tribes of Quraidha and An-Nadir, she befits none but you."[117]

This impressed Muhammad, whom Islamic tradition depicts as never being shy about asserting his prerogatives. Ibn Hisham says that Safiya b. Huyayy "along with another woman" was

---

112 Sunan Abi Dawud, bk. 20, no. 2967, https://sunnah.com/abudawud:2967. Accessed March 20, 2025.

113 Sahih Bukhari, vol. 1, bk. 8, no. 371, https://sunnah.com/bukhari:371. Accessed March 20, 2025.

114 Ibid.

115 Ibn Sa'd, *Kitab al-Tabaqat al-Kabir*, trans. S. Moinul Haq, (New Delhi: Kitab Bhavan, n.d.), II, 145; Sahih Bukhari, vol. 1, bk. 8, no. 371.

116 Sahih Muslim, bk. 8, no. 3329.

117 Sahih Bukhari, vol. 1, bk. 8, no. 371.

presented to Muhammad.[118] On their way to meet the prophet of Islam, they were led "past the Jews who were slain," a sight that greatly upset Safiya's companion: "when the woman who was with Safiya saw them she shrieked and slapped her face and poured dust on her head."[119] She was apparently still in a highly emotional state when she was brought before Muhammad, who disgustedly ordered: "Take this she-devil away from me."[120] Then he scolded his companion Bilal for leading them to him past the corpses of their own people: "Had you no compassion, Bilal, when you brought two women past their dead husbands?"[121]

Another version depicts Muhammad likewise scolding Bilal: "Has graciousness left you that you take a young girl past the dead?"[122] This version, that of another ninth-century biographer of Muhammad, al-Waqidi, also includes Bilal's explanation that he had taken that route quite purposefully: "O Messenger of God, I did not think that you would hate that. I wanted her to see the destruction of her people."[123] Muhammad is then depicted as comforting the terrorized young woman, saying to her, "This is only a devil."[124] Whether he meant Bilal or the spiritual entity that was upsetting her is unclear.

Ibn Hisham says that Muhammad treated Safiya in a markedly different manner from how he had reacted to the

118 Ibn Ishaq, *The Life of Muhammad: A Translation of Ibn Ishaq's Sirat Rasul Allah*, trans. A. Guillaume (Oxford: Oxford University Press, 1955), 514.

119 Ibid., 515.

120 Ibid.

121 Ibid.

122 Muhammad ibn Umar al-Waqidi, *The Life of Muhammad: Al-Waqidi's Kitab al-Maghazi*, ed. Rizwi Faizer, trans. Rizwi Faizer, Amal Ismail and AbdulKader Tayob, (London: Routledge, 2011), 331.

123 Ibid.

124 Ibid.

"she-devil": "He gave orders that Safiya was to be put behind him and threw his mantle over her, so that the Muslims knew that he had chosen her for himself."[125] He adds that Safiya had foreseen the Muslim destruction of the Khaybar oasis in a dream, in the course of which she saw the moon drop her lap. Ibn Hisham claims that Safiya's husband, Kinana ibn al-Rabi, heard about this and thought that it meant that Safiya was taken with the prophet of Islam: "This simply means that you covet the king of the Hijaz, Muhammad."[126] In a rage, Kinana supposedly "gave her such a blow in the face that he blacked her eye. When she was brought to the apostle the mark was still there, and when he asked the cause of it she told him this story."[127]

Having seen Safiya, Muhammad informed Dihya that he was taking her for himself, and gave him the opportunity to pick another woman: "Take any slave girl other than her from the captives."[128] Muhammad's ninth-century biographer Ibn Hisham states: "The apostle took captives from them among whom was Safiya d. Huyayy b. Akhtab who had been the wife of Kinana b. al-Rabi b. Abu'l-Huqayq, and two cousins of hers. The apostle chose Safiya for himself. Dihya b. Khalifa al-Kalb had asked the apostle for Safiya, and when he chose her for himself he gave him her two cousins. The women of Khaybar were distributed among the Muslims."[129] Ibn Hisham states that Muhammad prohibited "carnal intercourse with pregnant

---

[125] Ibn Ishaq, 511.
[126] Ibid.
[127] Ibid.
[128] Sahih Bukhari, vol. 1, bk. 8, no. 371.
[129] Ibn Ishaq.

women who were captured," but there was no prohibition regarding captive women who were not pregnant.[130]

As the victorious Muslims left Khaybar, Muhammad was impatient to experience the delights of his latest acquisition. Ibn Hisham says that he married Safiya "in Khaybar or on the way" out of the region.[131] Nothing is said about what Safiya might have been thinking and feeling after Muhammad had murdered her father and husband and then took her for his own. She may have not had time for such considerations, for she was being prepared to be Muhammad's bride: she was duly "beautified and combed, and got in a fit state for the apostle by Umm Sulaym d. Milhan mother of Anas b. Malik."[132]

Muhammad then "passed the night with her in a tent of his," before the caravan had even left the area that was littered with the corpses of the Jews of Khaybar. Muhammad and Safiya spent the night under heavy guard, but this was not so much because of lingering pockets of resistance among the vanquished, but because some of the Muslims were suspicious of Safiya. One of the Islamic prophet's trusted companions "passed the night girt with his sword, guarding the apostle and going round the tent until in the morning the apostle saw him there and asked him what he meant by his action. He replied, 'I was afraid for you with this woman for you have killed her father, her husband, and her people, and till recently she was in unbelief, so I was afraid for you on her account.'"[133] Moved, Muhammad called out to Allah: "O God, preserve Abu Ayyub, as he spent the night preserving me."[134]

---

130 Ibid., 512.
131 Ibid.
132 Ibid., 517.
133 Ibid.
134 Ibid.

According to al-Waqidi, Muhammad's other wives were unkind to Safiya: "I suffered his wives who looked down on me saying, 'O daughter of a Jew.' But I used to see the Messenger of God, and he was gracious and generous to me. One day when he visited me I was crying. He said, 'What is the matter with you?' I said, 'Your wives look down on me and say, "O daughter of a Jew."'" Safiya added: "I saw that the Messenger of God was angry. He said, 'When they speak to you or dismiss you, say, "My father is Aaron and my uncle, Moses."'"[135]

Safiya, however, was in that sense a special case. Most of the captured women were distributed among the Muslim warriors, used, and discarded.

QUR'AN-QUOTING RAPISTS

Modern-day Muslim rapists have on occasion made it clear that they were well aware of Islam's approval of such behavior. In India, a Muslim kidnapped and raped a fourteen-year-old Hindu girl, and forced her to read the Qur'an and Islamic prayers.[136] In Pakistan, a pious Christian woman recounted that her rapist was also religious: "He threw me on the bed and started to rape me. He demanded I marry him and convert to

---

135 Al-Waqidi, 332.

136 Swati Goel Sharma, "Forced To Read Namaz And Quran, Reveals Minor Hindu Girl Abducted By Married Muslim Man From Bengal," *Swarajya*, November 16, 2020, https://swarajyamag.com/politics/forced-to-read-namaz-and-quran-reveals-minor-hindu-girl-abducted-by-married-muslim-man-from-bengal. Accessed March 11, 2025.

Islam. I refused. I am not willing to deny Jesus and he said that if I would not agree he would kill me."[137]

In August 2013, *Paris Match* published a vivid recreation of a rape:

> We'll call her Elise. She walks over to her boyfriend's apartment. She is small, sweet, sociable. A young saleswoman who is about to go on vacation with her lover. In five short minutes, she has to meet him. In the distance, "a big and wide shadow" in a dark alley. Elise shivers. She's a brave girl, but this figure worries her. She accelerates, turns around several times. The specter is gone. Elise, relieved, sets off on rue Jacqueline-Auriol. This is where the man grabs her from behind. A hand grabs the girl's face. The other, "a greasy, clammy grip," covers her mouth. Massive, fierce, he grabs her by the hair, whispers in her ear the order to be silent, especially not to look at him. And throws her to the ground, between two vehicles, on the rough and cold concrete. He rips her pants off, rapes her. Twice. Then, to humiliate her further, he insults her and threatens her with his knife, quoting the Koran.[138]

---

137 John Pontifex, "PAKISTAN: Raped, punched, kicked and hit with a pistol – but undaunted," Aid to the Church in Need, June 7, 2021, https://acnuk.org/news/pakistan-raped-punched-kicked-and-hit-with-a-pistol-but-undaunted/. Accessed March 11, 2025.

138 Emilie Blachere, "Le 'monstre' de Colombes - Double aggression," *Paris Match*, August 22, 2013, https://www.parismatch.com/actu/faits-divers/le-monstre-de-colombes-double-agression-56925. Accessed March 11, 2025.

A survivor of a Muslim rape gang in the UK likewise recalled: "My main perpetrator quoted scriptures from the Quran to me as he beat me."[139] In a Paris suburb in 2019, two sixteen-year-old Muslim migrants raped a young girl while capturing her ordeal on video; they shared the video on social media. According to the Italian newspaper *Il Giornale*, "during the sexual violence, the attackers repeatedly cited Allah, the Qur'an and Mecca."[140] One of the rapists warned the victim: "I swear on the Qur'an of Mecca, shout and you will see the blows I give you."[141] The rapists later told the girl to follow them, or else: "In the name of Allah, I swear to you on the Qur'an of Mecca: it is better if you reflect in your mind and that you come with us, because a team is about to arrive…we are the best, those who are coming will make you regret…on my mother I swear to you: you will not come out alive. You will die."[142] Then they began to beat her.

A twenty-two-year-old Australian woman, Carmen Greentree, suffered a hauntingly similar ordeal. A professional surfer, she decided in May 2004 to travel to the Himalayas to study under the Dalai Lama. In New Delhi, however, she was abducted and taken to a houseboat, where she was raped multiple times, as well as beaten when she attempted to leave. "I didn't think I

---

139 Ella Hill, "As a Rotherham grooming gang survivor, I want people to know about the religious extremism which inspired my abusers," *Independent*, March 18, 2018, https://www.the-independent.com/voices/rotherham-grooming-gang-sexual-abuse-muslim-islamist-racism-white-girls-religious-extremism-terrorism-a8261831.html. Accessed March 11, 2025.

140 Federico Giuliani, "La stuprano inneggiando Allah. Poi postano il video dell'abuso sui social," *Il Giornale*, December 26, 2019, https://www.ilgiornale.it/news/mondo/parigi-due-giovani-africani-stuprano-minorenne-inneggiando-1803868.html. Accessed March 11, 2025.

141 Ibid.

142 Ibid.

was ever getting off that boat," Greentree recalled. "I thought I would die there one way or another."[143]

Greentree said of her captor, Rafiq Ahmad Dundoo: "I lost track of how many times he raped me. I've blocked it out so much I don't remember most of [the assaults] anymore. I was completely broken, I wasn't even me anymore. I was existing as a shell."[144] They were not the only people on the boat; Dundoo's parents, two brothers, wife, and child were there as well. They were utterly indifferent to Greentree's plight; when she told Dundoo's father that she was being held there against her will and repeatedly raped, "he was very dismissive straight away. I think his brothers and father knew [he was abusing me] but they thought it was normal, they just considered women to be property."[145]

Dundoo forced Greentree to don the traditional dress of Kashmiri Muslim women, and ordered her to help with the cooking, cleaning, and other tasks. She was, in short, treated as a slave. Greentree also added this telling detail: "They bought me a rug and heavily encouraged me to pray five times a day and gave me a Koran with English translations to learn. I read it cover to cover twice just to pass the time."[146]

In a major study of the beliefs and practices of the Islamic State regarding the sexual enslavement of non-Muslim women and girls, *The New York Times* was unusually forthright about

143 Nic White, "EXCLUSIVE: Australian surfer kidnapped and raped every night for two months on a squalid houseboat in India reveals how she escaped when her captor made one simple mistake - and why she fears there are other victims out there," *Daily Mail Australia*, July 4, 2020, https://www.dailymail.co.uk/news/article-8473721/Pro-surfer-abducted-raped-two-months-houseboat-India.html. Accessed March 11, 2025.

144 Ibid.

145 Ibid.

146 Ibid.

how Islamic State rapists believed that what they were doing was entirely justified in Islamic law: "In the moments before he raped the 12-year-old girl, the Islamic State fighter took the time to explain that what he was about to do was not a sin. Because the preteen girl practiced a religion other than Islam, the Quran not only gave him the right to rape her — it condoned and encouraged it, he insisted."[147] As if that weren't bad enough, "he bound her hands and gagged her. Then he knelt beside the bed and prostrated himself in prayer before getting on top of her. When it was over, he knelt to pray again, bookending the rape with acts of religious devotion."[148]

The girl added: "He told me that according to Islam he is allowed to rape an unbeliever. He said that by raping me, he is drawing closer to God."[149]

The *Times* noted that the Islamic State had abducted thousands of non-Muslim women, particularly Yazidis, and made them into sex slaves. It explained that "the Islamic State has developed a detailed bureaucracy of sex slavery, including sales contracts notarized by the ISIS-run Islamic courts. And the practice has become an established recruiting tool to lure men from deeply conservative Muslim societies, where casual sex is taboo and dating is forbidden."[150]

This being *The New York Times*, the article insisted that all this was based on "a narrow and selective reading of the Quran," without bothering even to attempt to explain how any of the

---

147 Rukmini Callimachi, "ISIS Enshrines a Theology of Rape," *New York Times*, August 13, 2015, https://www.nytimes.com/2015/08/14/world/middleeast/isis-enshrines-a-theology-of-rape.html?_r=1. Accessed March 11, 2025.

148 Ibid.

149 Ibid.

150 Ibid.

Islamic State's practice violated any Qur'anic tenet, but it was remarkable enough that any of this was in the *Times* at all.[151]

The *Times* article also engaged in the moral equivalence that is so often a favored practice of those who are embarrassed to be in the position of having to discuss crimes done in the name of Islam and in accord with its teachings: "In much the same way as specific Bible passages were used centuries later to support the slave trade in the United States, the Islamic State cites specific verses or stories in the Quran or else in the Sunna, the traditions based on the sayings and deeds of the Prophet Muhammad, to justify their human trafficking, experts say. Scholars of Islamic theology disagree, however, on the proper interpretation of these verses, and on the divisive question of whether Islam actually sanctions slavery. Many argue that slavery figures in Islamic scripture in much the same way that it figures in the Bible — as a reflection of the period in antiquity in which the religion was born."[152]

The Islamic State was troubled by the prospect of disagreement from other Muslims, not because its jihadis were afraid that they might be wrong, but because they were sure that the Muslims who disagreed were not being true to Islam. One wrote in the Islamic State's online magazine: "What really alarmed me was that some of the Islamic State's supporters started denying the matter as if the soldiers of the Khilafah had committed a mistake or evil. I write this while the letters drip of pride. We have indeed raided and captured the kafirah women and drove them like sheep by the edge of the sword."[153] Kafirah meant unbelieving.

---

151 Ibid.

152 Ibid.

153 Ibid.

One fifteen-year-old victim accordingly stated: "Every time that he came to rape me, he would pray. He kept telling me this is ibadah," that is, worship.[154] "He said that raping me is his prayer to God. I said to him, 'What you're doing to me is wrong, and it will not bring you closer to God.' And he said, 'No, it's allowed. It's halal.'"[155] She said of her captors: "They laughed and jeered at us, saying 'You are our sabaya.' I didn't know what that word meant." It meant "captive of the right hand," or sex slave.

The Islamic State's online magazine, *Dabiq*, emphasized that the seizure and sale of the Yazidi women was all done in accord with Islamic law, with a fifth of the slaves given to the leadership of the group, in accord with the Qur'an's rules regarding the distribution of the spoils of war (8:41). The magazine said: "After capture, the Yazidi women and children were then divided according to the Shariah amongst the fighters of the Islamic State who participated in the Sinjar operations, after one fifth of the slaves were transferred to the Islamic State's authority to be divided."[156]

Some of the women were auctioned off; at the auction, "the captives were also forced to answer intimate questions, including reporting the exact date of their last menstrual cycle. They realized that the fighters were trying to determine whether they were pregnant, in keeping with a Shariah rule stating that a man cannot have intercourse with his slave if she is pregnant."[157]

None of the Islamic State jihadis were concerned about the well-being of the slaves. One Yazidi woman recalled that in

154 Ibid.
155 Ibid.
156 Ibid.
157 Ibid.

the household where she was forced to live, there was another sex slave who was only twelve years old. Her captor repeatedly raped the little girl, despite the fact that she was bleeding heavily. "He destroyed her body," the older woman recalled. "She was badly infected. The fighter kept coming and asking me, 'Why does she smell so bad?' And I said, 'She has an infection on the inside, you need to take care of her.' I said to him, 'She's just a little girl.' And he answered: 'No. She's not a little girl. She's a slave. And she knows exactly how to have sex. And having sex with her pleases God.'"[158]

158 Ibid.

CHAPTER SIX
A LONG HISTORY OF ABUSE

SLAVES AS SPOILS OF WAR

In the early 630s, Arab armies under the leadership of the renowned military commander Khalid ibn al-Walid swept into the territory of one of the great powers of the day, the Persian Empire, and met surprisingly little resistance. The Persians, exhausted militarily after decades of inconclusive warfare with the Roman Empire, had no strength to resist the Arab advance. Khalid had one of the Persian leaders, al-Judi ibn Rabiah, beheaded.

At one point, according to the tenth-century Muslim historian al-Tabari, "the Muslims rushed in upon the enemy, killing the troops and making captives of the children, whom they kept with those who were left over." Imitating Muhammad's claiming of Safiya after massacring the Jews at Khaybar (if that incident actually had any historical foundation), "Khalid purchased the daughter of al-Judi, who[se beauty] was extolled."[159]

In the middle of the seventh century, the Arabs began their conquest of North Africa. The peerless eighteenth-century English historian Edward Gibbon recounted that some areas the Arabs entered had a reputation that was greater than their reality:

> The remote position and venerable antiquity of Tingi, or Tangier, have been decorated by the Greek and Arabian fables; but the figurative expressions of the latter, that the walls were constructed of brass, and that the roofs were covered with gold and silver, may be interpreted as the emblems of strength and opulence.[160]

They were emblems only; there was no actual strength and opulence there. Some of the areas the Arab warriors invaded were little-known and quite poor:

> The province of Mauritania Tingitana, which assumed the name of the capital, had been imperfectly discovered and settled by the Romans; the five colonies were confined to a narrow pale, and the more southern parts were seldom explored except by the agents of luxury, who searched the forests for ivory and

---

[159] Al-Tabari, *The History of al-Tabari*, vol. 11, *The Challenge to the Empires*, trans. Khalid Yahya Blankinship (Albany, New York: State University of New York Press, 1993), 59–60.

[160] Edward Gibbon, *The History of the Decline and Fall of the Roman Empire* (London: A. Strahan and T. Cadell, 1782), vol. 5, ch. 51, part 8, 256.

> the citron-wood, and the shores of the ocean for the purple shell-fish. The fearless Akbah [Uqba ibn Nafi] plunged into the heart of the country, traversed the wilderness in which his successors erected the splendid capitals of Fez and Morocco, and at length penetrated to the verge of the Atlantic and the great desert.[161]

While the Arabs managed to defeat warriors of vastly more advanced civilizations than their own, including Romans and Persians, they found in this remote area of northwest Africa only warriors who made them look as if they were the ones who were technologically and militarily advanced:

> The river Sus descends from the western sides of Mount Atlas, fertilizes, like the Nile, the adjacent soil, and falls into the sea at a moderate distance from the Canary, or Fortunate, islands. Its banks were inhabited by the last of the Moors, a race of savages, without laws or discipline or religion: they were astonished by the strange and irresistible terrors of the Oriental arms; and as they possessed neither gold nor silver, the richest spoil was the beauty of the female captives, some of whom were afterwards sold for a thousand pieces of gold.[162]

In 711, a warrior named Tariq ibn Ziyad crossed the Strait of Gibraltar and initiated the Arab conquest of Spain. A ninth-century Arab chronicler, Ibn Abd al-Hakam, notes that

161 Ibid.
162 Ibid.

Tariq set out on this venture "with his female slave of the name Umm Hakim."[163]

THE CONQUEST OF SINDH

Also in 711, less than a century after the traditionally accepted date of the death of Muhammad the prophet, the Umayyad caliphate was sent a military leader, Muhammad ibn Qasim, eastward to conquer Sindh. It was the first jihadist foray into the Indian subcontinent.

The governor of Iraq, Hajjaj ibn Yusuf, told Muhammad ibn Qasim to "kill anyone belonging to the combatants [*ahl-i harb*]; arrest their sons and daughters for hostages and imprison them."[164] Ibn Qasim this proceeded with great ruthlessness, murdering massive numbers of people and destroying numerous Hindu temples.

At Daybul, immediately after the Muslims defeated a Hindu force, they embarked upon a three-day-long massacre of Hindus, and enslaved all the young women they could apprehend.[165] The triumphant commander sent two of these enslaved women as a gift to the caliph al-Walid in Damascus, with a goodly share of the captured treasure. The women were carefully chosen, as they were royalty, daughters of Sindh's King Dahir. This would allow al-Walid to glory in the victory,

163 Ibn Abd al-Hakam, *Dhikr Fath Al-Andalus* (*History of the Conquest of Spain*), trans. John Harris Jones (London: Williams & Norgate, 1858), 18.

164 Derryl N. MacLean, *Religion and Society in Arab Sind* (Leiden: Brill, 1989), 37.

165 Arun Shourie, Harsh Narain, Jay Dubashi, Ram Swarup, and Sita Ram Goel, *Hindu Temples: What Happened to Them*, vol. 1, *A Preliminary Survey* (New Delhi: Voice of India, 1990), 264.

superiority and supremacy of Islam as he perpetuated their humiliation.

When the captive pair arrived, however, al-Walid found one of them, whose name was Janaki, to be particularly captivating. He quickly took her to bed, only for her to tell him, to his shock, horror, and rage, that Muhammad ibn Qasim had already had sexual relations with her. This gave the proud Walid the impression that Muhammad was deliberately insulting him, and that he had sent Janaki to him after having sex with her himself as a gesture of contempt. He ordered that ibn Qasim, regardless of his tremendous military success in Sindh, be sewn into a sack and delivered to him. By the time the general arrived, he had died.

This horrified the woman who had inadvertently sparked it all, the slave Janaki. She said: "The king has committed a very grievous mistake, for he ought not, on account of two slave girls, to have destroyed a person who had taken captive a hundred thousand modest women like us and who instead of temples had erected mosques, pulpits and minarets."[166] Those hundred thousand modest women suffered the same fate that innumerable women throughout the ages would suffer, up to and including the British girls whom the Muslim rape gangs, many of whom were comprised of Muslims from Sindh, would victimize.

SELLING NUNS INTO SEX SLAVERY

Not even nuns were spared. In the middle of the ninth century, the Roman Emperor Theophilos raided the territory of the Abbasid caliphate. According to the twelfth-century chronicler

166 Ibid., 207.

Michael the Syrian, when the caliph al-Mu'tasim heard about this, "he was infuriated and descended into Byzantine territory with two of his armies."[167] He seized Ancyra (the modern Turkish city of Ankara) and continued to Amorium, which Michael calls "a large and populous city, secure and lovely, unequalled in the country."[168] Al-Mu'tasim began a siege, which lasted for twelve days. Then the city "was captured through the betrayal of one of its princes, named George (Cho'r'ch'an). In that city were monasteries filled with thousands of virgins whom [al-Mu'tasim] gave to his servants."[169]

CRUELTY

The slaves were property. They had no rights. In the middle of the tenth century, the caliph of Córdoba, Abd al-Rahman III, had no hesitation about illustrating this. A Muslim historian of the eleventh century, Ibn Hayyan, recounted:

> I must say that I have heard from ulama, generationally close to that dynasty [the Umayyads], about the brutality of an-Nasir li-din [that is, "the defender of the faith of Allah," Abd al-Rahman III] towards the women that were under his protection and discretion, similar to what he showed in public toward men, according to the word of the principal ones among his most intimate servants—eunuchs who

[167] Michael the Syrian, *The Chronicle of Michael the Great, Patriarch of the Syrians*, trans. Robert Bedrosian (Sources of the Armenian Tradition, 2013), 154.

[168] Ibid.

[169] Ibid.

> lived in his house and witnessed his personal life: a female slave who was one of his most highly regarded favorites, but whose haughty personality did not bend easily to his vanity, having remained with him alone in one of his leisure days to drink in the garden of az-Zahra [a palace that Abd al-Rahman III had built for his favorite sexual slave that contained three hundred baths, four hundred horses, fifteen thousand eunuchs and servants, and a harem of 6,300 women], sitting by his side until drinking had an effect on him, and he threw himself upon her face to kiss and bite her, and she got disgusted by this and turned her face away, raining on his parade; this so provoked his anger that he ordered the eunuchs to seize her and put a candle to her face, burning and destroying her beauty…until they destroyed her face, burning her badly and finishing with her—one of his worst actions.[170]

Abd al-Rahman also made advances upon a thirteen-year-old Christian boy who was being held hostage. When the boy rejected him, the enraged caliph ordered him to be tortured and beheaded.[171]

Abd al-Rahman once even ordered his court executioner to murder one of his sex slaves, and rewarded him for doing so. Ibn Hayyim tells the story:

---

170 Darío Fernández-Morera, *The Myth of the Andalusian Paradise* (Wilmington, Delaware: ISI Books, 2016), 130–31.

171 Ibid.

His executioner, Abu Imran [Yahya], whom he always had at the ready with his "instruments," said that one night he called him to his room in the palace of an-Naura, where Yahya had slept with his sword and leather floor mat. [Yahya] then entered the room where [Abd al-Rahman III] was drinking and found him squatting, like a lion sitting on his paws, in the company of a girl, beautiful like an onyx, who was being held by his eunuchs in a corner of the room, who was asking for mercy, while he answered her in the grossest manner. He then told [Yahya] "Take that whore, Abu Imran, and cut her neck." [Yahya] said, "I procrastinated, asking him again, as was my custom, but he told me, "Cut it, so may *Allah* cut your hand, or if not, put down your own [neck]." And a servant brought her close to me, gathering up her braids, so that with one blow I made her head fly; but the strike of the blade made an abnormal noise, although I had not seen it hit anything else [but the neck].

Afterwards they took away the body of the girl, I cleaned my sword on my leather mat, I rolled up the mat, and I left; but when I entered my own room and I unfolded the mat, there appeared in it pearls big and shiny, mixed with jacinths and topazes that shone like red-hot coals, all of which I gathered in my hands and I hurried to take it to an-Nasir; he rejected it immediately and told me, "We knew they were

> there, but we wanted to give them to you as a gift; take it and may Allah bless it to you." And with it I bought this house.[172]

It wasn't just Abd al-Rahman. Spain under the Umayyads prospered in part because of its trading in slaves. Muslims could buy non-Muslim girls even when the girls were no more than eleven years old, and force them into sex slavery.[173] Blonde-haired girls were so sought after that some slavers would use makeup to make other slaves appear to be light-skinned. Then they would bring in substantial amounts of money.[174] In the twelfth century, an observer described the scene at a slave auction:

> The merchant tells the slave girls to act in a coquettish manner with the old men and with the timid men among the potential buyers to make them crazy with desire. The merchant paints red the tips of the fingers of a white slave; he paints in gold those of a black slave; and he dresses them all in transparent clothes, the white female slaves in pink and the black ones in yellow and red.[175]

In the fourteenth century, the Ottoman Sultan Orkhan concluded a dynastic marriage with the daughter of the Roman emperor, and immediately used it as to affect a series of humiliations of the Christians of the empire, which by then had been

---

172 Ibid., 131–32.
173 Ibid., 158.
174 Ibid., 159.
175 Ibid.

drastically weakened and reduced to little more than the city of Constantinople and some territories in Greece. Orkhan demanded, and received, permission to auction off slaves in Constantinople, despite the fact that the once-great city was the capital of the Christian empire and the slaves were themselves Christians. Gibbon described the scene: "A naked crowd of Christians of both sexes and every age, of priests and monks, of matrons and virgins, was exposed in the public market; the whip was frequently used to quicken the charity of redemption; and the indigent Greeks deplored the fate of their brethren, who were led away to the worst evils of temporal and spiritual bondage."[176]

A similar scene unfolded in India around the same time, as the Sultan of Delhi, Firuz Shah Tughlaq, in 1360 targeted the Hindu temple of Jagannath at Puri. The contemporary historian Ziauddin Barani recounted that after Firuz Shah Tughlaq had destroyed the shrine, he and his forces advanced to an island that was close by, for on it, "nearly 100,000 men of Jajnagar had taken refuge with their women, children, kinsmen and relations."[177] The Muslims then made the island "a basin of blood by the massacre of the unbelievers.... Women with babies and pregnant ladies were haltered, manacled, fettered and enchained, and pressed as slaves into service at the house of every soldier."[178]

In 1818, a British navy captain, G. F. Lyon, made his way to Tripoli. Once there, he saw that one Muslim warrior "waged

---

176 Gibbon, *The History of the Decline and Fall of the Roman Empire*, vol. 2, ch. 64, part 48, https://www.ccel.org/g/gibbon/decline/volume2/chap64.htm. Accessed March 16, 2025.

177 Sita Ram Goel, *The Story of Islamic Imperialism in India* (New Delhi: Voice of India, 1982), 51.

178 Ibid.

war on all his defenceless neighbours and annually carried off 4000 or 5000 slaves. From one of these slave hunts into Kanem he had just returned to Tripoli, with a numerous body of captives and many camels, and was, in consequence, in the highest favour with the Bashaw," the sultan of Tripoli, who was at that time Yusuf Karamanli.[179] Lyon said that the sultan had "about fifty young women, all black and very comely…guarded by five eunuchs, who keep up their authority by occasionally beating them."[180]

Throughout the centuries, and wherever the warriors of jihad went, it was much the same story. It was, indeed, a constant throughout Islamic history: When the warriors of jihad conquered a territory, they would capture women as part of the spoils of war. Those women would be made into sex slaves, in accord with the Qur'an's words and the example of Muhammad. This continues into modern times with the actions of Boko Haram, the Islamic State, Hamas, and others. This should surprise no one, as there has been no reformation or large-scale reevaluation in the Islamic world of the texts used to justify such behavior. In taking sex slaves, modern-day jihadis are not twisting, hijacking, or misunderstanding Islam; they are acting upon its tenets in good faith, without the slightest care about the rights of the women and girls they are using and destroying. If Allah doesn't care for them, why should they?

---

179 Ronald Segal, *Islam's Black Slaves: The Other Black Diaspora* (New York: Farrar, Straus and Giroux, 2001), 132.

180 Ibid., 133.

CHAPTER SEVEN

SO MANY HORROR STORIES

"HE DOES NOT TREAT THEM AS HUMAN BEINGS AT ALL"

It was a national self-immolation unparalleled in human history.

As British authorities stood by and watched, Muslim migrants, primarily from Pakistan, victimized young British girls on a truly staggering scale. For decades, clearly without fear of arrest or prosecution, these Muslim migrant gangs terrorized and raped tens of thousands of girls, often forcing them to engage in prostitution. The true number of victims may never be known, given the timidity, lassitude, and sympathy with the perpetrators that British authorities repeatedly displayed, but some have estimated that it could be as high as over a million British girls.[181]

There is no end to the horror stories, and many were widely reported, only to be received with indifference and inaction. The *Daily Mail* in December 2011 published the story of one seventeen-year-old girl, Laura Wilson, who was "groomed for sex by a string of British Pakistani men," and was eventually "stabbed and thrown into a canal to die after she brought 'shame' on an Asian family."[182] "Asian" is the British media's favored euphemism for Pakistani Muslim.

An eighteen-year-old Muslim, Ashtiaq Asghar, "repeatedly knifed" Wilson "then pushed her into the water, using the point of the knife to force her head below the surface as she fought to stay alive."[183] She was not successful.

Asghar murdered her because he was "furious after the young mother revealed details of their sexual relationship to his Muslim family and was on 'a mission to kill.'"[184] Asghar explained his perspective and motivations in a series of texts to his friend Ishaq Hussain, who had also had sexual relations with Laura Wilson. Asghar likely knew that Hussain would be sympathetic because, in the words of Lord Justice Davis when he tried Asghar for the murder of Laura Wilson, Hussain "seems

---

181 Mirror, "UK police hunt for child sex abuse gangs who could have assaulted over one million children," *The Standard*, February 6, 2015, https://www.standardmedia.co.ke/article/2000150764/uk-police-hunt-for-child-sex-abuse-gangs-who-could-have-assaulted-over-one-million-children. Accessed February 1, 2025.

182 Paul Sims, "Groomed for sex then thrown into a canal and killed: Life for man who murdered white girl for 'shaming' Asian family," *Daily Mail*, December 22, 2011, https://www.dailymail.co.uk/news/article-2077205/Teenage-mother-stabbed-death-thrown-canal-bringing-shame-family.html. Accessed February 25, 2025.

183 Ibid.

184 Ibid.

to have regarded girls, white girls, simply as sexual targets. He does not treat them as human beings at all. You got into that mindset yourself."[185]

Davis framed the contempt Asghar and Hussain had for Laura Wilson in racial terms, but it had a religious component as well. The day before he murdered Laura Wilson, Asghar told Hussain: "I'm gonna send that kuffar (non-Muslim) bitch straight to Hell."[186] He also wrote to Hussain: "I need to do a mission," and added that he was "making some beans on toast," a euphemism for shedding blood from a comedy film about jihad terrorists.[187]

The *Daily Mail* notes that Laura Wilson "was a troubled teenager who was first identified as being at risk of sexual exploitation by British Pakistani men when she was 12," in 2007.[188] "She had developed several links with Asian men in her home town of Rotherham, South Yorkshire."[189] Yet even though all this was known and "workers at a child sexual exploitation project later sent a report to social services," still "no action was taken to remove her from what became a continuing spiral of sexual abuse."

Shortly before Asghar murdered her on October 12, 2011, "she 'shamed' Asghar and Mr Hussain by informing their families of her relationship with both men." In Islamic culture, which is largely based on concepts of honor and shame, to bring shame upon someone is a monstruous crime. Wilson

---

185 Ibid.
186 Ibid.
187 Ibid.
188 Ibid.
189 Ibid.

committed it by telling Ashtiaq Asghar's mother that she was in love with her son and "wanted to have babies" with him.[190]

Laura Wilson was no doubt completely unaware of the nature of a shame/honor culture and of her status within it as a non-Muslim girl, and so was likely dismayed when Asghar's mother became enraged at her profession of love for Ashtiaq; she "attempted to hit Miss Wilson with a shoe, branding her 'a dirty white bitch' who should 'keep your legs closed.'"[191]

It was at this point, according to prosecutor Nicholas Campbell QC, that Asghar and Hussain concluded that Laura Wilson was "a loose cannon and they had to get rid of her."[192] They did so, and the price they had to pay could turn out not to be very steep at all. Ishaq Hussain was found not guilty of murdering Laura Wilson.[193] Ashtiaq Asghar was found guilty; however, the *Sheffield Star* reported on April 19, 2024, that Asghar "was ordered to serve a minimum of 17-and-a-half years behind bars when he was sentenced in December 2011, meaning he could be eligible for parole in mid 2028. However he could be released earlier if the time spent on remand waiting for his case to reach court is taken into account."[194]

Laura Wilson's mother, Maggie Wilson, said: "He'll be in his 30s when he's released – still young enough to have a life. He

---

190 Ibid.

191 Ibid.

192 Ibid.

193 "Man cleared of murdering Laura Wilson in Rotherham," BBC, December 1, 2011, https://www.bbc.com/news/uk-england-south-yorkshire-15992405. Accessed February 25, 2025.

194 Claire Lewis, "Murderer who stabbed teenage girl to death in Rotherham honour killing could be free in four years," *Sheffield Star*, April 19, 2024, https://www.msn.com/en-gb/news/world/murderer-who-stabbed-teenage-girl-to-death-in-rotherham-honour-killing-could-be-free-in-four-years/ar-AA1nhAYb. Accessed February 25, 2025.

could have children if he wanted – how is that fair?"[195] It wasn't fair at all. Nothing was fair about this entire phenomenon.

"I KILLED A GIRL…I WAS JUST ANGRY"

One of the most tragic victims of Muslim rape gang activity in Britain was fourteen-year-old Charlene Downes. According to the National Pulse, she disappeared in 2003 "after falling victim to Muslim groomers in the seaside resort of Blackpool."[196] It was not until four years later, in May 2007, that the trial began of Iyad Albattikhi, who faced accusations of killing Charlene, and his friend Mohammed Raveshi, who was charged with aiding Albattikhi by making efforts to ensure that no one would ever discover Charlene's body. Albattikhi and Raveshi hoped to convince anyone who came snooping around that Charlene had simply run away, and that they had no involvement or interest in her whereabouts.

This claim didn't fly. A 2009 report in the *Independent* stated that "during the trial, the jury was played taped conversations in which Mr Albattikhi, who ran a takeaway restaurant in the seaside town, joked that he killed the girl, that she was 'chopped up' and her body had 'gone in the kebabs'. In another excerpt, he said: 'I killed her, I killed a girl … I was just angry.'

---

195 Ibid.

196 Jack Montgomery, "Britons Mark 20 Years Since Grooming Gang Victim Charlene Downes 'Disappeared,'" National Pulse, November 1, 2023, https://thenationalpulse.com/2023/11/01/britons-mark-20-years-since-grooming-gang-victim-charlene-downes-disappeared/. Accessed February 23, 2025.

His co-accused was heard on the tapes saying: 'There is nothing left of her. She was here, she died, there really is nothing.'"[197]

Despite all this, "the jury failed to reach a verdict. A retrial was set for April 2008. However, while preparing for the second trial, senior police officers raised issues with the surveillance evidence, much of which had been obtained by a police informant, David Cassidy, who had worn a wire-tap device when speaking to Mr Albattikhi and Mr Raveshi."[198] It was the big break Albattikhi and Raveshi had been hoping for: "the second trial was abandoned when the CPS offered no evidence against the men. Mr Albattikhi and Mr Raveshi, who say they have never met Charlene, were released."[199]

Justice was served, supposedly, but some Britons refused to forget poor Charlene. The National Pulse said that "for some, such as National Pulse contributor 'Raw Egg Nationalist', the anniversary of Charlene's officially unsolved disappearance is marked as National Grooming Gang Day of Remembrance, when the suffering of as many as a million of mostly white, working-class victims of mostly Muslim groomers of South Asian heritage is commemorated – although the state does not observe the occasion."[200]

Of course the state does not observe the occasion. The state was invested, and had been for years, in denying that there was any problem at all, and hoping that it would all just eventually blow over. Charlene Downes didn't matter a whit to anyone in

---

[197] Mark Hughes, "Police errors mean girl's killer may never be found," *Independent*, October 16, 2009, https://www.independent.co.uk/news/uk/crime/police-errors-mean-girl-s-killer-may-never-be-found-1803647.html. Accessed February 23, 2025.

[198] Ibid.

[199] Ibid.

[200] Montgomery, "Britons Mark 20 Years."

the British government. What mattered was that the perpetually aggrieved and hypersensitive, as well as rapidly growing, Muslim community in Britain kept voting for the right people. The victims would have to fend for themselves.

The mind-boggling scale of these crimes leads to the inevitable question, which British officials to this day are doing all they can to avoid: How could Britain's law enforcement and judicial establishment have let this happen?

The answer is nearly as shocking and appalling as the crimes themselves. In the face of the wholesale victimization of a generation of their nation's young girls, British officials thought not of justice, much less of the future of their nation, but rather of the effect that acting decisively against this phenomenon could have on their careers. They were so afraid of being labeled "racist" or "Islamophobic," fears that leftists skillfully stoked for their own reasons and purposes, that they for the most part did nothing as the rape gangs ran wild. Even worse, on some occasions British authorities actually aided the gangs and punished their victims.

Journalist Dominic Green recounted, for example, that "one night in Oldham in 2006, for example, a 12-year-old girl named 'Sophie' entered a police station and reported that she had just been molested in a graveyard by a man named 'Ali.' A desk officer told her to come back with an adult when she was sober. Two men accosted her in the police station. Joined by a third, they raped her in their car. When they dumped her on the street, she asked a man named Sarwar Ali for directions. He took her to his home, raped her, and gave her money for bus fare home. A man named Shakil Chowdhury pulled up in his car and offered to take her home. He abducted her and took her to a house where he and four other men repeatedly raped her."[201]

"Sophie" had gone to the police station looking for relief, only to encounter others who were eager to victimize her. Her story epitomized the situation of modern Britain, in which the truth-tellers were demonized and vilified, the problem swept under the rug, and the stage set for many, many more British girls to be victimized.

NOT A SEX CRIME

When Azhar Ali Mehmood murdered Lucy Lowe in Telford, Shropshire, on August 5, 2000, she was sixteen years old and the mother of his child. She was also pregnant with his second child. Mehmood killed Lucy by setting fire to her home; also killed in the fire Mehmood set was Lucy's sister Sarah, who was one year older than she was and partially disabled, and the girls' mother, Eileen Linda Lowe. The girls' father, George Lowe, was also in the house, but managed to escape death by climbing out a bedroom window; he tried to save his family, but was unable to do so.

Lucy Lowe met Azhar Ali Mehmood when she was twelve years old, and not legally capable of consenting to sexual intercourse. Nevertheless, despite impregnating her twice, he was not charged with any sex crimes. He did get three murder charges and one charge of attempted murder, and was sentenced to life in prison, but officially, his manipulation and rape of a twelve-year-old was beneath the notice of the British legal system.

---

[201] Dominic Green, "The Biggest Peacetime Crime—and Cover-up—in British History," The Free Press, January 5, 2025, https://www.thefp.com/p/muslim-grooming-gangs-cover-up-keir-starmer-elon-musk. Accessed March 13, 2025.

Years later, in 2018, the daughter of Azhar Ali Mehmood and Lucy Lowe, Tasnim Lowe, said that her father had never expressed any sorrow for what he had done, and wondered why he hadn't been charged with sexually abusing her mother as well as killing her: "I would like to see that my dad shows remorse and that we can set up an investigation into why he was never charged with sex crimes."[202] Lowe asserted that British officials should have "taken charge" and stopped Mehmood from victimizing her mother: "They should have been like, 'This is wrong. This is illegal, we are going to do something about it.'"[203]

George Lowe also observed in 2018 that "the social services did nothing, schools did nothing and police did nothing, in a way. I had a word with her, but you know, you couldn't talk to her. She wasn't going to school for a start. They should have done something then. I can't understand it."[204]

They should have, but they did not. The BBC reported in September 2022, as Azhar Ali Mehmood was denied parole for a second time: "A recent inquiry into child sex abuse in Telford, which referenced the case, found crimes were ignored for generations, leading to more than 1,000 girls being abused. Agencies blamed children for the abuse they suffered, not the perpetrators, and exploitation was not investigated because of 'nervousness about race', its chairman Tom Crowther KC concluded."[205]

That nervousness about race was felt far beyond Telford.

---

202 "Lucy Lowe: Telford victim's daughter 'wants answers,'" BBC, March 20, 2018, https://www.bbc.com/news/uk-england-shropshire-43471241. Accessed March 13, 2025.

203 Ibid.

204 Ibid.

205 "Telford taxi driver who murdered family in fire refused parole again," BBC, September 17, 2022, https://www.bbc.com/news/uk-england-shropshire-62939177. Accessed March 13, 2025.

CHAPTER EIGHT

THE REAL PROBLEM

OFFICIAL INACTION—AND WORSE

As horrific and extensive as it was, there were innumerable indications that British authorities simply did not wish to deal with this problem, much less protect the victims of the rape gangs. Jayne Senior, an activist in the British city of Rotherham, which has become notorious for its Muslim rape gang activity, said: "There was physical, mental torture, trafficking and horrendous, horrendous abuse."[206] At the beginning, she said, "it tended to be predominantly girls 15 to 16, upwards. By 2012, what we saw is the majority of referrals were from about age 12."[207]

Senior went to the police and provided them with all the necessary information: "We'd share telephone numbers,

[206] James Pheby, "'Life's ruined' in U.K. town broken by grooming gangs," *The Japan Times,* February 4, 2025, https://www.japantimes.co.jp/news/2025/02/04/world/crime-legal/uk-town-grooming-gangs/. Accessed March 16, 2025.

[207] Ibid.

registration numbers, descriptions, names, dates of birth of those that we believed were harming, raping, trafficking our children."[208] Yet she got "very little response. We could have done so much more."[209]

For seven years, an eighteen-member Muslim rape gang in the English town of Walsall repeatedly raped a young girl, beginning when she was all of ten years old and continuing until she was seventeen. "It was pretty much wherever they saw me," she recounted later. "I could just be walking to the shop. They never cared if any children were watching, they never cared about stuff like that. As soon as one had finished the next was waiting, it was like a queue. They told me they would tell my family if I told anyone. Now looking back I don't believe they would have done that, but I was a child and I was so worried they would tell my family and I would get the blame."[210]

Eventually, however, when she was eighteen, she reported what had happened to the West Midlands Police, and gave them the names of fifteen of those who had victimized her for so long. Nine men were arrested, but the police later dropped the inquiry into this woman's claims altogether. In 2018, however, the victim read about some of the Muslim rape gang scandals that were beginning to get some coverage around the country, and asked that her case be reopened. The police initially refused, but finally agreed to do so under pressure; once their new investigation had officially begun, however, they dragged their feet and did little to pursue it. "In 19 months," according

---

208 Ibid.

209 Ibid.

210 Jeannette Oldham, "Police 'failed Walsall grooming gang victim after losing 30hrs of interview tapes,'" *Birmingham Mail*, February 7, 2021, https://www.birminghammail.co.uk/black-country/police-failed-walsall-grooming-gang-19777364. Accessed February 26, 2025.

to the *Birmingham Mail*, "the force have only recently interviewed two suspects in voluntary interviews."[211]

Even worse, after six months of desultory and unproductive investigation, "the force had seemingly LOST 30 hours of interview footage originally recorded in 2013, which contained details of her allegations."[212] The rape gang victim detailed how the police spent more time passing the buck than pursuing leads: "In 2013 the allegations I made about men and boys in Walsall were passed by Nottinghamshire Police to Walsall Police, Walsall then passed it to Wolverhampton, for whatever reason. I was never living in Wolverhampton, there was never any offending in Wolverhampton, so we don't know why any of the police documents went there. Then the case was sent to West Bromwich police which is where it is now at. Police dropped the case in 2015, didn't agree to reopen it in 2018 but then finally did so in June 2019."[213] Thinking about "every other investigation that had gone on and all the **** coming out about all the disgusting Asian men that were doing everything to these girls," the victim concluded with remarkable understatement, "I thought to myself, 'I know my investigation wasn't investigated properly.'"[214]

That was undisputable. But why were authorities so reluctant to apprehend the perpetrators of what were very public crimes, and to bring justice to the victims? That "nervousness about race" that had been noted in Telford went a very long way. In January 2020, a British police detective confirmed what everyone knew: As *The Telegraph* reported, "An Asian

---

211 Ibid.
212 Ibid.
213 Ibid.
214 Ibid.

grooming gang was free to roam the streets and abuse young girls because police officers were told to 'find other ethnicities' to investigate."[215]

Australia's *Catholic Weekly* reported in February 2025 that "one victim told the BBC in 2024 that as her abuse happened in early 2000s, she was 'let down' by police—an allegation to which the police responded with an apology and 'profound regret' for 'poor service.' The victim told the BBC that she was raped more than 100 times starting at age 12."[216]

The police's apology did not erase what had been done to the victim because both she and her abusers were of the wrong ethnicity to warrant British police attention in this age of diversity and multiculturalism.

THE CRIMES WERE NOT DONE IN SECRET

This craven betrayal was publicly known for years, and yet either the British people as a whole were ignorant about what happened, or powerless to do anything to dislodge the political establishment that had committed so heinous a crime. As far back as January 2011, *The Times* of London observed "a culture of silence that has facilitated the sexual exploitation of

215 Gabriella Swerling, "Asian grooming gang free to roam streets because officers were told to 'find other ethnicities' to investigate, detective claims," *Telegraph*, January 14, 2020, https://www.telegraph.co.uk/news/2020/01/14/police-officers-knowingly-neglected-girls-exploited-grooming/. Accessed March 14, 2025.

216 Jonathan Luxmoore, "British victim advocates demand courage, not fear of being labelled racist," *Catholic Weekly*, February 3, 2025, https://catholicweekly.com.au/british-victim-advocates-demand-courage-not-fear-of-being-labelled-racist/. Accessed March 16, 2025.

hundreds of young British girls by criminal pimping gangs."[217] These gangs consisted of "groups of older men," while their victims were generally "vulnerable girls aged 11 to 16."[218] *The Times* even went so far as to state "most of the victims are white and most of the convicted offenders are of Pakistani heritage, unlike other known models of child-sex offending in Britain, including child abuse initiated by online grooming, in which the vast majority of perpetrators are white."[219]

Three days after *The Times* article appeared, a Labour MP entered the controversy. Jack Straw, who served in the government of Prime Minister Tony Blair as home secretary from 1997 to 2001 and foreign secretary from 2001 to 2006, spoke with unusual forthrightness about what was going on, after first trying to insulate himself from charges of racism:

> Pakistanis, let's be clear, are not the only people who commit sexual offences, and overwhelmingly the sex offenders' wings of prisons are full of white sex offenders.
>
> But there is a specific problem which involves Pakistani heritage men… who target vulnerable young white girls.
>
> We need to get the Pakistani community to think much more clearly about why this is going on and to be more open about the problems that are leading to a number of Pakistani

---

217 "Revealed: conspiracy of silence on UK sex gangs," *The Times*, January 5, 2011, https://www.thetimes.com/article/revealed-conspiracy-of-silence-on-uk-sex-gangs-gpg5vqsqz9h. Accessed February 25, 2025.

218 Ibid.

219 Ibid.

heritage men thinking it is OK to target white girls in this way.

> These young men are in a western society, in any event, they act like any other young men, they're fizzing and popping with testosterone, they want some outlet for that, but Pakistani heritage girls are off-limits and they are expected to marry a Pakistani girl from Pakistan, typically.
>
> So they then seek other avenues and they see these young women, white girls who are vulnerable, some of them in care… who they think are easy meat.[220]

The response Straw received was all too predictable. Helen Brayley of University College London's Jill Dando Institute of Security and Crime Science attempted to divert the discussion into one about racism, implying that Straw was racist to have noticed that the crimes largely involved men of "Pakistani heritage": "When you jump in with thinking about race too quickly, you can miss a whole load of other things that are happening in other areas. So by racially stereotyping this early on without a national scoping project… we don't know what the situation is in other areas around the country… you might be leading to a self-fulfilling prophecy of if people are looking for Asian offenders, they will only find Asian offenders."[221]

---

220 "Jack Straw criticised for 'easy meat' comments on abuse," BBC, January 8, 2011, https://www.bbc.com/news/uk-12142177. Accessed February 25, 2025.

221 Ibid.

Another MP, Labour Party member Keith Vaz, who was chairman of the home affairs select committee, likewise criticized Straw for suggesting that the rape gang activity had something to do with the Pakistanis in Britain: "What I don't think we can do," Vaz advised, "is say that this is a cultural problem. One can accept the evidence which is put before us about patterns and networks but to go that step further I think is pretty dangerous. We can't ignore the facts of individual cases, but against what Jack says is what the judge said in the Derby case. [I] don't think you can stereotype an entire community." Vaz also complained that Straw was late to the party: "Why didn't Jack Straw say something about this (before)? He has represented Blackburn for 31 years, he's been the home secretary."[222] Why indeed?

The hints that Straw was being racist did what they had been intended to do: The focus of the public discussion was shifted, and nothing significant was done about the rape gangs. Late in 2012, Nick Lowles, a far-left campaigner against what he claimed was racism and fascism, hit upon the rape gang scandal as a chance to advance his claim that British society was under severe threat, not from the rape gangs, but from the supposed racists who opposed them.

THE THREAT OF RACISM

In the publication of his "anti-racism" organization, Hope Not Hate, Lowles wrote an article entitled "Grooming – an issue we cannot ignore," in which he tried to give the appearance of impartiality by writing: "Police and local authorities have been slow to protect these young girls. Leading figures in local

---

222 Ibid.

Muslim communities have often been too slow in speaking out on this issue, and in some cases simply dismissed it as Far Right propaganda. They have been joined in this by some on the left, who have been too quick to silence any discussion."[223]

As criticism of the inaction from British officials and the Muslim community on the rape gangs, this was tepid at best, but it was far too much for one of Lowles's fellow self-appointed "anti-hate" campaigners, Liz Fekete, who wrote an open letter to Lowles at the Institute of Race Relations website. "Like you," Fekete said to Lowles, "I am very concerned at the way in which the far Right is using the issue of sexual abuse, exploitation and violence towards young girls in Rochdale and other northern towns to further the cause of racism and Islamophobia."[224]

Fekete was annoyed that Lowles was playing into the hands of the very "far right" they both stood against so resolutely: "Given the current climate, in which the far Right accuses the anti-racist lobby of imposing a conspiracy of silence about Muslim involvement in 'on-street grooming', I was quite surprised to see you similarly accuse the 'left' and anti-racists of being 'too quick to try and silence any discussion' and of turning a blind eye to the fact that the bulk of perpetrators of what you describe as 'on-street grooming' come from the British-Pakistani community."[225]

---

223 Nick Lowles, "Grooming – an issue we cannot ignore," Hope not Hate (Nov/Dec. 2012), 21–2, in Nick Lowles, "Shining a Light on Child Sexual Abuse," Huffington Post, August 28, 2014, https://www.huffingtonpost.co.uk/nick-lowles/shining-a-light-on-child-sexual-abuse_b_5722214.html. Accessed February 28, 2025.

224 Liz Fekete, "Grooming: an open letter to Nick Lowles," Institute of Race Relations, November 15, 2012, https://irr.org.uk/article/grooming-an-open-letter-to-nick-lowles/. Accessed February 28, 2025.

225 Ibid.

Fekete needn't have worried. Lowles's principal point, however, was not about how British authorities had failed the rape gang victims. It was that it was important not to let racists instrumentalize the rape gangs for their own nefarious purposes, as he explained in the same article: "While the perpetrators of on-street grooming obviously have a low opinion of the white girls they abuse, they have a similarly poor opinion of all females. Grooming has more to do with misogyny rather than specifically religion/race."[226]

Lowles added: "I attacked the BNP and EDL for having us believe that grooming was a consequence of Islam as a religion as the facts simply do not back this up. The vast majority of perpetrators are from one specific community, rather than spread across all Muslim communities, so it is here we have to address the problem."[227] The British National Party and English Defence League were calling attention to the rape gangs as a problem with Islam; against this, Lowles oddly and with remarkable inconsistency argues that the rape gang activity had nothing to do with Islam, but only with Pakistani Muslims, which would have opened him up to charges of racism from his own side if they were interested in intellectual consistency and honesty. Luckily for Lowles, they were not.

STIGMATIZING THOSE WHO SPOKE OUT

Lowles's contention that seeing the rape gangs as a specifically Muslim or even a specifically Pakistani problem was "racist" became part of the mainstream discourse about the issue. In May 2013, the BBC asked: "Did concern over how exposure

[226] Lowles, "Grooming: an issue we cannot ignore."
[227] Ibid.

might inflame racial prejudice lead people to stay quiet when they should have spoken out? Far-right groups have been quick to suggest exactly that."[228] The Beeb referred to several government reports that acknowledged "high-profile court cases" had "mainly involved adult males of British Pakistani origin and white British female victims."[229] The reports claimed that the reason for this, however, was not because the perpetrators were predominantly Pakistanis, but because the "police and other agencies responded to publicity around previous trials by investigating whether the same problem existed in their area."[230] And also because authorities were racist: "Data is gathered more assiduously on perpetrators identified by professionals as Asian, Pakistani or Kurdish."[231]

These reports maintained, however, that contrary to all appearances, the rapists came "from all ethnic groups and so do their victims - contrary to what some may wish to believe."[232] The BBC noted that "of the victims who gave evidence to the inquiry, 42% were described as white British and 28% were from black and ethnic minority backgrounds."[233] No information was given on how many of the "white British" gang rapists were converts to Islam. Even to ask such a question would have been condemned as "racist" and "Islamophobic."

The racism narrative regarding the Muslim rape gangs became so pervasive that even a Pakistani Muslim, Nazir Afzal,

---

228 Mark Easton, "Uncomfortable truths of child exploitation in Britain," BBC, May 14, 2013, https://www.bbc.com/news/uk-22522232. Accessed February 28, 2025.

229 Ibid.

230 Ibid.

231 Ibid.

232 Ibid.

233 Ibid.

ran afoul of it when he prosecuted the rape gangs. "As the Chief Crown Prosecutor for the North West," Afzal wrote in August 2014, "I led the teams that brought the so-called Rochdale Grooming Gang to justice in 2012 for abusing up to 47 girls. My work saw me go up against not only the offenders, but those who tried to intimidate me for bringing abusers before the courts. They said I had given racists a stick with which to beat minorities – I said our communities should be carrying their own sticks."[234]

A home care worker in the city of Sheffield said that rape gang activity was rampant there, but that she had feared to speak out, preferring even to try to help the victims themselves rather than expose themselves to racism charges that could destroy their lives. This home care worker recounted: "Occasionally some of the care workers would go around in cars, which put us at great risk, but we were so desperate and frustrated with the lack of anything being done for the girls. It was endemic, totally endemic throughout. I wish I had said something at the time but if I had I would have probably been labelled a racist. I think the whole system completely and utterly failed the girls."[235]

---

[234] Nazir Afzal, "I was intimidated and branded a racist for bringing Rochdale abuse gang to justice, says prosecutor," *Daily Mail*, August 31, 2014, https://www.dailymail.co.uk/news/article-2738804/I-intimidated-branded-racist-bringing-Rochdale-abuse-gang-justice-says-prosecutor.html. Accessed February 28, 2025.

[235] Robin Cottle, "New abuse shocker! Sheffield hit by 'endemic' Asian gang child sex shame," *Daily Star*, September 19, 2014, in Robert Spencer, "Again in UK: Muslim rape gangs targeted girls in Sheffield, care worker kept mum, fearing being called racist," Jihad Watch, September 20, 2014, https://jihadwatch.org/2014/09/again-in-uk-muslim-rape-gangs-targeted-girls-in-sheffield-care-worker-kept-mum-fearing-being-called-racist. Accessed February 28, 2025.

THE PERSECUTION OF TOMMY ROBINSON

That it did. And those who tried to stand with the victims faced relentless persecution. On Friday, May 25, 2018, the controversial activist Tommy Robinson, whom the media endlessly vilified with its favorite Homeric epithet for those it hated and feared, "far-right," was arrested outside a courthouse where the trial of a Muslim rape gang was taking place. Robinson was discussing Britain's rape gang crisis on a livestream when the arrest took place; the arrest was shown on video.[236] Police claimed that he was arrested for "breaching the peace," but it was patently obvious that he was actually arrested for offending Islam.

A judge, clearly aware of how bad the arrest made the British justice system look, then imposed a gag order regarding the case. Robinson was given a thirteen-month prison sentence for violating reporting restrictions that had been placed upon the trial. He apparently received this harsh sentence because he was deemed to have violated the terms of an earlier probation, which apparently included a prohibition on making videos outside courthouses.

But the prohibition on him doing that was wrong and politically motivated in the first place. Clearly he was arrested, rather than simply given a warning, because of who he was and what he was doing. His arrest was of a piece with the government's desire to keep people ignorant and complacent regarding Muslim rape gangs and the high cost of mass Muslim migration.

---

236 "Orwellian Police arrest Tommy Robinson for journalism 25.5.2018," Cor Bestia, YouTube, May 25, 2018, https://www.youtube.com/watch?v=Owit-kPBsHdo. Accessed March 12, 2025.

Whatever one may have thought of Tommy Robinson and his work, style, or approach, he was being harassed and persecuted by the British government for calling attention to the activity of Muslim rape gangs, which British authorities had done everything they could to cover up, and to jihad violence and Sharia oppression in general.

The British government, in arresting Tommy Robinson, was showing itself willing to incarcerate people for having opinions that it considered unacceptable. Far-left activists such as Nick Lowles demonized as "Islamophobic," "hateful," and "bigoted" not only Tommy Robinson, but anyone and everyone who said that there were Muslim rape gangs at all, and that they had to be stopped.

As we have seen, when Lowles and other leftists wrote about the rape gangs, it was almost always from the standpoint of how the "far right" was using the issue in order to spread "hate." This alleged human rights campaigner showed scant concern for the actual victims of the rape gangs themselves. The lives of *tens of thousands* of British girls were ruined because of these "anti-hate" crusaders, and yet it was Tommy Robinson who went to prison.

CHAPTER NINE
A VERITABLE INDUSTRY

SEXUAL ABUSE ON AN INDUSTRIAL SCALE

In August 2014, a report was published on the gangs that demonstrated the astonishing magnitude of how British officials had failed the country and allowed the lives of a generation of girls to be destroyed. The report focused on only one city, Rotherham, and what it documented was damning. "At least 1,400 children," according to the BBC, "were subjected to appalling sexual exploitation in Rotherham between 1997 and 2013."[237] The author of the report, Alexis Jay, stated that the number of 1,400 victims was a "conservative estimate."[238]

The crimes involved "children as young as 11," who were "raped by multiple perpetrators, abducted, trafficked to other cities in England, beaten and intimidated."[239] Jay said: "It is

237 "Rotherham child abuse scandal: 1,400 children exploited, report finds," BBC, August 26, 2014, https://www.bbc.com/news/uk-england-south-yorkshire-28939089. Accessed February 26, 2025.

238 Ibid.

239 Ibid.

hard to describe the appalling nature of the abuse that child victims suffered."[240] Children were "doused in petrol and threatened with being set alight, threatened with guns, made to witness brutally violent rapes and threatened they would be next if they told anyone."[241]

The report noted, meanwhile, that Rotherham police "regarded many child victims with contempt."[242] This was because when they looked at them, they saw professional and possibly even personal ruin. "Several staff described their nervousness about identifying the ethnic origins of perpetrators for fear of being thought as racist; others remembered clear direction from their managers not to do so."[243] Staff members spoke about how hard it was to deal with matters that were "taboo," and so they ended up "ignoring a politically inconvenient truth" as they believed that dealing with it could harm "community cohesion."[244] And, of course, there was the ever-present "fear of being thought racist."

Some also didn't want to empower the "far right," as Jay noted: "Several councillors interviewed believed that by opening up these issues they could be 'giving oxygen' to racist perspectives that might in turn attract extremist political groups and threaten community cohesion."[245]

Rotherham officials knew all too well that arresting and investigating Pakistani Muslims for raping and sexually abusing

240 Ibid.

241 Ibid.

242 Ibid.

243 Ibid.

244 Katie Hall, "Real or imagined: Racism 'fear' over Rotherham child abuse," BBC, August 27, 2014, https://www.bbc.com/news/uk-england-south-yorkshire-28951612. Accessed February 26, 2025.

245 Ibid.

young English girls would open them to charges of stereotyping, "Islamophobia," hatred, and more. They could end up not only unemployed, but unemployable, subject to vilification in the media and threats from enraged Muslims.

The situation had not changed over five years later. The *Daily Mail* reported in January 2020 that according to a "damning" new report, "sex attacks on young girls by Asian grooming gangs were ignored by police fear of stoking racial tensions, a damning report has ruled."[246] Once again, "Asian" was used as British media code for "Muslim."

The Mail added that "a chief inspector from Rotherham was found to have admitted South Yorkshire Police force turned a blind eye to the harrowing cases of abuse...The unnamed senior police officer said: 'With it being Asians, we can't afford for this to come out.'" The father of one of the victims recounted: "She'd been missing for weeks and he [the chief inspector] was talking as though she was an adult doing it of her own free will. He said it had been going on for 30 years and that in his day they used to call them 'P*** shaggers'. I told him she was a child and this was child abuse."[247]

Indeed it was. But Muslims were to all intents and purposes a protected class in Britain, and could break laws with

---

246 Jack Elsom, "Rotherham sex gang victim says police should face criminal charges for 'aiding and abetting' abuse of hundreds of children as report reveals force ignored crimes for fear of stoking racial tensions," *Daily Mail*, January 18, 2020, https://www.dailymail.co.uk/news/article-7901731/Police-chief-admitted-force-ignored-sex-abuse-grooming-gangs-30-years.html. Accessed March 12, 2025.

247 Jack Elsom, "Rotherham sex gang victim says police should face criminal charges for 'aiding and abetting' abuse of hundreds of children as report reveals force ignored crimes for fear of stoking racial tensions," *Daily Mail*, January 18, 2020, original version, https://patria-uk.com/one-law-for-immigrants-and-another-for-us/. Accessed June 3, 2025.

impunity, as authorities were too worried about charges of "racism" and "Islamophobia" to go after them.

And so the girls would just have to suffer.

A PUBLIC FAILURE

They did before the eyes of the public. A journalist, Sean Thomas, was able to take for granted that the vast majority of British citizens knew exactly what had been going on. Writing just days after Alexis Jay's report was released, Thomas declared: "We don't need to rehearse the facts," Thomas wrote. "We've all read them, and reeled away in horror. The interesting question is how and why would any country allow the racialised gang-rape of its own daughters?"[248]

Then Thomas answered his own question: "Why? Because too many in that country, especially on the Left, most especially in the Labour Party, despise their own ordinary people: the white working classes.[249]

Thomas's assessment may have been correct, that the whole thing was a product of the cultural self-hatred that the left had worked so assiduously to instill in the masses on both sides of the Atlantic. That was likely to have been one reason why ordinary police officers were so afraid to incur charges of "racism" and "Islamophobia" by acting decisively against the rape gangs. They had been carefully and comprehensively indoctrinated

248 Sean Thomas, "The Self-Loathing of the British Left is Now a Problem for Us All," *Telegraph*, August 31, 2014. Quoted in Robert Spencer, "Who is responsible for Muslim rape gang scandal? Nick Lowles, Fiyaz Mughal & co.," Jihad Watch, August 31, 2014, https://jihadwatch.org/2014/08/who-is-response-for-muslim-rape-gang-scandal-nick-lowles-fiyaz-mughal-co. Accessed February 23, 2025.

249 Ibid.

with the idea that white Britons were fundamentally racist, and that this was one of the worst, if not the very worst, thing that someone could be. When confronted with the duty of apprehending criminals who were overwhelmingly members of a prominent racial minority, these officials could all too clearly see the prospect of the end of their careers and public disgrace.

This fear was longstanding. Shortly after the *Jay Report* appeared, it came to light that child protection officials in Yorkshire had produced an instructional video about the rape gangs as far back as 2007, when most people still had no idea that anything like the rape gang activity was occurring. According to the *Daily Mail*, "the 20-minute film, My Dangerous Loverboy, features an Asian man in his 20s grooming a younger white girl – lavishing her with gifts and getting her drunk before forcing her to have sex for money."[250]

Yet "despite winning plaudits at international media festivals, the video was hardly used as it was thought not to be politically correct." A female TV producer who was involved in the production of the video said: "The project was set up to specifically raise schoolkids' awareness of the dangers. The police and social workers were very clear it was Asian men who were seducing white British girls. I can't help wondering how many girls the film might have saved from being sexually exploited if the UKHTC [UK Human Trafficking Centre] and police had put their needs before political correctness."[251]

---

250 Sheron Boyle, "Educational video warning of Asian grooming gangs was made for schools seven years ago but was hardly used amid fears of appearing racist," *Daily Mail*, September 21, 2014, https://www.dailymail.co.uk/news/article-2763987/Educational-video-warning-Asian-grooming-gangs-schools-seven-years-ago-hardly-used-amid-fears-appearing-racist.html#ixzz3E1pZfU5K. Accessed February 28, 2025.

251 Ibid.

The UK Human Trafficking Centre, which is part of the National Crime Agency, commissioned *My Dangerous Loverboy*, and the film was a production of Eyes Open Creative, which was hoping to "open up people's eyes to the harsh realities of sexual exploitation."[252] When the film was released, the UKHTC stated: "We want this film to create awareness of the circumstances in which this kind of exploitation can occur, and encourage vigilance from everyone in a position to notice the behavioural and physical signs that indicate abuse."[253] A National Crime Agency spokesman explained in 2014 that "the film was officially launched in 2010 and the annual Safe and Sound conference. It was not suppressed. It was put on the UKHTC website, sent to every police force and to child protection agencies."[254]

The *Daily Mail* adds, however, that the National Crime Agency was "unwilling to offer a comment on why it was never made compulsory for schools and was only seen in a few classrooms."[255]

The answer to that was obvious enough.

Much the same thing happened even earlier, in 1990. The city council in Birmingham, England, asked Dr. Jill Jesson to research child prostitution in the city. She researched the problem for six months and then produced a report that, according to the *Birmingham Mail*, "highlighted claims that some Asian private hire drivers were linked to the sexual exploitation of young white girls in care, including some who had been

---

252 Ibid.
253 Ibid.
254 Ibid.
255 Ibid.

cautioned for prostitution offences."[256] Even in the early nineties, this was forbidden territory: She was asked to remove all references to the Pakistani drivers, and even after she did so, her report was never published, and the copies of it that existed were destroyed.

"I was employed to do the work because I think they thought I would be objective," Jesson recalled in November 2014. "I was told to reveal what I saw. I did – and some people didn't like it. There was a link between the sexual abuse of the girls and private hire drivers in the city. I thought at the time I did the work that there was an issue with race. Most of the girls were white. I was asked to take this link out, to erase it."[257]

Now, she said, "every time a news item has come on about sexual grooming of young girls and girls in care, and the link, too, between private hire drivers, I have thought 'I told them about that in 1991 but they didn't want to acknowledge it'. I think the problem has got worse and worse over time."[258] She added: "The sad part of this story is not the suppression of evidence but that the relevant organisations have failed to address this problem."[259]

At the time, Jesson recounted, "the role of the police seemed to be to find girls who were reported as missing. Their job was to find the girls, bring them back to the homes, but then the staff running the homes would just let them walk out again. The officers in charge of the homes would say 'Well, we

---

256 Jeanette Oldham, "Birmingham City Council hid links between Asian cabbies and child sex victims for 23 years," *Birmingham Mail*, November 19, 2014, https://www.birminghammail.co.uk/news/midlands-news/birmingham-city-council-hid-links-8131813. Accessed February 28, 2025.

257 Ibid.

258 Ibid.

259 Ibid.

can't lock them up. We can't stop them'. The homes and social workers knew the girls were coming back with new trainers and new coats, and the girls would just say their boyfriend had got them for them."[260]

Nevertheless, when her report was destroyed, Jesson saw that officials had a higher priority than the welfare of the young girls in the area: "The report was shelved, buried, it was never made public. I was shocked to be told that copies of the report were to be destroyed and that nothing further was to be said. Clearly, there was something in this report that someone in the department was worried about."[261]

The *Birmingham Mail* also noted that "an official West Midlands Police report – completed in August 2012 – had shown that 75 per cent of known on-street groomers in the region were Asian, while 82 per cent of girl victims aged 14 to 16 were white."[262]

THE NORM

Labour MP Ann Coffey issued her own report on the rape gangs in October 2014, saying: "My observations will make painful reading for those who hoped that Rochdale was an isolated case."[263] Coffey stated that the rape gang activity had not only become common, but had been normalized: "I have been concerned about the number of people who have told me that

---

260 Ibid.

261 Ibid.

262 Ibid.

263 Helen Pidd, "Report says child sexual exploitation 'normal in parts of Greater Manchester,'" *Guardian*, October 30, 2014, https://www.theguardian.com/society/2014/oct/30/child-sexual-exploitation-norm-greater-manchester-ann-coffey-report?CMP=twt_gu. Accessed February 28, 2025.

in some neighbourhoods child sexual exploitation had become the new social norm. They say there is no respect for girls: gangs of youths pressurising vulnerable young girls (including those with learning disabilities) for sex, and adults allowing their houses to be used for drinking, drug-taking and having sex."[264]

Coffey did not see the problem as having anything in particular to do with the Pakistani community, much less with Islam. Instead, she saw it as a byproduct of the mainstreaming of sexually explicit music videos and pornography, along with the pervasiveness of social media: "This social norm has perhaps been fuelled by the increased sexualisation of children and young people, involving an explosion of explicit music videos and the normalisation of quasi-pornographic images. Sexting, selfies, Instagram and the like have given rise to new social norms in changed expectations of sexual entitlement, and with it a confused understanding of what constitutes consent. I think we have lost the sense of what a child is. Sexual predators out there are having their quite unacceptable views confirmed through messages in the wider media: that children are just sexualised young adults."[265]

Maybe that was all there was to it, but America as well as Britain was awash in sexually explicit music videos and pornography, as well as saturated with social media, and yet the rape gang activity wasn't happening across the Atlantic. What accounted for the difference? No one dared look into that question.

---

264 Ibid.
265 Ibid.

CHAPTER TEN

ENTER ELON MUSK

PRIORITIZING MULTICULTURALISM

Fully ten years after Sean Thomas had noted that the British people knew what had happened and yet nothing was being done, the billionaire entrepreneur-turned-government-reformer Elon Musk shed more light on this phenomenon internationally than it had ever received before. By this time, the Labour Party that, according to Thomas, despised the "white working classes" of Britain, had won a landslide victory and was comfortably ensconced in power.

Musk dared to call attention to the Muslim rape gang scandal, and the world was treated to a new example of the fact that the Labour Party despised the people of the nation it was governing. According to a January 3, 2025, Fox News report, "SpaceX CEO Elon Musk is throwing his weight behind growing calls in the United Kingdom for a new investigation into the scandal of child abuse by grooming gangs, going so far as to back calls for King Charles III to intervene."[266] Musk posted about the scandal not once, but many times, and stated that the fact that the rape gangs had preyed upon British girls largely unhindered for decades was "the worst mass crime against the people of Britain ever."[267] Musk demanded a "national inquiry now!"[268]

This was a direct strike at the Labour government, for, as Fox News pointed out, "the scandal was seen by many as a prioritizing of multiculturalism and political correctness over the welfare of British children and the prosecution of criminals."[269]

Labour officials initially tried to defuse the controversy by paying lip service to the idea that there had been any kind of wrongdoing in the first place. Health Secretary Wes Streeting insisted that "this government takes the issue of child sexual exploitation incredibly seriously."[270] That would have been reassuring had it been true, but it was painfully clear that it wasn't true at all. Streeting said this while serving in the government of Prime Minister Keir Starmer; for five years as the rape gangs marauded all over the country, from 2008 to 2013, Starmer had been director of public prosecutions.

In those five years, Starmer had many chances to prosecute rape gang members, and yet he did not do so. Nor did

---

266 Adam Shaw, "Elon Musk demands UK act on grooming gang scandal amid growing calls for probe: 'National inquiry now!'" Fox News, January 3, 2025, https://www.foxnews.com/world/elon-musk-demands-uk-act-grooming-gang-scandal-amid-growing-calls-probe-national-inquiry-now. Accessed February 23, 2025.

267 Ibid.

268 Ibid.

269 Ibid.

270 Sam Francis, "Musk 'misinformed' on grooming gangs, says Streeting," BBC, January 3, 2025, https://www.bbc.com/news/articles/czxdzng92lno. Accessed February 23, 2025.

he become any kind of spokesman for the victims in the intervening years. And so in 2025, when he was prime minister, Starmer suddenly took "incredibly seriously" a problem he had ignored and denied for years? Streeting was straining credulity well beyond the breaking point; nothing was more obvious than the fact that he was simply doing damage control until the firestorm Musk had kicked up died down. Then Streeting and his colleagues could continue to ignore the Muslim rape gang victims and do nothing to stop the rapists, just as they had done for years.

Streeting also tried to impugn Musk's credibility on this issue, claiming that contrary to Musk's charge that nothing was being done, Starmer's government was actually getting "on with the job" of ending the rape gang activity.[271] Streeting said, with ostentatious understatement: "Some of the criticisms Elon Musk has made I think are misjudged and certainly misinformed."[272] He did not say, however, what he thought Musk was uninformed about, or what he had misjudged.

Streeting also professed to be happy to collaborate with Musk in confronting this problem: "But we're willing to work with Elon Musk who I think has got a big role to play with his social media platform to help us and other countries tackle these serious issues. If he wants to work with us and roll his sleeves up, we'd welcome that."[273]

Streeting may have fobbed off Musk, but he wasn't about to roll up his sleeves and tackle this problem, and the rest of Starmer's government wasn't, either. On January 8, 2025, five days after Musk had called for a national inquiry into the rape

---

[271] Ibid.
[272] Ibid.
[273] Ibid.

gangs and the official indifference to stopping and prosecuting them, the British parliament, in which Labour had a massive majority, voted 364 to 111 against establishing such an inquiry. Starmer remarked generously that "reasonable people could agree or disagree" about whether such an inquiry was needed at all.[274]

"I REALLY HOPE WE CAN PRESSURE HIM, PERSUADE HIM TO CHANGE HIS MIND AND DO THE RIGHT THING"

Conservative Shadow Home Secretary Chris Philp disagreed, charging that the overwhelming vote of Labour MPs against opening an inquiry was nothing less than "morally wrong."[275] Philp said he still had hope that such an inquiry would be opened: "We must have this inquiry and we… will do everything we can to keep the victims at the front of this debate and to try and get the government to do the right thing. It's not too late — Keir Starmer could still announce an inquiry and I really hope we can pressure him, persuade him to change his mind and do the right thing for victims."[276]

In March 2025, Philp renewed this call, charging that the local inquiries to which the Labour government had agreed "totally inadequate" to deal with the magnitude of what had happened all over Britain.[277] Philp declared: "It's a complete

---

274 Kate Whannel and Sam Francis, "MPs vote against Tory call for new grooming gangs inquiry," BBC, January 8, 2025, https://www.bbc.com/news/articles/clyvy4q82l9o. Accessed March 16, 2025.

275 Ibid.

276 Ibid.

277 David Williamson, "Survivors of grooming gang scandal 'betrayed' as 'cover-up' branded 'complete disgrace,'" *Express*, March 15, 2025, https://www.express.co.uk/news/politics/2027512/survivors-grooming-gang-scandal-have. Accessed March 16, 2025.

disgrace that they appear to be continuing to countenance a cover-up of some of these terrible events."[278]

Philp called for a considerably more searching and comprehensive inquiry than any that had been conducted up to that point: "We need a national inquiry which covers not just five towns but all the towns affected. It needs to be a statutory inquiry so it has the powers to compel the production of evidence and one of the key things the national inquiry should get to the bottom of is whether people in positions of public authority – whether that's local councillors, the police, the Crown Prosecution Service, which of course was run by Keir Starmer for some of this time – did they do their job properly, were they negligent? They certainly did ignore victims. Did they even actively cover this up for misplaced reasons of cultural or racial sensitivity?"[279] The answer to that was painfully obvious. He continued: "If any public officials did cover this up they should be investigated for the offence of misconduct in public office. These are the questions that a proper statutory national inquiry needs to get to the bottom of. Not a single public official – whether it's a councillor, the police, the CPS – nobody has been held accountable for these failures and it is wrong. Many victims have called for a proper national inquiry but the Labour Government has ignored those victims and it does constitute a betrayal."[280]

Indeed. Yet the Conservatives had been in power from 2010 to 2024, and had done no more than Labour was doing to understand why the rape gangs were operating, or to make any concerted effort to stop them. Starmer, meanwhile, insisted

---

278 Ibid.
279 Ibid.
280 Ibid.

that he would "call out" anyone who threatened or intimidated rape gang victims into silence.[281] Like Streeting's comments about Musk, this was designed to provide the appearance of action on the problem without any genuine action.

NEW INQUIRIES, OR NEW LIP SERVICE

The public outrage that Musk had stirred up, however, did not die down, and was rekindled by Labour's blasé refusal to open up a new inquiry. And so just over a week after parliament's resounding vote against such an inquiry, Home Secretary Yvette Cooper announced that the government planned to conduct what the BBC called a "nationwide review of grooming gang evidence," as well as launch "five government-backed local inquiries."[282] This fell short of the "statutory national inquiry" that Conservatives (and Musk) had called for, but at least it appeared to be something, and that was all that mattered. Philp complained that these limited inquiries were "wholly inadequate," as they would not be able to require witnesses to attend hearings, as a national inquiry would be able to do.[283]

Cooper also vowed a "rapid" investigation of "the demographics of the gangs and their victims," and even of the "cultural drivers" that led them into this activity.[284] "Rapid" for politicians, however, is not "rapid" for the rest of humanity, and so a month later, the mother of one of the victims drew attention to the "wholly inadequate" nature of the inquiries Cooper

---

281 Ibid.

282 Kate Whannel and Ed Thomas, "Cooper announces inquiries into grooming gangs," BBC, January 16, 2025, https://www.bbc.com/news/articles/c9w5l4vxv2qo. Accessed February 24, 2025.

283 Ibid.

284 Ibid.

had pledged to initiate. Karen Downes, the mother of the tragic murder victim Charlene Downes, asked again for an inquiry: "It would mean everything to get answers as we live in limbo, especially if it helped get justice for Charlene and all the other girls affected by grooming gangs."[285]

Karen Downes said that her family "cannot move on with our lives. We are hoping the inquiry would finally bring someone forward to finally end our nightmare, and give Charlene the justice that is rightfully hers." Cooper's inquiries promised only to give the British public and the world more obfuscation, deflection, and protection of the incriminated authorities, but at least they gave the Starmer government cover against attacks from the likes of Elon Musk.

Local inquiries had been held in the past, and spoke with relative forthrightness about the problem, but hadn't resulted in any effective action to end the rape gang activity. The "Independent Inquiry into Child Sexual Exploitation in Rotherham 1997-2013" noted the alarming fact that "no one knows the true scale of child sexual exploitation (CSE) in Rotherham over the years. Our conservative estimate is that approximately 1400 children were sexually exploited over the full Inquiry period, from 1997 to 2013."[286] The 2011 census recorded Rotherham's population as 109,691.

---

285 Yunus Mulla, "Missing teen's mum wants grooming gangs inquiry," BBC, February 17, 2025, https://www.bbc.com/news/articles/cj48rjxpxlvo. Accessed February 25, 2025.

286 Alexis Jay OBE, "Independent Inquiry into Child Sexual Exploitation in Rotherham 1997 – 2013," Rotherham Metropolitan Borough Council, October 2013, https://www.rotherham.gov.uk/downloads/file/279/independent-inquiry-into-child-sexual-exploitation-in-rotherham. Accessed February 23, 2025.

The report stated plainly what the rapists had done to their victims:

> It is hard to describe the appalling nature of the abuse that child victims suffered. They were raped by multiple perpetrators, trafficked to other towns and cities in the north of England, abducted, beaten, and intimidated. There were examples of children who had been doused in petrol and threatened with being set alight, threatened with guns, made to witness brutally violent rapes and threatened they would be next if they told anyone. Girls as young as 11 were raped by large numbers of male perpetrators.[287]

It was equally frank about how British officials had betrayed those whom they had been entrusted to protect:

> Within social care, the scale and seriousness of the problem was underplayed by senior managers. At an operational level, the Police gave no priority to CSE [child sexual exploitation], regarding many child victims with contempt and failing to act on their abuse as a crime. Further stark evidence came in 2002, 2003 and 2006 with three reports known to the Police and the Council, which could not have been clearer in their description of the situation in Rotherham. The first of these reports was effectively suppressed because some senior officers disbelieved the data it contained. This had

287 Ibid.

> led to suggestions of coverup. The other two reports set out the links between child sexual exploitation and drugs, guns and criminality in the Borough. These reports were ignored and no action was taken to deal with the issues that were identified in them.[288]

Here again, it was impossible for those officials to mount a plausible claim that they had been ignorant of what was going on: "Seminars for elected members and senior officers in 2004-05 presented the abuse in the most explicit terms. After these events, nobody could say 'we didn't know.'"[289] Nor could anyone say that they didn't know why the officials failed to act:

> By far the majority of perpetrators were described as 'Asian' by victims, yet throughout the entire period, councillors did not engage directly with the Pakistani-heritage community to discuss how best they could jointly address the issue. Some councillors seemed to think it was a one-off problem, which they hoped would go away. Several staff described their nervousness about identifying the ethnic origins of perpetrators for fear of being thought racist; others remembered clear direction from their managers not to do so.[290]

The report was explicit about why the fear of racism was a real problem: "In Rotherham, the majority of known

288 Ibid.

289 Ibid.

290 Ibid.

perpetrators were of Pakistani heritage including the five men convicted in 2010. The file reading carried out by the Inquiry also confirmed that the ethnic origin of many perpetrators was 'Asian'. In one major case in the mid-2000s, the convicted perpetrator was Afghan."[291]

All that was bad enough, but the Rotherham report also observed that "this abuse is not confined to the past but continues to this day."[292] How could it not have done so, when the fear of career ruin over charges of "racism" and "Islamophobia" continued to be a live possibility?

The city of Telford published its own report in July 2022: "Report of the Independent Inquiry Telford Child Sexual Exploitation." The compilers of the report attempted to head off the all too predictable moral outrage from the Left by going on record with the insistence that they opposed racism. The Telford report was calling attention to the activities of Muslim rape gangs who were overwhelmingly Pakistani, and so its author, Tom Crowther QC, maintained his ideological purity: "It would in my judgment be wholly wrong, and undoubtedly racist, to equate membership of a particular racial group with propensity to commit CSE."[293]

Crowther clearly hoped this would prevent outraged mobs from demanding his firing as an unacceptable member of the white racist establishment that supposedly held sway in Britain. He then proceed to tell the truth about the issue at hand:

> That said, on the papers disclosed by key stakeholders, it is an undeniable fact that a high

[291] Ibid., 92.

[292] Ibid., 1.

[293] Tom Crowther QC, "Report of the Independent Inquiry Telford Child Sexual Exploitation," July 12, 2022, vol. 1, 111.

> proportion of those cases involved perpetrators that were described by victims/survivors and others as being "Asian" or, often, "Pakistani". The Inquiry has itself also heard such accounts from victims/survivors. In considering the evidence, and in particular the disclosed material, I have been cautious not to infer too much from names, which may indicate wider geographical background and indeed religious heritage, but are wholly unreliable indicators of national background and (in particular) religious belief. Even bearing that in mind, however, the evidence plainly shows that the majority of CSE suspects in Telford during my Terms of Reference were men of southern Asian heritage.[294]

The Telford report doesn't dare venture into the question of why the majority of men engaged in the sexual abuse of children were South Asian; even going as far as it did was controversial enough in contemporary Britain. The report did point out, however, that in 2004, the Telford local Council heeded a national directive to create "locality teams," which were also known as "Clusters."[295] These were to be "groupings of agencies and services working together to support children and young people."[296] The support came with a breathtaking caveat: "Cluster staff were told that … detailed reports should not be shared by email, as the allegations could 'start a race riot.'"[297]

---

[294] Ibid.
[295] Ibid., 19.
[296] Ibid.
[297] Ibid.

Not only did officials fear a "race riot"; as dutiful leftist conformists, they were also terrified at the prospect of giving ammunition to those individuals and groups who were relentlessly demonized as "far right." In another English town, Oldham, according to Fox "a 2022 report into Oldham's actions between 2011 and 2014 found that children were failed by local agencies, but it also found that there was no cover-up despite 'legitimate concerns' that the far-right would capitalize on 'the high-profile convictions of predominantly Pakistani offenders across the country.'"[298]

So on the one hand, there was the prospect of enraged Muslims rioting; on the other, there was the risk of handing an issue to the "far right." And everywhere there was the fear of appearing "racist" and "Islamophobic." These were the reasons why hundreds of thousands of British girls had their lives destroyed. The Starmer government finally agreed in June 2025 to open a national inquiry, but there was little chance that it would be honest about what had really happened.

---

298 Shaw, "Elon Musk demands."

CHAPTER ELEVEN

ISLAMOPHOBOPHOBIA

CHARGES OF "ISLAMOPHOBIA" ONLY MADE MATTERS WORSE

In February 2025, a British think tank, the Policy Exchange, documented this phenomenon in a report, stating, according to the *Express*, that "the Rotherham grooming gang scandal was not stopped because people were 'afraid of being branded racist or anti-Muslim.'"[299] This report appeared as the Starmer government was preparing to criminalize "Islamophobia" with a statute that could be used to cover up or justify criminal activity, exactly as fears of "Islalmophobia" charges allowed the rape gangs to run rampant.

The effort to define and criminalize "Islamophobia" had gained tremendous impetus from an all-party parliamentary group report in 2018 that claimed that "Islamophobia" was

299 David Williamson, "Ministers urged not to adopt definition of 'Islamophobia' criminals could exploit," *Express*, February 25, 2025, https://www.express.co.uk/news/politics/2019391/ministers-not-adopt-definition-islamophobia. Accessed March 3, 2025.

"now so prevalent in society and dispersed across institutional, social, political and economic life that it deserves to be recognised at Britain's 'bigotry blind spot.'" That report claimed that a definition of "Islamophobia" was "vital" because of "age-old stereotypes and tropes about Islam" and "their modern-day iteration in the 'Asian grooming gangs' or 'Bin Laden' labels heighten 'vulnerability of Muslims to hate crimes.'"[300] It accordingly defined "Islamophobia" as "a type of racism that targets expressions of Muslimness or perceived Muslimness."[301]

The Policy Exchange report, on the other hand, stated that "the charge of 'Islamophobia' is often used by wrongdoers, criminals or bad faith actors who are Muslim to smear or deter those who seek to expose them." It added that this charge was "repeatedly used for this purpose in the Rotherham scandal and in other instances of grooming. It continued to be used in this way even years after the facts were established beyond doubt."[302]

That was true, and had been in Britain for many years. Even Nazir Afzal, despite having prosecuted many rape gang cases, was happy to join the chorus of those who complained about "Islamophobia," charging, according to GB News, that "the media's focus on the ethnicity of the perpetrators fanned the flames of anti-Muslim bigotry," and that rape gang activity was "better understood in the wider context of child sex abuse."[303] He insisted that "while the majority of perpetrators in these cases were of Pakistani heritage, the crimes were not

---

300 Ibid.

301 Ibid.

302 Ibid.

303 Adam Chapman, "EXCLUSIVE: Ex-policeman blows lid on senior officers prioritising 'wad of cash' over grooming gang abuses," GB News, February 16, 2025, https://www.gbnews.com/news/grooming-gangs-uk-rotherham-south-yorkshire-police. Accessed March 3, 2025.

religiously motivated but rather rooted in issues of male power and control."[304]

In this environment, stating unwelcome facts could mean career ruin.

OFFICERS "DIDN'T WANT ANY FLACK FROM COUNCILLORS"

One retired South Yorkshire Police officer revealed, according to GB News, that in Rotherham, "the scale and seriousness of the crimes were downplayed because officers 'didn't want any flack from councillors.'"[305] The whistleblower spoke of a "pervasive fear of being accused of racism and the political environment in which the officers operated within," which led to "a patchwork of failures that hindered the police investigations into the grooming gang abusers."[306]

Among these failures was a "'big push' towards appraisals and performance-related pay (PRP) at that time dictated which complaints were investigated and which were dropped."[307] PRP was supposed to give police officers incentive to be efficient and record successes quickly; this led to less priority being given to rape gang cases, for "busting a grooming gang ring is unlikely to produce quick results — given the manpower and resources such an investigation requires — so more straightforward cases and box-ticking exercises took priority."[308]

---

304 Ibid.

305 Adam Chapman, "EXPOSED: Ex-policeman blows whistle on politicians and mosques who influenced grooming gangs investigation," GB News, February 9, 2025, https://www.gbnews.com/news/uk/grooming-gangs-uk-rotherham-south-yorkshire-police. Accessed March 3, 2025.

306 Ibid.

307 Chapman, "EXCLUSIVE: Ex-policeman blows lid on senior officers."

308 Ibid.

The whistleblower stated that "if you're a superintendent — you're not going to get a wad of money if your violent crimes going through the roof, your staff appraisals aren't ticked off or training in the workplace slides. So there was more urgency put on those sorts of things than there ever was for anything else, particularly the Rotherham grooming gangs."[309]

As a result, he continued, "I can guarantee that at that time grooming gangs and sexual abuse of young children wouldn't be even looked at by the senior community. If somebody would have turned up at that time saying, 'I have information about how many girls were being taken away,' they [the girls] would probably be referred to as the 'naughty kids on the street.' Sure, they'll deal with them. But it wasn't a big push. The tick box culture meant they took their eye off the ball."[310] He also said that officers in charge had no reason to prioritize rape gang cases: "Those chief superintendents in those districts — what were their performance indicators for that year? I guarantee that abuse of women or girls wasn't featured."[311]

The whistleblower insisted: "I've got no gripe with the force. I've got no particular commander that I want to drop in it. I don't want anybody to get in trouble," but stated that "there are lessons to be learned."[312]

Those lessons had been obvious for years, but most of the British establishment steadfastly refused to learn them. The same whistleblower, speaking in 2025, said that the Muslim

309 Ibid.
310 Ibid.
311 Ibid.
312 Chapman, "EXPOSED: Ex-policeman blows whistle."

rape gangs were "still active" in Rotherham.[313] "I think it's still massive," he said of the rape gang activity.[314] Simon Morton of Thames Valley Police agreed, saying in January 2025 that it was "obvious" that rape gang activity was still "happening in every city around the country."[315]

Morton blamed the victims for this, complaining that they mistrusted authorities (which was perfectly understandable under the circumstances). The whistleblower, however, perhaps because he was protected by anonymity, was more forthright, saying: "It's ongoing because you've got a problem within the Muslim community defending their own. They get released from prison, go back home and then live within the community. If my dad was ever arrested for some sort of child sex offence, he wouldn't be coming back to the family. I think it's documented that it's acceptable to come back into the community. The faith is very protective. I'm sure that's going on."[316]

Even Nazir Afzal admitted that, saying that "the disproportionate involvement of Asian and Pakistani men in 'localised, street grooming' of predominantly white, working-class girls had to be addressed from within the community."[317] Afzal said: "We do have an issue with people of our ethnicity – it's not *the* issue but an issue – and we have to take care of it, we have to deal with it. The solution comes from within. It comes from

---

313 Adam Chapman, "EXCLUSIVE: Ex-policeman shares explosive assessment on grooming gangs 'protected' in Britain: 'It's massive,'" GB News, February 23, 2025, https://www.gbnews.com/news/grooming-gangs-news-south-yorkshire-police. Accessed March 3, 2025.

314 Ibid.

315 Chapman, "EXCLUSIVE: Ex-policeman blows lid on senior officers."

316 Ibid.

317 Ibid.

you," he said to a group of councillors and other officials in Bradford.[318]

Certainly the problem had come from them. The whistleblower said that "because of the Asian influence in Rotherham, there were a lot of people not touched because they were just absolutely sh*t scared, for want of a better word, of daring to question any sort of Asian activity, because at that time Rotherham council was heavily populated by people of the Asian community."[319]

And so the problem continued. GB News stated: "Reports support his assertion. Philip Marshall, who is leading Operation Stovewood—the National Crime Agency's inquiry into grooming gang activity in Rotherham from 1997 to 2013 — reported in January 2025 that his team has identified 324 men suspected of committing 1,142 crimes against 1,150 victims."[320]

According to Marshall, "of those crimes, 827 relate to the offence of rape — that is a startling figure. For one child to be raped is far too many. We're dealing with 827 rapes and another 600 crimes on top."[321] Yet, said GB News, "so far, this extensive criminality has only resulted in 39 convictions and prison sentences."[322]

The all-pervasive fear was obviously still paralyzing those who had the responsibility to act.

---

[318] Ibid.
[319] Ibid.
[320] Ibid.
[321] Ibid.
[322] Ibid.

THE COURAGE AND COWARDICE OF SARAH CHAMPION

Even when some British authorities showed that they were more courageous and less self-serving than their colleagues, they didn't exactly rise to Churchillian heights. They approached closer to the truth than others did, but were still miles away from it. On August 10, 2017, Sarah Champion, the Labour shadow secretary of state for women and equalities, who also happened to be the MP for Rotherham, ignited a fresh firestorm when she published an article in the English tabloid *The Sun*, asserting that "Britain has a problem with British Pakistani men raping and exploiting white girls."[323]

Having said this much, Champion showed that she knew how controversial her statement would be, adding: "There. I said it. Does that make me a racist? Or am I just prepared to call out this horrifying problem for what it is?"[324] She suggested, without elaboration, that the ethnicity of the attackers had something to do with their actions: "These people are predators and the common denominator is their ethnic heritage."[325]

Maybe Champion was prepared, as she said, to call out the problem as she saw it or claimed to have seen it, but she doesn't seem to have been prepared for the outrage her remarks provoked. Soon she was resigning from the shadow cabinet and issuing an abject apology, blaming the UK's *Sun*, which had published her piece, for editing it without her approval.

---

323 Sarah Champion, "British Pakistani men ARE raping and exploiting white girls… and it's time we faced up to it," *The Sun*, August 10, 2017, https://www.thesun.co.uk/news/4218648/british-pakistani-men-raping-exploiting-white-girls/. Accessed February 23, 2025.

324 Ibid.

325 Ibid.

The Sun's editors, she said, had published the piece "stripped of any nuance about the complex issue of grooming gangs, which have exploited thousands in my constituency."[326] She claimed that all she had wanted to do was "open the debate about a very specific form of child abuse," but that "the Sun decided to make the headline and opening sentences highly inflammatory and they could be taken to vilify an entire community on the basis of race, religion or country of origin."[327]

Champion added: "The article should not have gone out in my name and I apologise that it did."[328]

The Sun denied the disgraced MP's accusations, saying: "Sarah Champion's column, as it appeared on Friday, was approved by her team and her adviser twice contacted us thereafter to say she was 'thrilled' with the piece and it 'looked great'. Indeed, her only objection after the article appeared was her belief that her picture byline looked unflattering. Her office submitted five new pictures for further use."[329] That was before, however, Champion discovered how resolute her Labour colleagues were in their determination not to confront this issue as forthrightly as she had done.

Champion herself, however, did not get to the heart of the matter. After her article appeared, *The Sun*'s Trevor Kavanagh declared that British authorities had to take on what he called "the Muslim Problem," and commended Champion for having

---

326 Jessica Elgot and Graham Ruddick, "Sarah Champion distances herself from Sun article on British Pakistani men," *Guardian*, August 16, 2017. https://www.theguardian.com/politics/2017/aug/16/sarah-champion-complaint-sun-article-british-pakistani-men. Accessed February 23, 2025.

327 Ibid.

328 Ibid.

329 "Sarah Champion quits Labour front bench over rape article," BBC, August 17, 2017, https://www.bbc.com/news/uk-politics-40952224. Accessed February 23, 2025.

had the courage to take her stand.[330] Horrified, Champion said that Kavanagh had written a "repulsive and extreme Islamophobic" piece, and disavowed any connection with his perspective: "I am ashamed that he made positive reference to my own piece. We must always stand up against racism and prejudice, whatever form it takes."[331]

Labour leader, Jeremy Corbyn said unctuously that "attempts to brand communities or ethnic or religious groups, wittingly or unwittingly, will only make that more difficult. In recent days, *The Sun* has published statements that incite Islamophobia and stigmatise entire communities. That is wrong, dangerous and must be condemned, as Naz Shah's public letter does in the clearest possible terms. The interests of victims of sexual abuse and the rigorous investigation into the underlying causes of that abuse are damaged by this kind of bigotry and prejudice."[332] Corbyn was referring to another Labour MP, Naseem "Naz" Shah, who had written an open letter to *The Sun*, signed by 107 other MPs, expressing outrage at Kavanagh's "Nazi-like terminology."[333]

No doubt Muslim communities in Britain that formed a significant part of Labour's constituency were grateful for the support from Jeremy Corbyn. Yet there was one problem with Champion's apology and Corbyn's righteous indignation: What if there really was a connection between the behavior of the

---

330 Elgot and Ruddick, "Sarah Champion distances herself."

331 Ibid.

332 Ibid.

333 Ben Lazarus, "'SHUT YOUR MOUTH': Corbyn ally shares message telling Rotherham sex abuse victims to be quiet 'for the good of diversity,'" *The Sun*, August 22, 2017, https://www.thesun.co.uk/news/4299167/corbyn-ally-shares-message-telling-rotherham-sex-abuse-victims-to-be-quiet-for-the-good-of-diversity/. Accessed February 27, 2025.

rape gangs and Islam? What if it really weren't simply a bizarre coincidence that the rapists were almost always Muslims?

If there were a connection between Islam and the rape gang activity, wouldn't it have behooved British authorities to investigate that link as part of their efforts to eradicate this activity? Such an investigation did not happen, of course, and instead, the British left, which dominates the culture just as American leftists dominate the culture on the other side of the Atlantic, was instead busy constructing a fantasy scenario in which the real victims of Muslim rape gang activity were Muslims themselves.

"SHUT UP FOR THE GOOD OF DIVERSITY"

Despite issuing her humiliating Maoist-style public self-incrimination, retraction, and apology for having dared to depart from the party line, Sarah Champion was fired. Labour distanced itself from such "racism." The contrast couldn't have been sharper with the experience of Naz Shah, who had organized the open letter criticizing Trevor Kavanagh. Just days after Champion's humiliating self-abnegation, Shah retweeted and liked a tweet from a parody account purporting to be that of the far-left political commentator Owen Jones. The fake Jones said: "Those abused girls in Rotherham and elsewhere just need to shut their mouths. For the good of diversity."[334]

Shah later deleted the retweet and unliked the "Jones" post. A spokesperson for her office explained: "This was a genuine accident eight days ago that was rectified within minutes. To suggest otherwise is absolute nonsense. Her record speaks for itself. Naz has been working for over 20 years on the issues of

---

334 Ibid.

child abuse, violence against women and grooming, which is well documented. She has and will continue to advocate for all victims, and work towards eradicating this evil from society."[335]

Maybe, but nothing in that statement gave any indication that Shah, who was herself a Muslim of Pakistani descent, was willing to face, much less expose, the involvement of Pakistani Muslims in these rape gangs, or to explore the reasons why they were so overrepresented. In fact, Shah had not only protested against Trevor Kavanagh's column, but had been a leader of the outrage mob that had successfully removed Sarah Champion from the shadow cabinet.

Eleven months after liking and retweeting a statement telling victims of horrific sexual abuse that they should "shut their mouths for the good of diversity," Labour appointed Naz Shah to be shadow minister of state for, of all things, women and equalities. Her claim that the retweet had been an "accident" was implausible in light of the fact that Shah both liked and retweeted the statement, which are two separate motions; thus Shah couldn't claim that her hand had simply slipped. Nevertheless, she was on the side of the leftist establishment, unlike Sarah Champion, and so she remained in line for promotion and preferment. The rape gang victims, meanwhile, had been forgotten once again.

335 Ibid.

CHAPTER TWELVE

LIFE IN THE NEW EUROPE

A NEW YEAR'S EVE IN THE NEW EUROPE

What happened in Britain was a multidimensional scandal of towering proportions. There were all the girls whose lives had been ruined. There were innumerable officials who had betrayed their public trust in allowing it all to happen. There were the leftist "anti-racism" advocates who demonized and stigmatized those who dared to call attention to the real problem. There was the establishment media, which followed the leftist line readily instead of having an ounce of concern for the victims.

All of it added up to a society and a civilization in tremendous crisis and steep decline. And Britain was not alone. Although in most cases it has taken place on a much smaller scale, the same phenomenon has played out in other countries as well. As this behavior was, at least in the eyes of some Muslims, sanctioned in Islam, this was not surprising.

Such was the ethnic makeup of twenty-first century Europe as these crimes were committed. In 2015, as German Chancellor

Angela Merkel opened the doors of her country to millions of Muslim migrants, she repeatedly proclaimed to her people: "*Wir schaffen das!*" that is, "We can do this!" It was extremely unlikely, however, that any significant number of Germans had any idea of what exactly she was saying that they could do. It wasn't even clear that Merkel herself knew, either. On December 31, 2015, however, Germany, and the world, found out one of the things that could happen when a massive influx of Muslim migrants entered a non-Muslim country.

On New Year's Eve 2015, Muslim migrants whom Merkel had just invited into Germany joined others in committing the staggering number of roughly two thousand rapes and sexual assaults in several cities, including Cologne, Dusseldorf, Dortmund, and Bielefeld. On the same night, mass rapes took place also in Stockholm and other cities of Europe.[336] Germany Justice Minister Heiko Maas was sure that it was a premeditated action: "For such a horde of people to meet and commit such crimes, it has to have been planned somehow. No one can tell me that this was not coordinated or planned. The suspicion is that a specific date and an expected crowd was picked."[337]

---

[336] Ivar Arpi, "It's not only Germany that covers up mass sex attacks by migrant men… Sweden's record is shameful," *The Spectator*, December 27, 2016, https://www.spectator.co.uk/article/it-s-not-only-germany-that-covers-up-mass-sex-attacks-by-migrant-men-sweden-s-record-is-shameful/. Accessed March 9, 2025. Oliver JJ Lane, "REVEALED: Full List Of 1,049 Victims, Crimes Committed During Cologne New Year's Sex Assaults," Breitbart, January 21, 2016, https://www.breitbart.com/europe/2016/01/21/revealed-full-list-of-1049-victims-crimes-committed-during-cologne-new-years-eve-sex-assaults/. Accessed March 9, 2025.

[337] "Cologne violence was likely planned: German justice minister," *Hurriyet Daily News*, January 10, 2016, https://www.hurriyetdailynews.com/cologne-violence-was-likely-planned-german-justice-minister--93681. Accessed March 9, 2025.

Maas had good reason for this suspicion. The news agency Agence France-Press noted that according to the German newspaper *Bild am Sonntag*, "some North Africans had sent out calls using social networks for people to gather in Cologne on New Year's Eve."[338] These calls were heeded: "Young men not only from Cologne, but as far as France and Belgium responded to the call to travel to the western German city."[339]

A January 2016 report from Germany's national police stated that on that night, "Women, accompanied or not, literally ran a 'gauntlet' through masses of heavily intoxicated men that words cannot describe."[340] The police were overwhelmed: "Security forces were unable to get all of the incidents, assaults, crimes, etc. under control. There were simply too many happening at the same time."[341] There were so many "fights, thefts, sexual assaults against women, etc.," that even identifying the suspects "was unfortunately no longer possible," as there were just too many incidents for police to be able to keep track of all of them.[342]

The Muslim migrants also displayed utter disdain for the police, who were "bombarded with fireworks and pelted with glass bottles."[343] One officer said that he encountered a level of contempt "like I have never experienced in my 29 years of public service."[344] This likely stemmed from the Qur'an's char-

---

338 Ibid.

339 Ibid.

340 "Police Report Outlines 'Chaotic and Shameful' New Year's Eve," *Spiegel International*, January 7, 2016, https://www.spiegel.de/international/germany/cologne-attacks-on-new-years-produced-chaos-say-police-a-1070894.html. Accessed March 9, 2025.

341 Ibid.

342 Ibid.

343 Ibid.

344 Ibid.

acterization of non-Muslims as the "most vile of created beings" (98:6), but was also a manifestation of the general sentiment among the migrants that they occupied a privileged position in German society. One of them said as much on that New Year's Eve, telling police: "I'm a Syrian! You have to treat me kindly! Ms. Merkel invited me."[345] As they were apprehended, some of the migrants gleefully tore up their residence permits before the eyes of the police, saying: "You can't touch me. I'll just go back tomorrow and get a new one."[346]

HELL IN HELSINKI

Similar scenes unfolded in Zurich, Salzburg, and Helsinki, among other cities.[347] In the Finnish capital, around one thousand asylum seekers, mostly from Iraq, came together at the city's central railroad station. The action was on a much smaller scale than in Cologne. Helsinki police said that they had "received information about three cases of sexual assault, of which two have been filed as complaints."[348] Helsinki deputy police chief Ilkka Koskimaki revealed that "the suspects were asylum seekers. The three were caught and taken into custody on the spot."[349]

The Helsinki police revealed information that confirmed Heiko Maas's suspicion that this was a coordinated action,

---

345 Ibid.

346 Ibid.

347 "New Year's Eve sex assaults also reported in Finland, Sweden and Austria," News.com.au, January 8, 2016, https://www.news.com.au/world/europe/new-years-eve-sex-assaults-also-reported-in-finland-sweden-and-austria/news-story/ce603ac27e5ebb4479874096fe299b97. Accessed March 9, 2025.

348 Ibid.

349 Ibid.

announcing in a statement that "ahead of New Year's Eve, the police caught wind of information that asylum seekers in the capital region possibly had similar plans to what the men gathered in Cologne's railway station have been reported to have had."[350] Koskimaki, however, continued the ever-expanding tradition of willful ignorance among European officials, saying that "police did not see a link between the Cologne and Helsinki incidents."[351] He also added: "There hasn't been this kind of harassment on previous New Year's Eves or other occasions for that matter … This is a completely new phenomenon in Helsinki."[352]

Koskimaki didn't expatiate on what had changed to create the new situation. It had started, in Germany at least, before New Year's Eve 2015. In February 2020, the German newspaper *Bild* told the tragic story of an eleven-year-old girl who was "looking for tenderness, closeness, affirmation. But the innocent feelings of the girl were badly exploited by young men: they abused the child!" One of the perpetrators, an Afghan Muslim migrant named Khudai R., confessed to his crimes. He insisted that he had been quite clear about what he wanted from the girl: "I just asked her if she wanted to have sex with me."[353] She agreed, and so he proceeded to rape her.

"There were three sex meetings," says *Bild*; "at two of them, Khudai's buddies Ezatullah N. and Siya A. (both 19 at that time) from Hessen participated. The last time, Khudai and

---

350 Ibid.

351 Ibid.

352 Ibid.

353 Mirko Voltmer, "Flüchtling gesteht Missbrauch von Elfjähriger," *Bild*, February 17, 2020, https://www.bild.de/regional/hannover/hannover-aktuell/maedchen-schwer-missbraucht-fluechtling-gesteht-sex-mit-elfjaehriger-68860346.bild.html. Accessed March 14, 2025.

Ezatullah took turns taking porn photos on their cell phones. The duo later took a selfie with their tongues out in front of the minor. One of them is said to have thrown a stone at her."[354] These young migrants knew exactly what they were doing: "According to Khudai's lawyer, the defendant believed that the girl was under the age of 14."[355]

Distraught, "the learning-disabled student turned to her guidance counselor. Her mother (36, a single parent and geriatric nurse) told the judge: 'She was a happy girl before. After that, no more.' Her daughter had been suicidal, had cut herself, and is now living in a therapeutic living group."[356]

A MAYOR OFFERS A REMEDY

Nevertheless, after the mass sexual assaults in Cologne, that city's Mayor Henriette Reker had an idea for a remedy. Reker thought that the problem of mass rape could be solved once and for all if women simply stopped provoking the migrants to attack them. Said Reker: "The women and young girls have to be more protected in the future so these things don't happen again."[357]

That was certainly true, but Reker wasn't referring to protection from the police. She explained that "this means they should go out and have fun, but they need to be better prepared, especially with the Cologne carnival coming up. For

---

354 Ibid.

355 Ibid.

356 Ibid.

357 Oliver JJ Lane, "Cologne Mayor: Women Should Be More Careful After Migrant Mass Rapes, Promises 'Guidance' So They Can 'Prepare,'" Breitbart, January 5, 2016, https://www.breitbart.com/europe/2016/01/05/cologne-mayor-women-careful-migrant-mass-rapes-promises-guidance-can-prepare/. Accessed March 14, 2025.

this, we will publish online guidelines that these young women can read through to prepare themselves."[358]

So it was the potential victims who had to prepare themselves. Reker didn't suggest educating the new arrivals in Western values. They were going to act the way they were going to act, and it was up to German women to adapt to the new parameters of society. The Qur'an says: "O prophet, tell your wives and your daughters and the women of the believers to draw their veils close around them. That will be better, so that they may be recognized and not molested. Allah is always forgiving, merciful." (33:59) This was the underlying assumption behind calls for woman to cover themselves entirely, except for their face and hands: controlling men's desires was the responsibility of women, and it was they who had to change their behavior in the face of male temptation. If women failed to prevent men from being tempted, even if she covered herself completely, any attack or rape was her fault.

This wasn't just the thinking of all too many in the Islamic world. It was the thinking of Henriette Reker. She was playing into the idea that a rape victim must have been "asking for it," or, as one Islamic website put it, "the semi-naked styles of dress in which women go out…lead to the commission of this reprehensible crime" of rape.[359]

Thus Cologne's mayor slipped easily, without many people even noticing, into the Sharia mindset. Reker's recommendations were more of the official denial and obfuscation that has become so common all over Europe. She ignored, among other things, the fact that an official report established that the attackers were "almost exclusively" Arab migrants from North

358 Ibid.

359 "Punishment for Rape in Islam," Islam Question & Answer.

Africa.[360] To recognize that would have been to call into question the entire mass migration enterprise, and no mainstream German politician who wanted to have a political future was willing to do that.

MISTAKES WERE MADE

In Cologne, a report on the mass sexual assaults noted that the police made "serious mistakes."[361] These mistakes likely stemmed from the same wellsprings that led British officials to make so many "mistakes": the fear of charges of "racism" and "Islamophobia."

German authorities were generally no more willing to discuss the issues involved in these crimes than were their counterparts in Britain and France. The British paper the *Express* said in January 2016 that "Angela Merkel's government is under increasing pressure to come clean over the true numbers of sex crimes linked to migrants after it emerged that authorities deliberately withheld the nationalities of the Cologne attackers for several days. They also 'covered up' similar incidents in other cities including Dusseldorf and Hamburg, Munich and Berlin."[362]

Ultimately, however, the public outcry forced authorities to appear to be doing something about the crisis. Cologne's police

---

360 "Cologne attackers were of migrant origin - minister," BBC, January 11, 2016, https://www.bbc.com/news/world-europe-35280386. Accessed March 14, 2025.

361 Ibid.

362 Nick Gutteridge, "Migrant Sex Attack 'Cover-Up': Welcome party for Cologne refugees turned into mass groping," *Express*, January 16, 2016, https://www.express.co.uk/news/world/634815/Cologne-attacks-fury-migrant-sex-cover-up-refugee-event-groping-Germany. Accessed March 16, 2025.

chief, Wolfgang Albers, was fired for covering up the mass sexual assaults that had taken place there.[363] The real culprit, however, was the stigma of charges of "racism" and "Islamophobia" that the left used to silence any honest discussion of these incidents.

ASSUMPTIONS OF SUPERIORITY

Another byproduct of the migrants' theology and culture was the fact that the attackers generally regarded their victims with contempt. In Germany in August 2024, a thirty-one-year-old Afghan Muslim migrant known in the German media only as Mohammad S., in accord with laws designed to protect those accused of crimes, convinced two eighteen-year-old girls to come to his apartment in Erfurt. Then he pulled out a machete and announced: "You won't get out of here until one of you has sex with me."[364] He raped one of the girls.

When Mohammad S. was arrested, police discovered evidence on his cell phone that beginning in March 2022, he had a sexual relationship with an eleven-year-old girl, named in media reports as Emily K., raping her on a daily basis. Mohammad S. claimed implausibly that Emily's family approved of this, but her father told a different story: "We wanted to stop it, we told

---

363 Erik Kirschbaum, "Police chief in Cologne, Germany, is fired amid criticism tied to assaults on women," *Los Angeles Times*, January 8, 2016, http://latimes.com/world/europe/la-fg-germany-assaults-20160108-story.html. Accessed March 17, 2025.

364 Janek Könau, "'In Deutschland gibt es keine guten Menschen,'" *Bild*, February 25, 2025, https://www.bild.de/regional/thueringen/vergewaltigung-in-erfurt-afghane-fuehrte-beziehung-mit-11-jaehriger-67bc57d67bb4d33b4af24a21?t_ref=https%3A%2F%2Fm.bild.de%2Fregional%2Fthueringen%2Fvergewaltigung-in-erfurt-afghane-fuehrte-beziehung-mit-11-jaehriger-67bc57d67bb4d33b4af24a21. Accessed March 13, 2025.

him that it was a criminal offense."[365] Nevertheless, "as soon as she left the house, we couldn't do anything."[366]

Mohammad S., meanwhile, had utter contempt for his German hosts, who had given him refuge from the Afghan war zone and generously gave him welfare benefits. "There are no good people in Germany," he declared.[367] "Animals are better than them. And if a human is an animal, it must be slaughtered."[368]

This idea comes straight from the Qur'an: "Already we have created many of the jinn and mankind for Gehenna, having hearts with which they do not understand, and having eyes with which they do not see, and having ears with which they do not hear. They are like cattle, no, they are worse. These are the neglectful." (7:179) And: "Indeed, the worst of animals in Allah's sight are the ungrateful who will not believe." (8:55)

The Brandenburg police on January 30, 2020, noted what was in Germany, as in France, an all too typical incident: "The police were called to Tschirschdamm on Wednesday evening. A young man is said to have come too close to two children there. When the officers arrived on the scene, they were able to meet both the teenagers and the adult suspect. According to the girls, the suspect first grabbed them by the buttocks and then held a lighter over their heads. In addition, the man, in broken German and with gestures, apparently made them understand that he wanted to set them on fire. The two girls were then placed in the care of their parents and interviewed by criminologists. At the same time, the 22-year-old suspect, an Afghan,

---

365 Ibid.
366 Ibid.
367 Ibid.
368 Ibid.

was taken into custody by the Brandenburg Police Department. After they had clarified his identity there without a doubt and he underwent identification checks, he was released today. The criminal police are now investigating charges of sexual harassment and threats against the 22-year-old."[369]

A RAPE GANG IN AUSTRIA

The stories were similar from country to country. Remix News reported in November 2024 on a series of incidents that took place in Austria, but could have happened virtually anywhere among non-Muslims: "In an explosive trial in Vienna, 19 migrants — along with Austrians with a migration background — are accused of blackmailing and gang raping a 12-year-old girl over the course of months, with the first one already confessing to his crimes."[370]

One of the accused, a seventeen-year-old Muslim from Syria named Ahmad, claimed, as did so many accused Muslim rapists, that he "did not know how young the victim was but said she wanted to have sexual relations with him."[371] He also insisted: "I thought she was my age, 14 or something."[372] There were nineteen accused rapists in all, accused of "gang raping Mia for months and using videos of the gang rapes taken between

369 "Teenager belästigt und bedroht," Polizei Brandenburg, January 30, 2020, https://polizei.brandenburg.de/pressemeldung/teenager-belaestigt-und-bedroht/1811101. Accessed March 17, 2025.

370 "Austria: 19 migrants standing trial for allegedly gang raping a 12-year-old girl in Vienna over the course of months," Remix News, November 29, 2024, https://rmx.news/article/austria-19-migrants-standing-trial-for-gang-raping-a-12-year-old-girl-in-vienna-over-the-course-of-months/. Accessed March 14, 2025.

371 Ibid.

372 Ibid.

February and June 2023 as blackmail material to coerce her into having further sex, sometimes multiple times a week."[373]

The blackmail value of these videos may have been limited, for in one of them, "she is seen being abused by eight of the migrants while screaming, 'Stop!'"[374] State Criminal Police Major Florian Finda said that the victim "had been abused once using violence. The perpetrator was a 16-year-old Syrian. After that, the others constantly put pressure on her to sleep with them… She showed us chat messages saying that there was a video of her having sex with them and that if she didn't want it to be published, she should sleep with them."[375]

The accused were Syrians, Turks, an Italian, a Bulgarian, a Serb, and Austrians, and included four minors.[376] As always, there was no way to tell whether the Italian, Bulgarian, Serb, and Austrians were Muslims, whether converts or native-born.

373 Ibid.
374 Ibid.
375 Ibid.
376 Ibid.

CHAPTER THIRTEEN

SWEDEN SUCCUMBS

SWEDEN'S RAPE EPIDEMIC

On February 19, 2017, President Trump unleashed a torrent of ridicule when he said: "Here's the bottom line, we have to keep our country safe. When you look at what's happening in Germany, when you look at what's happening last night in Sweden — Sweden. Who would believe this? Sweden. They took in large numbers, they're having problems like they never thought possible."[377]

After numerous leftists ridiculed Trump and pointed out that nothing in particular had happened the previous night in Sweden, he issued a clarification: "My statement as to what's happening in Sweden was in reference to a story that was

[377] "Trump's remarks about Sweden create debate and confusion," ABC News, February 19, 2017, https://abcnews.go.com/Politics/trumps-remarks-sweden-create-debate-confusion/story?id=45596087. Accessed March 9, 2025.

broadcast on @FoxNews concerning immigrants & Sweden."[378] And on the following day: "Give the public a break -The FAKE NEWS media is trying to say that large scale immigration in Sweden is working out just beautifully. NOT!"[379]

Trump was referring to an interview on Fox News of documentary filmmaker Ami Horowitz, who was releasing a film about migrant violence, including a sharp increase in rape, in Sweden. This was just part of a much larger problem. Just two weeks before Trump's words sparked this faux controversy, the UK's *Express* reported of Sweden that "in February 2016, the National Criminal Investigation Service was forced to admit more than 50 areas in [sic] were now labelled as 'no-go zones' as sex crimes, attacks on police, drug dealing and children carrying weapons were common occurrences."[380] The situation was so bad that Malmö, the third-largest city in Sweden, had been "so hard hit by crime and car fires, the Social Democrats demanded soldiers should be sent in to reestablish law and order."[381] Malmö was (and still is) Sweden's most Muslim-dominated area.

On December 31, 2016, a year after the mass rapes in Cologne and elsewhere, Muslim mobs in Malmö fired rockets

---

378 Donald Trump, @realDonaldTrump, Twitter (X), February 19, 2017, https://x.com/realDonaldTrump/status/833435244451753984. Accessed March 9, 2025.

379 Donald Trump, @realDonaldTrump, Twitter (X), February 20, 2017, https://x.com/realDonaldTrump/status/833681539997253636. Accessed March 9, 2025.

380 Lizzie Stromme, "SWEDEN ON EDGE: Now MPs DEMAND billion pound investment into police amid growing crisis," February 5, 2017, *Express*, https://www.express.co.uk/news/world/763096/Sweden-MPs-demand-billion-pound-investment-police-growing-crisis. Accessed March 9, 2025.

381 Ibid.

at crowds and police.[382] The *Express* reported in November 2016 that Muslim migrants were carrying out sexual assaults and rapes with impunity, and that this could increase: "Migrant sex attacks against children in the Swedish city of Malmö could increase following a spate of incidents in broad daylight, police have warned. The city of Malmö has seen a huge rise in migrant crime in recent months."[383]

Malmö area police spokesperson Ewa-Gun Westford took the characteristic stance of European officials all over the continent: "Some cases concern rapes while in other cases it's sexual molestation, and we think [this situation] could escalate. We do not want to create a rancorous atmosphere among the public but want to tread carefully. The information we have leads in a certain direction, but it is very sensitive and [these are] difficult issues for the vulnerable."[384]

What was the "sensitive," "difficult" nature of fighting back against rape? Westford is referring only to the fact that Muslim migrants were perpetrating these crimes—and no one wanted to discuss the implications of that. The perpetrators appeared aware of this, behaving as if they didn't have a care in the world. In January 2017, two Afghan Muslim migrants kidnapped a

---

382 Lizzie Stromme, "Battlefield Sweden: Police admit Malmo isn't safe as thugs send fireworks into crowds," *Express*, January 3, 2017, https://www.express.co.uk/news/world/749735/Sweden-police-malmo-not-safe-NYE-thugs-grenade-attack. Accessed March 9, 2025.

383 Will Kirby, "Migrant sex attacks against children in Sweden could escalate, officials warn," *Express*, November 11, 2016, https://www.express.co.uk/news/world/731127/Migrant-sex-attacks-increase-Sweden-police-Malmo-Ewa-Gun-Westford-child/1000. Accessed March 9, 2025.

384 Ibid.

Swedish woman and streamed their repeated rapes of her live on Facebook.[385]

As a result of that incident and many more like it, in February 2017, a Swedish publication began an article by stating: "Welcome to Sweden, the rape capital of the world. Not only is our country at the top of Europe's list of the highest number of reported rapes, according to the OECD [Organisation for Economic Co-operation and Development], only Australia has had more reported rapes than Sweden."[386]

Malmö, once a calm Scandinavian city, had become an epicenter of criminal activity. Around the time that Trump called attention to the problems in Sweden, one Malmö high school student complained: "You have to look over your shoulder when you go out at night now. I don't let my little brother go out at night any more. I hope that the politicians actually view this as a serious problem and start to solve this in Malmö."[387]

Justice and Migration Minister Morgan Johansson offered some recommendations about how the crime wave could be ended: "We have to get rid of the weapons, we need tighter punishment so that those who are held for serious gun crime

---

385 Patrick Knox, "GANG RAPE ARRESTS: Two Afghan migrants revealed as those arrested over horrific three-hour rape streamed on Facebook Live in Sweden," *The Sun*, January 26, 2017, https://www.thesun.co.uk/news/2709224/two-afghan-migrants-revealed-as-those-arrested-over-horrific-three-hour-rape-streamed-on-facebook-live-in-sweden/. Accessed March 9, 2025.

386 Evelyn Schreiber, "Opinion: Welcome to Sweden, the rape capital of the world," *NA*, February 28, 2017, https://www.na.se/2017-02-28/opinion-welcome-to-sweden-the-rape-capital-of-the-world. Accessed March 13, 2025.

387 Michael Qazvini, "How Muslim Migration Made Malmo, Sweden A Crime Capital," Daily Wire, January 16, 2017, https://www.dailywire.com/news/how-muslim-migration-made-malmo-sweden-crime-michael-qazvini. Accessed March 13, 2025.

can be arrested immediately and not just be released a few days later."[388]

Maybe that would do it, but as the Daily Wire observed, "What Johansson failed to mention, however, was the fact that the bulk of the violence stems from one community. The Muslim immigrant community has a crime problem. It's a truism that Swedish (and European) politicians have denied in bold-faced lies and assurances to the public. Malmo, like Molenbeek, its sister city in Belgium, has become a breeding ground for criminals. Thousands of Muslim immigrants have fled their war-torn homes in the Middle East to settle in quaint European cities filled with naïve and welcoming townspeople. This has been true in France, England, Germany, Belgium, Denmark, and Sweden. Since the great migration into Europe, crime, largely committed by migrants, has gone up manifold, leaving many to reassess their naïveté about hosting duties."[389]

There were good reasons for such a reassessment. The Danish psychologist Nicolai Sennels has noted that in Sweden, "92 percent of all severe rapes (violent rapes) are committed by migrants and refugees. 100 percent of all attack rapes (in which the victim and the attacker had no previous contact) are committed by that same group. In other words, thousands of Swedish women would not have been raped and thereby traumatized for life had it not been for the influx from Islamic countries."[390]

---

388 Ibid.

389 Ibid.

390 Nicolai Sennels, "Dangerous refugees: Afghan Muslim migrants 79 times more likely to rape," Jihad Watch, July 1, 2017, https://jihadwatch.org/2017/07/dangerous-refugees-afghan-muslim-migrants-79-times-more-likely-to-rape. Accessed March 13, 2025.

Sennels also pointed out that in Sweden, "Afghans are 79 times more likely to commit a sexual crime than men who are born of Swedish citizens," and that "the top-10 list of rapists' national backgrounds shows only one non-Islamic country (Chile). Most rapists have an Iraqi background, followed by refugees and migrants from Afghanistan, Somalia, Eritrea, Syria, Gambia, Iran, Palestine, Chile and Kosovo."[391]

Swedish police officer Peter Springare said in 2017: "Here is what I have been handling last week: rape, rape, severe rape, attack rape, extortion, extortion, violence, illegal threats, violence against the police, threats against the police, drug dealing, severe drug dealing, attempted murder, rape, extortion, and violence. The criminals' country of origin: Iraq, Iraq, Turkey, Syria, Afghanistan, Somalia, Somalia, Syria, Somalia, unknown country, unknown country, Sweden. With half of the suspects we do not know the country of origin because they have no valid papers. This usually means that they are lying about their nationality and identity."[392]

Sennels also stated that Sweden was not singular in this: "Since Denmark caved to UN pressure in 2015 and started taking in thousands of asylum seekers from Islamic countries, rapes soared 163 percent in just one year."[393]

Although Elon Musk didn't say anything about the situation in Sweden, the migrant rape epidemic, after being largely ignored for years, suddenly became a topic of widespread public discussion in January 2025, around the same time that Musk sparked new discussion of the Muslim rape gangs in Britain.

391 Ibid.
392 Ibid.
393 Ibid.

The Swedish publication Fria Tider stated: "That immigrants are extremely overrepresented in rape statistics has been known for a very long time and it is something that Fria Tider has reported on since its inception in 2009. However, the phenomenon has been completely covered up in public Sweden – until now, when it is starting to be described as a problem. Recently, Expressen," a major Swedish newspaper, "has suddenly started reporting on the overrepresentation of immigrants in sex crime statistics."[394]

TEACH THEM RAPE IS WRONG

Sweden's Integration Minister Mats Persson had an idea about how to deal with this problem: teach migrants "liberal values."[395] He maintained that it was "possible to get them to stop raping," and said that "'patriarchal structures' and a different view of gender equality" were the explanations for why Muslim migrants were so vastly overrepresented in rape statistics.[396]

Persson recommending increasing the minimum prison sentence for rape, which was three years, and emphasized the importance of educating the new arrivals about Western values: "We must be clear from day one that anyone who comes here needs to support our view on women's and homosexual rights."[397]

That was much more realistic than most European politicians were willing to be, but if Persson was unaware that the

394 "Ministern: Invandrare ska få gå kurs om att det är fel att våldta," Fria Tider, January 20, 2025, https://www.friatider.se/ministern-invandrare-ska-fa-ga-kurs-om-att-det-ar-fel-att-valdta. Accessed March 13, 2025.

395 Ibid.

396 Ibid.

397 Ibid.

Muslim migrants in Sweden were virtually certain to reject Western values as "manmade" and hence inferior to what they considered to be divine law, the Sharia, he was whistling in the dark. The migrants had grown up in an environment that assumed that as Muslims, they were "the best of peoples" on earth (Qur'an 3:110), while non-Muslims were "the most vile of created beings" (Qur'an 98:6). The overwhelming majority of them weren't likely to exchange Qur'anic values for a value system that they considered to be inherently flawed and inferior.

NO DEPORTATIONS FROM SWEDEN

Much the same situation prevailed in Sweden. In one Swedish city, Östersund, police echoed Henriette Reker by cautioning women not to venture out alone at night. Said Regional Police Chief Stephen Jerand: "Now the police are going out and warning women against travelling alone in the city. We have seen a worrying trend. This is serious, we care about the protection of women and that is why we are going out and talking about this."[398]

To her credit, Östersund Mayor Ann-Sofie Andersson took umbrage at this, saying: "The solution can never be to not go out because of such a warning. We have very many women who work in home and social care at night for example. What are they supposed to do?"[399] And Johan Hedin of Sweden's Centre Party declared: "It's wrong if it calls on women to adapt to the

---

398 "Police defend warning for solo women in northern Sweden," The Local, March 8, 2016, https://www.thelocal.se/20160308/backlash-begins-after-swedish-women-told-not-to-go-out-alone. Accessed March 17, 2025.

399 Ibid.

criminals. It risks leading people the wrong way, if the victims must adapt to the perpetrators."[400]

On April 29, 2023, in the Swedish city of Örebro, a Somali Muslim migrant, Mohamedamin Ibrahim, murdered his Swedish/Thai girlfriend Saga Forsgren Elneborg, who was seven months pregnant with his son. Prosecutor Elisabeth Anderson explained: "The suspect's family has not accepted that he was with a white girl."[401] In line with the Qur'an's command to "strike the necks" of the unbelievers, Ibrahim killed Elneborg, according to Anderson "by suffocating and strangling her by means of pressure on her neck with an impact on the trachea and the blood supply to the head."[402]

Ibrahim did this because of his mother's rage upon discovering that her son was in a relationship with a non-Muslim woman. Ibrahim's mother sent him a text telling him not to return home: "Don't come to me. I am no longer your mother. I am Islamic and Somali."[403] Dismayed, Ibrahim lied, responding: "I'm also Muslim and Somali and I don't go home to a white person."[404]

Ultimately, Ibrahim murdered his girlfriend, killing her unborn child in the process, in order to cover up the relationship. Anderson explained: "I mean that the murder took place in an honor context because the man wanted to preserve or

---

400 Ibid.

401 "Hovrätten slår fast: Livstid för mord på "för vit" gravid kvinna," Fria Tider, October 9, 2024, https://www.friatider.se/hovratten-slar-fast-livstid-mord-pa-vit-gravid-kvinna. Accessed March 13, 2025.

402 Yaron Steinbuch, "Somali refugee allegedly strangles pregnant Swedish girlfriend in honor killing," *New York Post*, April 4, 2024, https://nypost.com/2024/04/04/world-news/somali-refugee-allegedly-strangles-swedish-girlfriend-in-honor-killing/. Accessed March 13, 2025.

403 "Hovrätten slår fast."

404 Ibid.

restore his and his family's honor by killing the woman who was carrying his child."[405]

Saga Forsgren Elneborg's mother said of her daughter: "She was so happy. She would move to a new apartment and start her life as a mother. This is the worst thing imaginable."[406]

Because he has been given a Swedish passport, Mohamedamin Ibrahim cannot be deported.

Two Muslim migrants from Iraq, Mazin Al-Sharash and Akar Bajorani, also won't be deported. In December 2023, a Swedish court sentenced Al-Sharash to six years in prison, and Bajorani to five years and three months, for gang-raping and urinating upon a Swedish woman on a cruise ship during a twenty-four-hour cruise between the Swedish cities of Stockholm and Mariehamn.

The court noted that Al-Sharash and Bajorani had "acted with particular recklessness and brutality" during their rapes, but Al-Sharash had become a Swedish citizen and so could not be deported back to Iraq, despite not speaking Swedish and needing an Arabic translator at his trial, although he had been in the country for five years. Bajorani, meanwhile, had "integrated" well into Swedish society, at least in the judgment of the court, and so wouldn't be deported, either.[407]

---

405 Steinbuch, "Somali refugee allegedly strangles."

406 Ibid.

407 Thomas Brooke, "Iraqi duo who urinated on and gang raped woman on cruise ship to remain in Sweden as court says they have 'integrated,'" Remix News, December 6, 2023, https://rmx.news/crime/iraqi-duo-who-urinated-on-and-gang-raped-woman-on-cruise-ship-to-remain-in-sweden-as-court-says-they-have-integrated/. Accessed March 13, 2025.

JUVENILE PERPETRATORS AND AN UNDERAGE VICTIM

They would have plenty of company in Sweden. In one sadly typical case in September 2022, three Muslim migrants from Syria, two who were seventeen years old and one who was eighteen, were charged with raping a girl who was herself underage.

The three young men cornered the girl in a public toilet at the Garden Association in Linköping, locking the door to keep their victim from running away. They then took turns raping her. Remix News reported that "police obtained footage of one of the rapes, which one of the suspects recorded with his smartphone and sent to a contact on Snapchat. This suspect has therefore been also charged with transmitting child pornography."[408]

None of the accused rapists spoke Swedish; they all needed an Arabic interpreter for their court proceedings, in which they would be tried as juveniles and no doubt out on the streets again in no time.

---

408 "Sweden: 3 Syrian migrants charged with locking underage girl in bathroom and raping her, posting child pornography to Snapchat," Remix News, January 4, 2024, https://rmx.news/crime/sweden-3-syrian-migrants-charged-with-locking-underage-girl-in-bathroom-and-raping-her-posting-child-pornography-to-snapchat/. Accessed March 18, 2025.

CHAPTER FOURTEEN

FRANCE LOSES ITS WAY

A TRIVIAL MATTER

It was difficult to deport Muslim migrant rapists from France as well. In December 2024, three Algerian Muslim migrants who were in France illegally attacked and gang-raped a woman who was visiting an apartment next door to the one in which they were squatting. Both had already been ordered to be deported, but had ignored the order. Remix News reported that this was not unusual: "Deportation rates for Algerians in France with a deportation order are an abysmal 0.2 percent. In other words, only 2 out of every 1,000 Algerians with a deportation order are ever actually sent back. This data came to light following the rape, torture and murder of 12-year-old Lola in Paris by an Algerian woman with a longstanding deportation order, a case that shocked the nation in 2022."[409]

---

409 "France: 3 Algerians gang rape Polish mother inside squatted apartment in city of Gap," Remix News, December 19, 2024, https://rmx.news/article/france-3-algerians-gang-rape-polish-mother-inside-squatted-apartment-in-city-of-gap/. Accessed June 3, 2025.

The case of Lola Daviet was unusual in that the main perpetrator was a woman, and yet even in this case, the victim was raped. It appeared as if in this case as well as so many others, sexual violation was seen as a reliable way to humiliate the infidel. An Algerian Muslim migrant, Dahbia Benkired, who was in France on an expired student residence permit, abducted Lola, forced her to perform oral sex on her, tortured her, and ultimately stabbed her multiple times in the neck.[410] The fact that the attack centered on Lola's neck was another indication of Dahbia Benkired's cultural and religious background. Said anti–mass migration politician Éric Zemmour: "Of Algerian nationality and in an irregular situation, it's official: The assassin of Lola should never have crossed her path. Once again."[411]

For Dahbia Benkired, Lola Daviet's life was clearly of no importance. She was no better than an animal, and her death was a trivial matter.

"I KNOW YOU'RE NOT MUSLIM"

Meanwhile, life in France had become just as precarious for young women as it had become elsewhere. In a type of story that had come to be all too commonplace, Remix News reported in October 2024 that "two Latvian tourists were sexually assaulted

---

410 William Molinie, "INFO EUROPE 1 – Meurtre de Lola : ce que la principale suspecte a déclaré en garde à vue," Europe 1, October 18, 2022, https://www.europe1.fr/faits-divers/info-europe-1-meurtre-de-lola-ce-que-la-principale-suspecte-a-declare-en-garde-a-vue-4141440. Accessed March 14, 2025.

411 Thomas Brooke, "Algerian migrant indicted for rape and murder of Parisian schoolgirl Lola had been ordered to leave France upon expiry of residence permit," Remix News, October 18, 2022, https://rmx.news/crime/algerian-migrant-indicted-for-rape-and-murder-of-parisian-school-girl-lola-had-been-ordered-to-leave-france-upon-expiry-of-residence-permit. Accessed March 13, 2025.

in Paris by a group of seven men on the Champ de Mars, near the Eiffel Tower on Saturday night leading to the arrests of four foreign nationals."[412] The foreign nationals in question were "two Algerian and two Egyptian males."[413]

The women would have suffered even worse were it not for the fact that as the assault was going on at around 2:30 a.m., "officers from the Parisian anti-crime brigade patrolling the area spotted the two women being surrounded by the group. One man was seen trying to undress one of the victims and kissing her breasts, according to a police source. Both women were subjected to inappropriate touching."[414]

The victims were disinclined to pursue the matter: "Initially, the two victims expressed their intent to file a formal complaint. However, due to the trauma and shock from the attack, they later changed their minds, opting to return to their accommodation to rest."[415] Authorities, however, vowed to continue the investigation, but as they had so many others like it, apprehending the culprits and bringing them to justice was unlikely.

Another victim in France, meanwhile, received from her tormenters a brisk lesson in the Islamic motivations for such attacks that authorities in Britain in particular but also all over the West were determined to deny. Three teenagers, who were reported as being between twelve and fourteen years old gang-raped a twelve-year-old girl in a hangar in Paris.

---

412 Thomas Brooke, "Latvian tourists sexually assaulted on Champ de Mars: 4 migrants arrested," Remix News, October 7, 2024, https://rmx.news/article/latvian-tourists-sexually-assaulted-on-champ-de-mars-4-migrants-arrested/. Accessed March 14, 2025.

413 Ibid.

414 Ibid.

415 Ibid.

They then allowed her to depart from the scene of the crime, but according to her mother, "before letting her leave, they made her swear on Allah not to say anything, and that she should not tell anyone, neither her parents nor the police."[416] One of the rapists asked the girl: "I know you're not Muslim… So, what religion are you?"[417] When the rapists found out the girl was Jewish, they began speaking disparagingly of Jews and asked her to convert to Islam.[418] Clearly, they didn't see any incongruity in asking this of a girl just after they had raped her.

When they were apprehended, one of the boys claimed that they had raped her because he was in a relationship with her and she had not disclosed that she was Jewish. Investigators found antisemitic material on his cell phone. One of the other rapists, meanwhile, explained that he had participated in the rape of the girl "because she said bad things about Palestine."[419] Once again, he showed no sign of thinking it odd that someone who did such a thing should be punished by being raped.

A similar incident took place on December 12, 2023, in the Paris suburb of Val-de-Marne, when a man brandishing a six-inch knife walked into Les Mini Kids, a Jewish daycare center,

---

416 "'Swear on Allah': French antisemitic rape victim told to convert to Islam - report," *Jerusalem Post*, June 25, 2024, https://www.jpost.com/breaking-news/article-807650. Accessed March 17, 2025.

417 Ibid.

418 Ibid; Itzik Brandwein, "France: 12-year-old Jewish girl raped in suspected antisemitic attack," Israel National News, June 18, 2024, https://www.israelnationalnews.com/news/391738. Accessed March 17, 2025.

419 Brandwein, "France: 12-year-old Jewish girl raped."

and said to female director: "You're a Jew, you're a Zionist. Five of us are going to rape you, cut you up like they did in Gaza."[420]

"I'm afraid," the director said afterward. "I can't tell myself that I'm going to reopen a nursery where I welcome babies, parents. We're going to see psychologists, to see how it evolves and that this trauma does not end in depression, or even more. For now, parents do not want to come back at all; there are some who want to remove the children from the nursery altogether."[421] "Striking terror in the enemies of Allah," as per the Qur'an (8:60) was one of the guiding principles at play in such incidents.

On the morning of October 12, 2023, a man in Marseille began shouting, according *to Ouest-France*, "that he belonged to Hamas, that he wanted to 'rape' women and children and kill 'everyone.'"[422] An investigation was duly opened.

BRAZEN

Many of the migrants were so unconcerned about the French authorities that they didn't even hesitate to rape women, or attempt to do so, in the middle of the street. At least one of them failed: On February 3, 2023, according to Remix News,

420 Ben Cohen, "'Zionist, We Are Going to Rape You!' Knife Wielding Intruder Threatens Director of Jewish Daycare Center Near Paris," *Algemeiner*, https://www.algemeiner.com/2023/12/14/zionist-we-are-going-rape-you-knife-wielding-assailant-threatens-director-jewish-daycare-center-near-paris/. Accessed March 17, 2025.

421 Ibid.

422 "Marseille. Il hurlait dans la rue qu'il appartenait au Hamas et voulait tuer « tout le monde »," *Ouest-France*, October 16, 2023, https://www.ouest-france.fr/provence-alpes-cote-dazur/marseille-13000/marseille-il-hurlait-dans-la-rue-quil-appartenait-au-hamas-et-voulait-tuer-tout-le-monde-6406cbc4-6bfe-11ee-b2ff-3bb9482842ad. Accessed March 17, 2025.

"a French teenager saved a 13-year-old French schoolgirl from being raped on the street by an Algerian migrant."[423]

The girl was talking to her mother on the phone as she walked down a street in the southwestern French city of Cenon. Frédérique Porterie, the public prosecutor of Bordeaux, explained that the would-be rapist, who was forty-nine years old, "came running towards her, grabbed her, pushed her and made her fall before pulling her by the hair and putting his hand in her pants."[424] The Algerian "straddled her, unzipped his fly, and began to try forcing her to perform fellatio on him in the middle of the street."[425]

However, at that point "another teenager, who was approximately the same age as the victim, tackled the Algerian migrant, allowing the girl to get away. The Algerian then attempted to attack the teen who had tackled him, but the teen's efforts bought enough time for the girl to get away from danger and for others from the area to arrive to help stop the ongoing attack."[426]

When the police arrived, the attacker "bit two of them on the hand, with one of the bites resulting in a severe injury that could lead to lasting nerve damage. He also hit a third officer with a strong blow. The vicious attack led one officer to require 10 days of hospital treatment, while the other two required five days."[427] And not surprisingly, given the state of French justice

---

423 John Cody, "French teenager saves 13-year-old girl from rape by Algerian migrant with 11 convictions," Remix News, February 7, 2023, https://rmx.news/france/french-teenager-saves-13-year-old-girl-from-rape-by-algerian-migrant-with-11-convictions/. Accessed March 17, 2025.

424 Ibid.

425 Ibid.

426 Ibid.

427 Ibid.

regarding migrants, the accused was found to have eleven prior convictions.

The Algerian is also a drain on the resources of the French welfare state: He is "unemployed, habitually smokes marijuana, and lives on welfare. During his court hearing, he denied he had anything to do with the case and "does not remember anything."[428]

"VERY RELIGIOUS"

"The attack," reported *Le Figaro* on September 1, 2023, was the handiwork of a "young man, aged 21, of Algerian nationality and in an irregular situation."[429] An "irregular situation" meant that he was an illegal migrant. Clearly unafraid of French police, he raped a woman "in the middle of the street at the entrance of the Castel Club, a nightclub, in a business area of La Roche-sur-Yon."[430]

Initially, the accused denied that he had done anything at all. Then, he began to claim that he and the victim had "a consensual sexual relationship."[431] He "admitted 'traveling with false papers,' under two identities known to the police. His lawyer, Meriem Abkoui, made it clear that his client's record 'is blank for both identities.'"[432] Under the circumstances, this was hardly reassuring, but in trying to make her case, Abkoui revealingly explained that the accused rapist was "very reli-

---

428 Ibid.

429 Pauline Darrieus, "Une jeune femme violée en pleine rue en Vendée, un suspect incarcéré," *Le Figaro*, September 1, 2023, https://www.lefigaro.fr/faits-divers/une-jeune-femme-violee-en-pleine-rue-en-vendee-un-suspect-incarcere-20230901. Accessed March 17, 2025.

430 Ibid.

431 Ibid.

432 Ibid.

gious and was afraid that his brother would judge him for this relationship outside marriage."[433]

Another attacker, apparently a convert to Islam, was likewise "very religious." *L'Est Républicain* reported that "on April 18, 2022, Fabio Califano, a 25-year-old from Dijon, came to ask for the hand of a resident of Étupes. He brought her a traditional garment from Turkey ('on a pleasure trip') as well as other gifts that all women dream of, a packet of flour, incense, spices."[434]

The happy occasion was not what it appeared to be. The intended bride's father recounted later: "I was not there. If the cops hadn't arrested him, what would have happened?"[435] He asked this because on the night before he showed up to propose marriage, Fabio Califano had called the seventeen-year-old girl he now said he wanted to marry and said to her: "I am going to burn you all, I am going to cut your throats. You and your mother, I will rape you because I have the right to do so."[436]

Once he was on trial, Califano insisted that he had shown up to propose marriage to make up for his boorish behavior the night before: "I wanted to apologize for my behavior."[437] *L'Est Républicain* notes, however, that "this was not the suspect's first outburst. When he returned from a trip a few days earlier, the follower of a radical ('Salafist') Islam had sent a frightening message to the young woman with whom he had been chatting

---

433 Ibid.

434 Aude Lambert, "Apologie du terrorisme et menaces de mort contre une famille d'Etupes : trois ans de prison pour l'inquiétant croyant," *L'Est Républicain*, May 11, 2023, https://www.estrepublicain.fr/faits-divers-justice/2023/05/11/apologie-du-terrorisme-trois-ans-de-prison-pour-l-inquietant-croyant. Accessed March 17, 2025.

435 Ibid.

436 Ibid.

437 Ibid.

on Facebook for three weeks. What was the reasoning? She refused – even then – to marry him: 'Soon we will cut your throats and play football with your heads.' The text was accompanied by a video showing a beheading scene."[438]

The girl's father, meanwhile, was most angry about the fact that the image of Islam had been besmirched: "Islam is not what I have been told for two hours. The religion stands for peace, tolerance and respect…We have been living in fear for a year."[439]

This disingenuousness or willful ignorance, combined with the denial of authorities, meant that women and girls in France and elsewhere would continue to be vulnerable.

"I DID NOT KNOW YOUR LAWS"

Boys were not exempt. "On June 25, 2021," reported the French-language publication Actu, "the Assize Court of Saint-Brieuc sentenced a 30-year-old Afghan to 15 years' imprisonment for the rape of a 12-year-old boy."[440] Over a year later, the Afghan "was taken from his cell in Brest to explain himself regarding other acts of sexual assault, committed 4 years ago in the same city."[441]

He seemed altogether happy to do so: "It is in complete relaxation, with a smile on his face, accompanied by his interpreter, that the defendant comes to explain himself at the bar of

---

438 Ibid.

439 Ibid.

440 "Saint-Brieuc : il agresse deux mineures et se défend : 'Je ne connaissais pas les lois de votre pays,'" Actu, July 8, 2022, https://actu.fr/bretagne/saint-brieuc_22278/saint-brieuc-il-agresse-deux-mineures-et-se-defend-je-ne-connaissais-pas-les-lois-de-votre-pays_52326942.html. Accessed March 17, 2025.

441 Ibid.

the Saint-Brieuc criminal court. He is accused of acts of sexual assault and harassment of two underage girls in 2018. Facts that occurred a few days before the rape of the little boy."

The Afghan explained: "In my country, it is normal to have sex with young boys because women are inaccessible. When I arrived in France I did not know your laws, but since I learned that it was prohibited."[442]

Apparently he was a late learner. He came to France in 2016, but didn't commit his first sexual assault until 2018. On April 16 of that year, he approached "a young underage girl on rue Mansart in St-Brieuc. Claiming to need help in broken English, he manages to lure her into his room in a home, taking care to lock the door."[443]

His victim recounted: "He slammed me against the wall holding me down with his knee, he was way too strong, I was trying to resist, but I couldn't get away, he was trying to kiss me and tear my clothes off, I was terrified, he ended up telling me that if I wanted to leave I had to touch his penis. When I told him I would call the police, he immediately opened the door."[444]

Her attacker blamed his intended victim: "I wanted to touch her a little, but she wouldn't. If she was a decent girl, she wouldn't have come up to my room."[445]

A few weeks later, he approached another woman, who recalled: "He told me, 'Miss, Miss, come and have sex with me.' He was insistent and chased me, I was very scared, I warned my parents who called the police."[446] The Afghan admitted this, while confessing to a certain puzzlement about it all: "It's true,

---

442 Ibid.

443 Ibid.

444 Ibid.

445 Ibid.

446 Ibid.

I said that, but she was shouting 'Get out, get out!', but I didn't understand that word."[447]

The prosecutor noted that one of his victims had attempted suicide five times: "The defendant reacts to the five suicide attempts of the victim with a broad smile, and this is unacceptable, he has no remorse, no regrets."[448]

Why should he have any remorse or regrets? He knew that what he had attempted to do was not in violation of his religion, and that was really all that mattered. In the mainstream Muslim view, Islamic law is divine and perfect, and superior to any manmade law such as the French legal code. Islamic law forbids men to have sexual relations with other men, but often this is understood as meaning that a Muslim must not declare himself "gay" and pursue a life of sexual relations only with men. If he marries and has children but has sex with men on the side, there is no problem. A common expression puts it succinctly: "Men are for pleasure, women are for children."

"THIS ONE IS THE PRODUCT OF A PATRIARCHAL SYSTEM"

On September 9, 2024, the French-language Actu-Juridique reported on yet another sexual assault case involving a Muslim migrant: "Mr. M. is brought before the judges of the Créteil Judicial Court for sexually assaulting a woman in Choisy Park and beating her husband. Despite his clean record, he is being brought before the court immediately due to his irregular status in France and faces a high risk: the prosecution is requesting a

---

447 Ibid.

448 "Saint-Brieuc : il agresse deux mineures et se defend."

ten-month prison sentence with a committal warrant."[449] Ten months! A high risk indeed.

The victim said that "after spending some time with relatives in Choisy Park, she decided to go home and began walking out of the park. After a few steps, she felt followed and turned around when Mr. M. allegedly touched her genitals with his hand, focusing on her buttocks, without penetration. She claims to have punched him in the shoulder, to which he allegedly replied, 'I want you.' Mrs. G. immediately called her husband, who had remained in the park. He ran over and was allegedly hit by Mr. M.: 'He continued to come towards my husband, who pushed him away with his fists.' The couple called the police, who arrested Mr. M., who was very drunk (0.83 mg of alcohol per liter exhaled when he blew into the balloon)."[450]

The defendant's version differed markedly from this. He said that he had happened upon a woman who was "dressed very scantily" and that he gallantly told her that she was "very beautiful."[451] Who could object to that except the most churlish onlooker? Then, however, he added: "Maybe I touched her, I was drunk."[452] He decided to affect a posture of victimhood, saying: "I'm leaving the park because I had to catch the bus. I'm

---

449 Adèle Cailleteau, "TJ de Créteil : « Il reste beaucoup de chemin à parcourir dans l'éducation des hommes, surtout quand ils viennent du Pakistan »," Actu-Juridique, September 9, 2024, https://www.actu-juridique.fr/penal/tj-de-creteil-il-reste-beaucoup-de-chemin-a-parcourir-dans-leducation-des-hommes-surtout-quand-ils-viennent-du-pakistan/. Accessed March 18, 2025.

450 Ibid.

451 Ibid.

452 Ibid.

on my phone, and a guy comes up from behind. He asks me if I touched his wife and punches me."[453]

Asked what he was doing on his phone, he answered, "I was watching a song on YouTube."[454] When police searched his phone, however, they found pornography. His defense attorney decided to attempt a defense based on culture: "There's still a long way to go in educating men, especially when they come from Pakistan. This one is the product of a patriarchal system, of this culture where forced marriage is still practiced."[455] Actu-Juridique adds that this inventive attorney elaborated upon this "line of defense for several minutes, focusing on the cultural gap between the laws of the country where Mr. M. is being tried and the customs of his country of origin."[456]

In addition, in order to "generate empathy for his client, he also evokes his 'frustrated sex life' based on very concrete facts: he was 25 when he had his first sexual encounter—with a prostitute—and his last intercourse was several months ago. The lawyer assures that his client has now fully understood the lesson, which he clumsily summarizes: 'You have to approach the person first before touching them.'"[457] He added that he was "requesting a less severe sentence, with a simple suspended sentence for which his client is eligible, and an acquittal concerning the violence against Mr. G. To help Mr. M. better 'control his sexual urges' and treat his alcohol addiction, he is also requesting compulsory treatment."[458]

453 Ibid.
454 Ibid.
455 Ibid.
456 Ibid.
457 Ibid.
458 Ibid.

M.'s alcohol abuse may have indicated that he was learning to fit into his new environment, but if what his attorney said about the cultural differences between France and Pakistan was true, as it obviously was, it would take more than compulsory classes to help him learn to control his sexual urges. For he would need to learn also why he should discard practices that Allah commanded for ones that mere human beings developed.

CHAPTER FIFTEEN

'ALWAYS THE MAGHREBI TYPES'

A MIGRATION ACTIVIST EXPERIENCES THE EFFECTS OF MIGRATION

Such incidents pointed yet again to the folly of mass Muslim migration into France and elsewhere in the West, as well as of the leftist embrace of and advocacy for that migration. Even if the girl's attackers had been born in France, their parents almost certainly had not been; France's large and growing Muslim population was of relatively recent vintage. As Muslims flooded into France, at one point a French advocate for mass migration found herself face-to-face with the recklessness and irrationality of what she had done as a migration advocate: she became the victim of a migrant rapist.

A fifty-eight-year-old migrant in Bordeaux, Yero Ba, raped twenty-three-year-old Océane Decan at knifepoint. "Yero" is a Fulani name meaning "fourth-born son," the Fulani are a predominantly Muslim tribe in West Africa, particularly Nigeria, that is engaged in a particularly virulent and bloody jihad in that country and its neighbors. Yero Ba raped Decan in 2021, and was duly arrested. In September 2023, however, two months before his trial for the rape was scheduled to begin, he was released from pre-trial detention, and was completely free, with the understanding that he would appear for his trial. He was released over the strenuous objections of the prosecutor, who strongly believed that Ba should stay behind bars until his trial began.

Once released, Yero Ba had no job to go to; nor did he have a home. What he did have was a lengthy criminal record, including convictions for acts of violence and sexual assault. The French publication Infos Bordeaux revealed that the case had a special piquancy because of the victim's activities: "If feminist associations, usually very silent in the face of this type of rape, have decided to publicize the case, it is because Océane Decan is one of them. Very committed to the left, she has fought for the cause of migrants since her youth."[459]

Infos Bordeaux said that Decan had a lengthy record of aiding migrants and opposing "fascists"; whether it was longer than Yero Ba's criminal record, the paper did not say. "A high school student in Jean-Brito (Ille-et-Vilaine)," Infos Bordeaux reported, "she was already mobilizing her classmates to help migrants through food drives. Before entering Sciences Po Bordeaux, she was involved in numerous organizations that help foreigners (Amnesty International, Utopia 56, Sos Racisme, etc.)."[460]

---

459 "Engagée auprès des migrants… et violée par l'un d'entre eux !" Infos Bordeaux, December 12, 2023, https://www.infos-bordeaux.fr/2023/actualites/engagee-aupres-des-migrants-et-violee-par-lun-dentre-eux-12602. Accessed March 17, 2025.

460 Ibid.

Océane Decan has been passionate about her pet cause: "On her Facebook profile, 'Océane Lelostec,' compares the fate of migrants to that of Jews during the Second World War. She remains strongly committed to opposing 'police violence, the deportation of migrants, and fascists.'"[461]

Despite all her work for migrants, there was one migrant Decan did not want to see. And yet there he was: "One day in October, I was walking in the center of Bordeaux and I ran into him on Rue Sainte-Catherine: he was playing guitar and begging. It was a shock. It woke everything up. I'm having panic attacks, I don't dare leave my house anymore. As soon as I have to go into town, I have to be accompanied."[462] Remix News reported: "French media reports that she is on sick leave and suffers from 'post-traumatic stress disorder,' according to her psychologist.[463]

In France, she wasn't the first to suffer from that malady, and will by no means be the last.

"THE MONSTER OF CHERBOURG"

Among them are a woman named Mégane and her friends and family. On August 4, 2023, when Mégane was twenty-nine, a Muslim migrant named Oumar Ndiaye broke into her apartment and raped her with a broomstick. The rape was so brutal that doctors put Mégane into an artificial coma, in which she remained for more than a month. Remix News reported that

461 Ibid.

462 Ibid.

463 John Cody, "France: Pro-migrant activist raped by homeless migrant is 'shocked' to see her rapist on the street," Remix News, December 13, 2023, https://rmx.news/crime/france-pro-migrant-activist-raped-by-homeless-migrant-is-shocked-to-see-her-rapist-on-the-street/. Accessed March 17, 2025.

"after the victim was transported to the hospital, doctors diagnosed her perforation of the colon, small intestine, peritoneum and diaphragm, pneumothorax, rib fractures and a high risk of septic shock. The injuries were so extreme that hospital staff were moved to tears over the attack."[464]

Even the emergency responders who arrived at the scene of the crime began to weep when they saw the condition Mégane was in. One observer said: "Investigators are shocked, they have never seen so much barbarity."[465] The French newspaper *Le Figaro* called the rape an "act of torture." Politician Damien Rieu called Ndiaye "the monster of Cherbourg."[466] But why was Oumar Ndiaye in Cherbourg in the first place?

Mégane's father, Ludovic Loir, was angry over the French government's apparent indifference to the crime. He said: "Mégane came out of a coma a few days ago, but her state of health remains fragile. This is obviously excellent news, but it will take her a long time to recover from all that she has suffered. (The government) not communicating about this attack gives credit to all these sexual predators and other parasites of society who plague the streets. A wake-up call to the government about the fact that we leave this kind of individual, with a heavy

---

464 "'Sexual predators and other parasites' – Father slams French government's silence after brutal rape of his daughter that left her in a coma," Remix News, September 8, 2023, https://rmx.news/crime/sexual-predators-and-other-parasites-father-slams-french-governments-silence-after-migrant-tortured-and-raped-his-daughter-megane-into-a-coma-with-a-broomstick/#8216i-dream-of-a-france-where-a-young-woman-is-not-in-danger-of-ending-up-in-a-coma-after-being-robbed-raped-and-horribly-tortured8217. Accessed March 17, 2025.

465 Ibid.

466 Ibid.

criminal past, in complete freedom, would be welcome. 'Trust in justice,' we were told… We only want that."[467]

For the French government to take any serious notice of what Oumar Ndiaye had done to Mégane, however, it would have had to repudiate its entire stance on mass migration, or at very least call it into question, and it wasn't about to do that.

According to Remix News, Oumar Ndiaye was, like Yero Ba, a serial offender, with "a long and violent criminal record consisting of 17 offenses involving physical assault, theft, and the incestuous sexual assault of his younger sister."[468]

Ndiaye had a history of getting the kid-gloves treatment from French authorities. A prosecutor noted that "a procedure for the rape of a minor initiated in 2019 was dismissed by the prosecution in 2020, on the grounds that the offense was not sufficiently characterized. And a sexual assault procedure against his sister is currently under investigation, without it being possible at this stage to determine whether or not these facts have been established."[469] Ndiaye's lengthy rap sheet was despite the fact that at the time he raped Mégane, he was only eighteen years old. And when he was arrested for raping and brutalizing Mégane, he showed "neither empathy nor remorse."[470]

Jordan Bardella, president of the National Rally, was forthright about what mass migration had done to France: "Courage to the 29-year-old victim, the umpteenth life shattered by the barbarism that is gaining in France."[471] Éric Zemmour stated: "I dream of a France where a young woman is not in danger of ending up in a coma after being robbed,

---

[467] Ibid.
[468] Ibid.
[469] Ibid.
[470] Ibid.
[471] Ibid.

raped and horribly tortured by Oumar, a repeat offender, in her own home."[472]

Yet in an indication of the fix France was in and the left's willful blindness regarding issues of mass migration and crime, particularly rape, Socialist Party Secretary General Olivier Faure professed outrage that Zemmour went out of his way to point out that the name of the rapist and torturer was Oumar. Faure insisted that it made no difference what the offender's name was: "A criminal must be condemned for his crimes, whether his name is Oumar, Francis, Michel, Emile, Guy or Patrice. Barbarism, perversion and vice have no skin color or nationality. Using a heinous act to imply that immigrants are rapists is racist."[473]

Faure did not, however, show any awareness of the fact that a young man named Oumar was likely to have been the product of a culture that reveres a religion that allows for such activity, whereas Francis, Michel, Emile, Guy, or Patrice were extremely unlikely to have done so.

The French authorities, meanwhile, made it abundantly clear that they were in no mood to tolerate anyone drawing too many unwelcome conclusions from what Oumar Ndiaye had done to Mégane. On September 9, 2023, a French patriotic group called Argos announced:

> Argos supports Mégane and her family as she comes out of a coma.

---

472 Ibid.

473 "Viol barbare à Cherbourg : Olivier Faure préfère parler de racisme plutôt que de la victime," *Valeurs Actuelles*, August 13, 2023, https://www.valeurs-actuelles.com/politique/viol-barbare-a-cherbourg-olivier-faure-prefere-parler-de-racisme-plutot-que-de-la-victime. Accessed March 17, 2025.

> Savagely attacked and raped by Oumar N. last August, Mégane finally came out of the coma today but remains in a fragile state. The Argos activists therefore went to the hospital in Cherbourg where she is being treated in order to show her our support. A donation was also made via a fund set up recently.
>
> In a society where the state and Justice do their job, Mégane would not have had to suffer the barbarity of Oumar. In a society where young people do not have such a wait-and-see attitude, Oumar could not have committed these crimes. Support for Mégane,
>
> People's Self-Defense for our own![474]

The Argos activists held up banners saying: "The state doesn't defend us, get ready."[475] This was quite obviously true, but the French state did not want the news aired about, and so twelve members of the group were arrested and held for two days. Prosecutor Pierre-Yves Marot told them: "You are appearing for having, through speeches made at an undeclared demonstration, incited willful harm to a person's integrity by calling for self-defense."[476] In diverse, multicultural France, defending oneself was a crime.

---

[474] "French activists face up to 5 years in prison for protesting outside house of migrant accused of brutal rape of 29-year-old Mégane," Remix News, September 14, 2023, https://rmx.news/france/self-defense-a-crime-french-activists-face-up-to-5-years-in-prison-for-protesting-outside-house-of-migrant-accused-of-raping-29-year-old-megane-until-she-entered-a-coma/. Accessed March 17, 2025.

[475] Ibid.

[476] Ibid.

Yet that self-defense was increasingly necessary. French women, in particular, had to defend themselves from migrants. France's Interior Ministry revealed in January 2025 that 63 percent of those who were guilty of sexual assault were foreigners.[477] As the ministry did not record the offenders' religious identity, there was no way to tell what percentage of the remainder were committed by Muslims who were born in France. There were 34,588 reported rapes in France in 2022, up from 22,770 in 2020 and 12,820 in 2016.[478] It was during this period, of course, that there was a mass influx of Muslim migrants into France.

"THE PEOPLE WHO ATTACK US DAILY ARE MOSTLY NON-NATIVES"

In June 2023, feminist group Collectif Némésis published a video in which women spoke forthrightly about what their daily lives were like now that Muslim migrants had flooded into France. Collectif Némésis says of itself: "We are a group of young Parisian women, most of whom are fed up with being harassed, assaulted, raped, killed because of our sex, the way we dress or even our origin. We do not recognize ourselves in the post-modern feminism that dominates in the media. This feminism refuses to name and describe its aggressors, thus inflicting a double penalty on the victims. Our goal is above all to free the

---

477 "France: 63% of those arrested for sexual assault and 92% for petty theft in public transport were foreigners," Remix News, January 14, 2025, https://rmx.news/article/france-63-of-those-arrested-for-sexual-assault-and-92-for-petty-theft-in-public-transport-were-foreigners/. Accessed March 17, 2025.

478 S. Galan, "Number of cases of woman rape recorded by the police in France from 2016 to 2022, by age of the victim," Statista, August 15, 2024, https://www.statista.com/statistics/1103661/rape-on-woman-age-victim-france/. Accessed March 17, 2025.

voice of French women and to highlight the role that migration policies play in the problems that women experience."[479]

The group was forthright about what those migration policies had done to France, as well as to Britain: "We have all made the same observation: The people who attack us daily are mostly non-natives. We created Nemesis because mainstream feminist organizations are very reluctant to talk about cases like the Cologne sexual assaults (caused by people of Middle Eastern or North African origin) or large-scale rape and pimping of female British minors in Rotherham, Telford, Rochdale, Derby, Oxford, etc. (organized exclusively by members of the Indo-Pakistani community). But also because street harassment is mainly the work of men from a different culture, and feminist associations try to hide this fact by masking our very concrete problems with abstract concepts such as 'patriarchy.'"[480]

The group had plenty of incidents it could use to show the foolishness of those migration policies. "Personally," one woman said in the Collectif Némésis video, "it is always the Maghrebi types who follow, whistle at and insult me."[481] She recounted one typical incident: "There was this Maghrebi type who accosted me, asks whether I want drugs, crack, or coke. I refuse, but he insists for another 10 minutes and then asks me whether we could spend the night together. I say no. I want to catch the subway, then he asks whether he can join me. I say

[479] "'It is always the Maghrebi types who follow, whistle at, and insult me' – French women recount their experience with sexual harassment from foreigners," Remix News, June 10, 2023, https://rmx.news/crime/it-is-always-the-maghrebi-types-who-follow-whistle-at-and-insult-me-french-women-recount-their-experience-with-sexual-harassment-from-foreigners/. Accessed March 17, 2025.

[480] Ibid.

[481] Ibid.

no."[482] The Maghreb is the western part of the North Africa, including the former French colonies of Algeria, Morocco, and Tunisia, from which many migrants enter France.

Not only did her pursuer not take no for an answer, but he started following her, along with a growing number of other men: "Heading for the tram station, when I see these two individuals together with six others, and I find myself all alone with them in the station. The tram arrives, I board it and remain in front, right next to the driver, so at least if there is a problem, he is right beside me. All of them also board (the tram), stationing themselves at the doors, and at that moment, I don't feel very reassured. I pull up the (hood) of my sweatshirt so they cannot see me, and the first individual stands right next to me."[483]

As one of the men inched ever closer to her, she confronted him, asking him forthrightly, "Are you going to keep doing this?"[484] No clear answer was forthcoming: "But in fact he did not understand what I was saying, trying to explain that he doesn't speak French."[485]

When she tried to get out of the tram, the men blocked her way. She told one of them that she was going to miss her stop if they didn't let her get through, but "instead of stepping aside to let me pass, he pushes up his pelvis into me so that I bump into him."[486]

Another woman recounted a similar experience:

> Hello, my name is Mathilda. I'm 25 years old.
> I lived in Lyon for three years before moving

---

[482] Ibid.
[483] Ibid.
[484] Ibid.
[485] Ibid.
[486] Ibid.

> to Paris. In Lyon, I lived for a year in the Guillotière district, which traumatized me a bit from street harassment, because every time I had to go home late at night, I had to take a VTC or an Uber. I didn't dare take the metro or walk home for fear of running into the people who hang out in Guillotière, especially on Place Gabriel-Péri, as I lived right next door.
>
> Several times, I've been insulted, spat on, when I refused to give a cigarette, when I didn't respond to compliments. And I lived above a shisha bar. So every time I passed in front of it on my way home, I'd get a lot of stares, insults, whistles or catcalls. This also happened to me in Lyon.[487]

She said that one night, a migrant approached as she was on her way home: "When I got on the escalator, he was right behind me on the escalator. He actually started stroking my hair. So I turned around and got scared when I saw that it was him."[488] She started running. "I can't even remember exactly what happened during my maybe 30 seconds of running, but actually, I shouted at him behind me as I ran too, and he was screaming for me to turn around. And in fact, he ran behind me until I got to the front of my building. I had my electronic door key, and I managed to get in, but so did he. In fact, there were two staircases in the building. I took one, and I think he

487 Ibid.

488 Ibid.

made a mistake. Luckily for me, he took the other. So he didn't find me."[489]

After this, she said, "I was terrified, I was crying, and I was really extremely shocked. So there you have it, a very, very bad experience in Lyon. I obviously learned (to take) all the precautions I could. I was shocked. Obviously, I moved out. I never went home alone on the metro again, and I was very scared at night when I was alone in the street and it was dark."[490]

That woman was fortunate. On September 16, 2023, an illegal migrant from Mali, which is 90 percent Muslim, raped a student at a prominent French school, École Supérieure des Sciences Economiques et Commerciales, which is commonly known as ESSEC Business School. The migrant attacked his victim as she was returning home from a nightclub, pushing her up against a car and raping her right out in the open. A pair of police officers spotted the scene and arrested the man, where he insisted that there was no rape, as the woman had consented to the sexual activity.

Remix News reported that this was yet another example of the failure of the French authorities' approach to the migrants they had brought into the country: "The 31-year-old migrant, known as Mady. T., was already known to the authorities for a previous allegation of rape at the same nightclub back in August 2022. He was not charged at that time and was subsequently released from police custody."[491]

---

489 Ibid.

490 Ibid.

491 Thomas Brooke, "France ravaged by migrant rapes as spate of sexual assaults targeting elderly women sweep the nation," Remix News, September 25, 2023, https://rmx.news/crime/france-ravaged-by-migrant-rapes-as-spate-of-sexual-assaults-sweeps-the-nation. Accessed March 17, 2025.

Around the same time, two Muslim migrants, identified as Adel A. and Mohamed E., were arrested on "multiple counts of gang rape, acts of torture, and barbarity and extortion following the rape of a 30-year-old woman in an underground car park in the French city of Nice." They were accused "torturing their victim before forcing her to withdraw money from an ATM, stealing her bank card, and fleeing the scene."[492]

These kinds of stories were all too common. Remix News reported that "another victim, also 67, also suffered an attempted rape in the French town of Tours."[493] This time the offending migrant was from Sudan: "A police source told the publication how an intoxicated Sudanese asylum seeker had been interrupted by a neighbor lying on top of his victim with his pants undone. The victim's underwear had been ripped off and she had been hit in the face."[494]

Not even elderly women were spared, as the guiding idea behind the rapes was to humiliate the infidel and express dominance, not to achieve sexual gratification. Also in September 2023, *Le Figaro* reported that "at midnight on Wednesday [September 20], as a 67-year-old woman was returning home in Versailles, in the Yvelines department, not far from the Gonards cemetery, a man was waiting for her, hidden in the courtyard of her building. Taking her by surprise, he forced her into her home before tying her up, *Le Figaro* learned from a police source. An endless night of physical and sexual violence ensued: according to our information, the sexagenarian woman was repeatedly punched in the face before being raped, continuing until dawn. It was only in the early hours of the

492 Ibid.
493 Ibid.
494 Ibid.

morning that the victim managed to escape her tormentor, taking refuge at a neighbor's house. The neighbor immediately contacted the police."[495]

According to Remix News, the attacker was an Algerian national.[496] The victim died of her injuries.

495 "Versailles : une femme de 67 ans séquestrée et violée durant toute une nuit," *Le Figaro,* September 22, 2023, https://www.lefigaro.fr/faits-divers/versailles-une-femme-de-67-ans-sequestree-et-violee-durant-toute-une-nuit-20230922. Accessed March 17, 2025.

496 Brooke, "France ravaged."

CHAPTER SIXTEEN
NOT SAFE DOWN UNDER

A RAPE GANG DOWN UNDER

The Skaf gang terrified all of Australia. *The Age* vividly described this gang's activity in a 2002 profile:

> A mobile phone calls them together. Into cars they jump, and race around the corner to a local park. It's their back yard, turf they have marked out as their own over years of theft, vandalism and menacing behaviour, young years spent thumbing noses at authority.
>
> But that was all prelude. Tonight, August 10, 2000, is not the gang's usual go of hot cars, stolen mobile phones or drugs. Out goes the call: We've got a slut, bro.[497]

[497] "When race and rape collide," *The Age*, September 17, 2002, https://www.theage.com.au/national/when-race-and-rape-collide-20020917-gdulki.html. Accessed March 3, 2025.

The Australian gang members converge upon a sixteen-year-old girl who has been "lured from home by a boy she trusts." Two of the gang members "rape her before she flees."[498] This was just one of many such incidents "in which young girls were raped by groups of up to 14 men in and around Bankstown." *The Age* noted that the crimes involved both ethnicity and religion: "In the space of two months, seven teenage girls who identify as Australian — although two have Italian parents, one has Greek parents and one is part Aboriginal — were abducted and pack-raped by members of a group of youths their own age. Three others escaped the boys' clutches. At least 19 youths were involved in the attacks, though not all were present at every one. One girl was assaulted by four, another by two."[499]

Of the fourteen boys who were apprehended in connection with these rapes, "all were born, raised and educated in Australia and identify as Lebanese Muslims, or just 'Lebs', although two had mixed parentage."[500] Many enjoyed taunting their victims with this in mind: "The teenager raped on August 30 was called an 'Aussie pig', told she would be raped 'Leb-style' and asked 'does Leb cock taste better than Aussie cock?' by three of her assailants. Another girl was asked her nationality and concluded: 'The world isn't what I thought it to be — it isn't safe and females are punished for being Australian.'"[501]

Maybe they were punished for being non-Muslim, but few people had that in mind in Australia any more than they did anywhere else. The whole thing was framed almost exclusively in racial terms, only a handful dared to note that the assailants

---

498 Ibid.
499 Ibid.
500 Ibid.
501 Ibid.

were not just Lebanese, but Muslim. New South Wales Premier Bob Carr said, with extreme caution, on an Australian TV show in September 2001: "The incidents had a similar MO, in that males of Middle Eastern appearance aged between 15 and 19 years old would operate in this fashion, that is entice girls into the car and effectively, in some cases at least, kidnap them."[502]

A reporter on the same show seemed less inclined to conform to politically correct sensibilities, daring to point out that "the victims were all Caucasian women aged between 13 and 18, those convicted all Lebanese Muslim youths."[503] She did add, however, that "the rape trials coincided with a wave of anti-Muslim sentiment. There were the horrors of September 11 and stories of boatloads of asylum seekers heading for Australia."[504]

And on the other hand, Christina Radburn of the Bankstown Multicultural Youth Service suggested that the whole thing was just a wild weekend: "They stopped along the way; they had every opportunity to escape. Nobody accepts rape and I'm not saying what was done was right. If they picked up girls offering them marijuana, did the girls expect nothing in return? No one gets something for nothing these days. We were finding that both sexes, not just males, had really warped ideas on how to approach the opposite sex."[505]

Maybe that was all there was to it. Yet there were so very many cases of this kind, in so many different places. One of them was in Australia itself, where in 2002, what *The Sydney Morning*

---

502 Australian Broadcasting Corporation TV Program Transcript, July 15, 2002, https://web.archive.org/web/20070108091135/http://www.abc.net.au/7.30/content/2002/s607757.htm. Accessed March 3, 2025.

503 Ibid.

504 Ibid.

505 "When race and rape collide."

Herald called "the most violent, prolific gang rapists Sydney has known" embarked upon "a six-month rampage, luring girls as young as 13 to their home in Ashfield to rape them."[506] In this case, the perpetrators were "four brothers from Pakistan" who "came to Australia from Pakistan around 2000."[507]

The brothers behaved much the way that Muslim rape gang members in the UK behaved: "The rapes of at least eight girls took place mostly in the brothers' Ashfield home between January and July 2002. The girls were invited to a 'party', but would arrive at the house, which was strewn with rubbish and plastered with posters of semi-naked girls, to find no other females there. Some victims were repeatedly raped at knifepoint and told they would be killed if they went to police. The brothers videotaped their rapes, and the tapes show another dozen possible victims. The police have not been able to find them all and some did not want to come forward."[508]

They seemed to enjoy being cruel to their victims: "The brutality of the crime, the last to go to trial, was typical. Before raping the girl, MSK [one of the accused] told her he had strangled a girlfriend and hung her from a balcony in Iraq - though he was from Pakistan."[509] During the trial, MSK "jumped the dock and threw broken glass at the victims' mothers."[510]

Although the brothers were relatively recent arrivals to Australia, they quickly demonstrated that they knew how the

---

506 "In the open: rapists' campaign of vicious assaults," *Sydney Morning Herald*, July 22, 2005, https://www.smh.com.au/national/in-the-open-rapists-campaign-of-vicious-assaults-20050722-gdlqc9.html. Accessed March 3, 2025.

507 Ibid.

508 Ibid.

509 Ibid.

510 Ibid.

game was played in Anglophone societies: they "claimed in the face of damning DNA evidence that they were the victims of an anti-Muslim conspiracy."[511] One of the brothers even "feigned mental illness, they sacked numerous lawyers and aborted trials to ensure delays as they tried to wear down the victims who had agreed to testify."[512]

"ALL AUSTRALIAN WOMEN ARE SLUTS"

Years after the Skaf gang terrorized Australia, other Muslims there demonstrated that they held much the same outlook as the Skaf rapists who had so gleefully tormented Australian women. Afzal Nazir, a native of Pakistan who was a cab driver in Sydney, was found in October 2016 to be not a "fit and proper person" to drive a cab.[513] This ruling from the New South Wales Civil and Administrative Tribunal came after five of Nazir's passengers testified about how he had sexually harassed them in various ways.

One woman recounted that when she entered his cab, Nazir was "highly agitated" and lectured her at immense length, declaring "that all Australian women are sluts and deserve to be raped because of the way they dress."[514] This recalled once again the Qur'an's counsel (33:59) to women to don the veil so that

---

511 Ibid.

512 Ibid.

513 Daniel Piotrowski, "'All Australian women are sluts and deserve to be raped': Vile rantings of Pakistani migrant 'cabbie from hell' who pretended to shoot an AK47 at passengers and accused one of being a lesbian for wearing PANTS," *Daily Mail Australia*, October 5, 2016, https://www.dailymail.co.uk/news/article-3822937/A-Pakistani-migrant-taxi-driver-declared-Australian-women-sluts-vile-rant-tribunal-hears.html. Accessed March 18, 2025.

514 Ibid.

they are not molested, with the implication that if they do not don the veil, they deserve molestation. Tribunal senior member Geoffrey Walker recounted in his ruling on the case that Nazir "said his wife would never dress like Aussie women do as she is a respectable person and has studied for many years."[515]

Walker related that Nazir had also told his luckless passenger that he had gained entry into Australia by paying $2,000; in other words, he "had not simply arrived on a boat and people should respect him."[516] Once down under, however, Nazir was less than happy: "He said Australians do not care about true relationships, they all want to f*** each other and then f*** them off."[517] Nazir's lecture fired him up. As he grew progressively angrier, he started to hit the steering wheel while "yelling about how dumb Australian people are as they constantly mix up his race and said how stupid they could be, that they could not tell where he was from."[518]

He told the woman about an encounter he had with someone who was drunk, and said that "if that happened in his country he would pul [*sic*] out his AK 47 and put 14 bullets in his head."[519] As he said this, he pantomimed firing a gun at his startled passenger.

That was not a singular incident. According to the *Daily Mail Australia*, "four other women made serious complaints against Mr Nazir about his behaviour while driving cabs in Newcastle in August and September 2011."[520] After picking up two women from a nightclub, he asked them why they had

515 Ibid.
516 Ibid.
517 Ibid.
518 Ibid.
519 Ibid.
520 Ibid.

remained virgins (which he was apparently assuming about them). "When they asked him to stop talking about 'sexual relations… he simply laughed and kept talking about it.'"[521]

For his part, Nazir denied all the accusations, but the tribunal did not find his version of events convincing. Walker observed: "He has accepted no responsibility for his misconduct."[522]

NOT MORALLY WRONG IN HIS HOMELAND

In his refusal to take any responsibility for his actions, Afzal Nazir was like many other Muslim migrants accused of sexual assault and rape in non-Muslim countries; another Muslim migrant in Australia likewise repeated a claim many others in situations similar to his had made: what he did wasn't considered wrong back home.

Mufiz Rahaman was a Rohingya Muslim who fled Bangladesh and made his way to Australia, where he ended up facing charges of aggravated sexual assault of another Rohingya refugee, a 10-year-old boy. Rahaman, 20, lived in the same house with the boy and other refugees, and one night, according to the *Daily Mail*, "he crept into the child's bedroom – which he shared with his father – as he slept and took off the boy's underpants. He then raped the boy, who arrived in Australia in 2013, while his father was in another room preparing lunch."[523]

---

521 Ibid.

522 Ibid.

523 Belinda Cleary and Belinda Grant Geary, "Muslim refugee, 20, who raped a boy, 10, in his Sydney home says what he did 'is not a crime because it is acceptable in his homeland,'" *Daily Mail Australia*, August 31, 2016, https://www.dailymail.co.uk/news/article-3767301/Muslim-refugee-20-raped-10-year-old-boy-bedroom-claimed-culturally-acceptable-sexually-assault-children-homeland.html#ixzz4J1PjEpsJ. Accessed March 18, 2025.

As the victim's father was returning to the room, he heard Rahaman say to the boy: "I'll give you money for this."[524] The boy replied: "My father will hit me."[525] The father then hurried into the room, only to find Rahaman "lying on top of his son who was face down on the bed with his pants around his knees."[526] Appalled and angered, the boy's father said to Rahaman: "What are you doing to this little boy? You're an adult."[527] The attacker denied having done anything, but the boy told his father the truth: Rahaman had raped him.

When he was on trial, Rahaman "told the court he had been a victim of sexual abuse as a child before he moved to Australia."[528] He also said that "he thought sexual assault was not seen as morally wrong in his homeland."[529] On top of all that, he "had not accepted responsibility for his actions and demonstrated a 'lack of morality.'"[530] Judge Andrew Scotting observed: "There is a need for specific deterrence … The offence appears to have been (viewed) as being culturally acceptable conduct in the offender's childhood."[531]

While there was no doubt some truth to this claim, Rahaman's victim was from his homeland, and his father didn't seem to be prepared to take the whole thing in stride as "culturally acceptable conduct." And whether or not his behavior would have been considered acceptable among the Rohingya, Rahaman

524 Ibid.
525 Ibid.
526 Ibid.
527 Ibid.
528 Ibid.
529 Ibid.
530 Ibid.
531 Ibid.

committed his crime in Australia. He should have been prepared to take the responsibility for violating Australian law.

"UNCOVERED MEAT"

Long before Mufiz Rahaman arrived in Australia, however, it was clear that many Muslims had vastly different ideas regarding sexual morality and mores from those that prevailed among non-Muslims in the country. In October 2006, the Mufti of Australia, Sheikh Taj Al Din Al Hilaly, preached a sermon in Sydney in which he placed the blame for rape squarely upon the victims:

> When it comes to adultery, it's 90 percent the woman's responsibility. Why? Because a woman owns the weapon of seduction. It's she who takes off her clothes, shortens them, flirts, puts on make-up and powder and takes to the streets, God protect us, dallying. It's she who shortens, raises and lowers. Then, it's a look, a smile, a conversation, a greeting, a talk, a date, a meeting, a crime, then Long Bay jail. Then you get a judge, who has no mercy, and he gives you 65 years.[532]

As if to emphasize that this was not simply his own eccentric opinion, Al Hilaly invoked the twentieth-century Egyptian poet Mostafa Saadeq Al-Rafeie:

---

532 Peter Fredson, "Why Cats Eat Uncovered Meat," Daily Kos, October 26, 2006, https://www.dailykos.com/stories/2006/10/26/262016/-. Accessed March 18, 2025.

> But when it comes to this disaster, who started it? In his literature, writer al-Rafee says, if I came across a rape crime, I would discipline the man and order that the woman be jailed for life. Why would you do this, Rafee? He said because if she had not left the meat uncovered, the cat wouldn't have snatched it.[533]

But the cats would naturally be quick to snatch any uncovered meat:

> If you get a kilo of meat, and you don't put it in the fridge or in the pot or in the kitchen but you leave it on a plate in the backyard, and then you have a fight with the neighbor because his cats eat the meat, you're crazy. Isn't this true?
>
> If you take uncovered meat and put it on the street, on the pavement, in a garden, in a park, or in the backyard, without a cover and the cats eat it, then whose fault will it be, the cats, or the uncovered meat's? The uncovered meat is the disaster. If the meat was covered the cats wouldn't roam around it. If the meat is inside the fridge, they won't get it.
>
> If the woman is in her boudoir, in her house and if she's wearing the veil and if she shows modesty, disasters don't happen.[534]

---

533 Ibid.

534 Ibid.

Behind the woman who dared to venture out uncovered was Satan himself:

> Satan sees women as half his soldiers. You're my messenger in necessity, Satan tells women you're my weapon to bring down any stubborn man. There are men that I fail with. But you're the best of my weapons.
>
> ...The woman was behind Satan playing a role when she disobeyed God and went out all dolled up and unveiled and made of herself palatable food that rakes and perverts would race for. She was the reason behind this sin taking place.[535]

After receiving condemnation and ridicule from all over the world, Al Hilaly backtracked, and issued an apology of sorts, while blaming the newspaper The Australian and defending his words: "I unreservedly apologise to any woman who is offended by my comments. I had only intended to protect women's honour, something lost in The Australian presentation of my talk. I would like to unequivocally confirm that the presentation related to religious teachings on modesty and not to go to extremes in enticements, this does not condone rape, I condemn rape and reiterate that this is a capital crime. Women in our Australian society have the freedom and right to dress as they choose, the duty of man is to avert his glance or walk away."[536]

---

535 Ibid.
536 Ibid.

Apology or no apology, many Muslim leaders denounced Al Hilaly. Ali Roude of the New South Wales Islamic Council said that Al Hilaly had "failed both himself and the Muslim community…As a father, brother and son myself, I take offence at the portrayal of both men and women in the alleged published comments."[537]

"Yet at the same time, Al-Hilali had defenders. Abduljalil Sajid of the Muslim Council of Britain said that al-Hilali's remarks had been taken out of context, and affirmed that 'loose women like prostitutes' encourage immorality in men. As for al-Hilali, Sajid said that 'he is a great scholar and he has a great knowledge of Islamic jurisprudence…. I respect his views. His intentions are noble in order to make morality and modesty part of our overall society.'"[538]

"It was also somewhat surprising that Al-Hilali's remarks generated any uproar at all. After all, the idea that a woman is responsible if she is raped did not originate with him, and this was not the first time it has been enunciated in the West. One notorious example occurred in September 2004 in Denmark, when the mufti Shahid Mehdi of the Islamic Cultural Center in Copenhagen said on the Danish television program Talk to Gode that women who venture outside without a hijab are 'asking for rape.'"[539]

Another Muslim leader in Australia, Tanveer Ahmed, acknowledged that "in a large number of Muslim households, young men will be taught that white women are cheap and easy. It is extrapolated to a much bigger scale, for it symbolises

---

537 Robert Spencer, "Muslim Rape? They Were Asking For It," Jihad Watch, October 31, 2006, https://jihadwatch.org/2006/10/spencer-muslim-rape-they-were-asking-for-it. Accessed March 18, 2025.

538 Ibid.

539 Ibid.

for them a moral corruption endemic in free societies, the kind they believe has led to a breakdown in families. Their views have some overlap with social conservatives in general, who see human freedoms, especially with regard to sexuality, as having gone too far."[540]

"Even more significantly, Ahmed conceded that 'what Hilali says is consistent with a strict, conservative interpretation of Islam. This remains the fundamental difficulty with Islam's attempts to sit with modernity. As long as Muslims view their religion as sitting above history and culture — with the Koran as the literal word of God, which in their view makes Islam undebatable — there will always be Hilalis who can point to certain texts and argue for a social and legal structure consistent with 7th-century Arabia.... This is a man who knows the Koran in intimate detail and his views are consistent with a strict reading of the Muslim holy book.'"[541]

That was the heart of the problem.

540 Ibid.
541 Ibid.

CHAPTER SEVENTEEN

THE SAME STORY BACK HOME

CHRONIC BEHAVIOR IN PAKISTAN

Incidents of this kind didn't happen only in the West. They were frequent in the countries from which the migrants had come. In those countries, however, Muslims who victimized non-Muslims sexually didn't generally have to worry about running afoul of the law, however toothless and cowed the law was in the West. Instead, they could count on the sympathy and Islamic loyalty of the authorities. On January 5, 2025, a thirty-five-year-old Muslim in Pakistan named Muhammad Ali abducted his Christian neighbor's daughter, Saba Shafique, who was twelve years old, from their neighborhood in Lahore Cantonment, Punjab Province. Ali took Shafique to Shaheed Benazirabad city in Sindh Province, where he forced her to convert to Islam and married her.

Saba Shafique's father, Shafique Masih, noted that on the marriage certificate, his daughter was listed as being eighteen years old, when actually she was only twelve. "Saba's physical appearance also doesn't match the age stated in the alleged marriage and Islamic conversion certificates," said Masih.[542] "Whoever facilitated this sham conversion and marriage should be equally punished along with Ali."[543]

The police were no help, either: "The police deliberately misstated Saba's age, but when I protested, they told me that it would help in strengthening my case. My lawyer, Rana Irfan, has filed an application to rectify her age as per her birth certificate." Nor did the authorities show any inclination to act upon the case: "The police told me that they needed official permission to go to Sindh Province to recover Saba, but three weeks have passed and there's no progress in the matter. I'm visiting the police station on a daily basis to plead with them to act, but it seems now that they are not serious in finding my minor daughter."[544]

A Christian lawmaker in Punjab, Ejaz Augustine, explained that "forced conversions and marriages of minor girls have become a serious crisis for the Christian community. A bill criminalizing child marriages is pending in the Punjab Assembly since April 2024, but it is very unfortunate that despite our repeated demands for its passage, there's been no movement in this regard."[545] Augustine spoke of powerful forces blocking such legislation, saying: "These vested interests have already blocked a federal legislation seeking criminalization of forced conversions in 2021, and they are now again active to stop

---

542 "Christian Girl, 12, Forcibly Converted/Married in Pakistan," Morning Star News, February 7, 2025, https://morningstarnews.org/2025/02/christian-girl-12-forcibly-converted-married-in-pakistan-2/. Accessed March 4, 2025.

543 Ibid.

544 Ibid.

545 Ibid.

Punjab from raising the legal age for marriage for both boys and girls to 18."[546]

Four days after Saba Shafique was abducted, four Muslims seized another Pakistani Christian girl, fourteen-year-old Saneha Sharif. Saneha's father, Sharif Masih, recounted: "Saneha was lured out of the house by a Muslim girl whose family had recently moved to our neighborhood. A neighbor, Rehan Razaque, saw her being bundled into a van by the accused, which included two women, one of whom was the mother of the girl who had brought Saneha out of her home."[547]

According to Morning Star News, Sharif Masih said that one of the suspects, Muhammad Dildar, "had been making unwelcome advances toward his daughter that she always discouraged."[548] Yet the police had been no help. Masih stated: "The police registered a case but arrested only two accused, including Samina Usman and Shabbir Ahmed. Samina has been sent into judicial custody, while Ahmed is still in police custody, but both the accused have not yet provided any lead that could help recover Saneha. Despite repeated pleas to the police, they are not making any effort to recover Saneha or arrest the other accused. We even gave them some cell phone numbers to trace the whereabouts of Dildar, but nothing has been done to find him."[549]

Eleven days after the abduction of Saneha Sharif, three Muslims in the Okara District of Pakistan's Punjab Province abducted yet another Christian girl. According to Morning

---

546 Ibid.

547 "Five Muslims Abduct Christian Girl, 14, in Pakistan," Morning Star News, January 21, 2025, https://morningstarnews.org/2025/01/five-muslims-abduct-christian-girl-14-in-pakistan/. Accessed March 4, 2025.

548 Ibid.

549 Ibid.

Star News, Ariha, a twelve-year-old Christian girl, was seized from her home at gunpoint. Ariha's mother, Sumera Gulzar, a Catholic, said that the perpetrator was one of the family's neighbors, Sajjad Baloch, who was forty years old.

Gulzar recounted: "I immediately contacted Baloch's family, and they asked me to give them two to three days to recover my daughter from his custody. The next day I received a phone call from Baloch in which he threatened to rape Ariha and to sell her to sex traffickers if we pursued the matter."[550]

In a December 2024 report on the persecution of Christians in Pakistan, the persecution watchdog Open Doors International reported that "Christian girls as young as 7 — primarily from poor families and including girls with physical disabilities — are kidnapped, forcibly married and, despite being underage, sexually assaulted and forced to convert to Islam on pain of death. In addition to abduction, reports indicate that Christian girls have been seduced as a means of converting them to Islam."

Christian girls in Pakistan have been victimized in this way for many years. On occasion, the victims have even been killed. On November 30, 2020, Sonia Bibi, a twenty-four-year-old Christian woman, was waiting at a bus stop in Rawalpindi to take her to her place of employment when she was killed by a shot in the head. The suspected killer was a Muslim named Muhammad Shehzad; Sonia Bibi's father, Allah Rakha Masih, said that Shehzad had been stalking and harassing Sonia after she declined his marriage proposal. Shehzad was even said to have threatened to kill her if she didn't relent and marry him; he also pressured her to convert to Islam. Shehzad's entreaties,

---

550 "Muslims Kidnap 12-Year-Old Christian Girl in Pakistan," Morning Star News, February 5, 2025, https://morningstarnews.org/2025/02/muslims-kidnap-12-year-old-christian-girl-in-pakistan/. Accessed March 4, 2025.

however, fell on deaf ears: Allah Rakha Masih said that Sonia "was a true Christian and strong in her faith and she was killed for following her Christian faith."[551]

The police generally offer little no help. In April 2014, according to the Roman Catholic news agency Agenzia Fides, "on Easter Day, Saira, a 7-year-old Christian girl was raped by a Muslim man, Mohammad Alam Fakhar, in a village in the district of Sialkot, Punjab. The girl, who after the violence suffered a hemorrhage, was hospitalized just three days after the abuse and is still in critical condition in the hospital in Sialkot, while some Muslims have asked Saira's family not to press charges against the perpetrator. Despite the fears and obstacles, a complaint was filed on April 22 against the rapist and two other people. The police ordered a medical examination which confirmed the rape."[552]

AsiaNews added that not just Mohammad Alam Fakhar, but "a 'clan' of four Muslim men" raped Saira."[553] Yet the police, "instead of arresting the culprits, helped the local clan to kidnap the girl's father; Iqbal Masih was taken and hidden in a secret place to 'force the family not to report the story, to reach an agreement with the criminals and to avoid a dispute of a

551 "Pakistan: sexual violence and forced conversion," Aid to the Church in Need International, April 21, 2021, https://acninternational.org/religiousfreedomreport/news/Pakistan-sexual-violence-and-forced-conversion. Accessed March 4, 2025.

552 "ASIA/PAKISTAN – A 7-year-old Christian Girl raped on Easter Sunday," Agenzia Fides, April 28, 2014, https://www.fides.org/en/news/35620-ASIA_PAKISTAN_A_7_year_old_Christian_Girl_raped_on_Easter_Sunday#.U8hE-PldVqU. Accessed March 4, 2025.

553 Jibran Khan, "Punjab: clan gang rapes seven year old Christian and kidnaps father to stop him reporting them," AsiaNews, April 24, 2014, https://www.asianews.it/news-en/Punjab:-clan-gang-rapes-seven-year-old-Christian-and-kidnaps-father-to-stop-him-reporting-them-30906.html. Accessed March 3, 2025.

religious background.' The Christian community has attempted every possible means to negotiate with police, with no success. The police seem reluctant to punish the rapists and free Masih, in the hands of the torturers who abused daughter."[554]

"RAPED WHILE SHE WAS PLAYING IN THE STREET"

This kind of incident was all too common; Agenzia Fides listed some other examples, including that of "a 15-year-old Christian, Fouzia Bibi, raped in January 2013 in the district of Kasur by two Muslims; and that of another Christian student, who was raped in July 2013 by a Muslim boy under the supervision of two armed men. In addition, in December 2012, a 6-year-old Hindu girl Wijenti Meghwar, was raped while she was playing in the street in the town of Ghulam Nabi Shah, in Sindh province: the case is still open."[555]

In 2012, Agenzia Fides published an article entitled "The long trail of Christian children raped or killed," full of examples of Muslims sexually abusing Christians.[556] These included Amaria Masih, "an l8-year-old Catholic" who was "raped and murdered on November 27, 2011 in the village of Samundari (Punjab) by the young Muslim Arif Gujjar, who wanted to marry and convert her."[557] Anna was "a 12-year-old Christian girl" and the daughter of a poor scavenger in the town of Shahdra; she was "kidnapped and raped repeatedly for eight

---

554 Ibid.

555 "ASIA/PAKISTAN – A 7-year-old Christian Girl raped on Easter Sunday."

556 "ASIA/PAKISTAN - The long trail of Christian children raped or killed," Agenzia Fides, August 24, 2012, https://www.fides.org/en/news/32088-ASIA_PAKISTAN_The_long_trail_of_Christian_children_raped_or_killed. Accessed March 4, 2025.

557 Ibid.

months by a gang of Islamic militants."[558] Ultimately, after enduring this trauma, she was forced to convert to Islam and marry a Muslim.

Another girl, Farah Hatim, was likewise "forced to marry and convert to Islam in the city of Rahim Yar Khan, in Punjab. Some non-governmental Organizations in Pakistan and outside the country officially brought the case to the United Nations," but of course nothing was done.[559] Rebbecca Masih and Saima Masih were "two Christian girls kidnapped by a group of Muslims in the district of Jhung, in Faisalabad (in Punjab), and forced to convert to Islam and forced to marry a rich local businessman."[560]

An even worse fate awaited Shazia Bashir, "a 12-year-old Christian girl, who was raped and murdered in January 2010."[561] To add insult to injury, "Chaudhry Naeem, the rich Muslim lawyer, responsible for the crime, was acquitted."[562] A twelve-year-old girl, Lubna Masih, was "raped and murdered by a group of Muslims in Rawalpindi."[563] Kiran George, "a girl from Sheikhupura (Lahore) who died on March 10, 2010 from burns all over her body, after the Muslim Ahmad Raza, a police officer, poured gasoline on her and lit her on fire. The young woman had been enslaved by a woman, Sama, a dealer of youth to be sold as prostitutes or slaves to wealthy Muslim families."[564]

On August 9, 2024, another Muslim abducted yet another twelve-year-old Christian girl. Muhammad Asad abducted

---

558 Ibid.
559 Ibid.
560 Ibid.
561 Ibid.
562 Ibid.
563 Ibid.
564 Ibid.

Fairy Shaukat, in Pakistan's Punjab Province. Fairy's mother, Parveen Shaukat, explained: "Fairy had gone to a nearby shop to buy groceries in the afternoon, but she did not return home. My sons started searching for her but could not find her. We then filed a complaint with the police, but their attitude was not welcoming. Instead of helping us, they delayed the registration of a First Information Report [FIR]."[565] Morning Star News reported that Parveen Shaukat "said that a neighbor later informed the family that he had seen Asad abduct Fairy."[566]

Parveen Shaukat accused the police of delaying action until Muhammad Asad could complete the action he had set out to do: convert Fairy to Islam and make her his wife. "We informed the police about the accused, but they still did not take any action, giving sufficient time to Asad to convert the minor child and contract an Islamic marriage with her."[567]

Finally, the Shaukat family found out what had happened to Fairy by means of a WhatsApp message. Parveen Shaukat recounted: "On Aug. 13, my sons received the *Nikahnama* [Islamic marriage certificate] of Fairy through WhatsApp from an unknown number. We were shocked to see the document and urged the police to take action against this underage marriage. When the police finally raided the house of the accused, he was not there. It's nearly 20 days now that I haven't seen my child, and we have no information about her safety."[568]

565 "Christian Girl, 12, Forcibly Converted/Married in Pakistan," Morning Star News, August 28, 2024, https://morningstarnews.org/2024/08/christian-girl-12-forcibly-converted-married-in-pakistan/. Accessed March 14, 2025.

566 Ibid.

567 Ibid.

568 Ibid.

Parveen Shaukat ruled out the possibility that her daughter had willingly gone off with Muhammad Asad: "Fairy is just 12 years old. She had no access to a cell phone and rarely went out of the home by herself. She was abducted by Asad, who we have heard is a loafer. He targeted my child for sexual exploitation, and my heart sinks every time I think of how she is being treated in captivity."[569]

Even all those incidents were just the tip of the iceberg. In April 2014, as little seven-year-old Saira was violently raped, a coalition of organizations called the Movement for Solidarity and Peace, which included "Justice and Peace" Commission of the Pakistani Roman Catholic Bishops, published a report, "Forced marriages and forced conversions in the Christian community of Pakistan."[570]

This report stated, according to Agenzia Fides, that "each year about a thousand girls belonging to Christian and Hindu religious minorities are kidnapped, converted and forced into Islamic marriage."[571] This included around seven hundred cases involving Christian girls and three hundred involving Hindus, and the actual number was likely even higher: the report pointed out that "the true extent of the problem is probably much bigger, since many cases are not reported."

This was because these cases involved "girls between 12 and 25 years of age, from poor families and low social classes. The

---

569 Ibid.

570 ASIA/PAKISTAN - Every year, thousands of Hindu and Christian girls kidnapped and forced into Islamic marriage: new Report," Agenzia Fides, April 9, 2014, https://www.fides.org/en/news/35548-ASIA_PAKISTAN_Every_year_thousands_of_Hindu_and_Christian_girls_kidnapped_and_forced_into_Islamic_marriage_new_Report#.VAdIqvldVqV. Accessed March 4, 2025.

571 Ibid.

few cases, because very often complaints are not filed for fear of threats, that come to court, the girls who are intimidated and abused, claim to have converted and married freely, and the case is closed."[572] Yet in reality, none of this was done freely, for "under the custody of the kidnapper, she may suffer sexual violence, forced prostitution, domestic abuse and beatings, if not human trafficking."[573] One Muslim rapist, gleefully unashamed of his actions, told his nine-year-old Christian victim "not to worry because he had done the same service to other young Christian girls."[574]

Fr. James Channan of the "Peace Center" in Lahore explained: "The phenomenon has been verified. It is really very alarming and disturbing for Christians and Hindus, who feel very insecure and vulnerable. We have dealt directly with several cases of forced marriages: the young people belonging to poor social class and often rich Muslim landowners take advantage of such abuse. In Pakistan, it seems to me that Christians and Hindus suffer social, religious and political discrimination, which is getting worse."[575]

"CHRISTIAN GIRLS ARE CONSIDERED GOODS TO BE DAMAGED AT LEISURE"

Nine years after that Movement for Solidarity and Peace report appeared, nothing had changed. In 2023, it repeated essentially the same assessment it had made in 2014, calculating that in

572 Ibid.

573 Ibid.

574 "Christian women under terror grip in Pakistan," *Business Standard*, January 28, 2017, https://www.business-standard.com/article/news-ani/christian-women-under-terror-grip-in-pakistan-117012800099_1.html. Accessed March 4, 2025.

575 "ASIA/PAKISTAN - Every year, thousands of Hindu and Christian girls."

Pakistan, "up to 1,000 young Christian and Hindu girls and young women aged between 12 and 25 are abducted by Muslim men every year. The research, which suggests that Christians make up 70 percent of these cases, found that the scale of the problem 'is likely to be much greater as a number of the cases are never reported and do not progress through the law enforcement and legal systems.' Many of the girls suffer rape, forced prostitution, human trafficking and domestic abuse."[576]

In one notorious incident, three Christian girls of the ages of seventeen, eighteen, and twenty were walking home when four Muslims began following them in a car. When the girls rejected their advances and began to run away from them, the Muslims hit them with their car. According to *Business Standard*, "two girls fell to the ground: one's hip was broken, the other's ribs were shattered. The youngest, Kiran Masih, aged 17, flew up in the air and crashed into the speeding car's windshield."[577] One of the men declared: "Christian girls are only meant for one thing, the [sexual] pleasure of Muslim men."[578] The police, meanwhile, were sympathetic to the attackers, as was so often the case, and dragged their feet on apprehending the attackers.

Wilson Chowdhry of the British Pakistani Christian Association (BPCA), according to ANI, "said that violence against Christians is rarely investigated and highly unlikely to be met with justice. Women have a low status in Pakistan, but none more so than Christian women who find themselves under the grip or terror, especially after this attack. Chowdhry added that accounts like this — including the claim that it is a Muslim man's right to rape Christians and other 'infidels'

576 "Pakistan: sexual violence and forced conversion."
577 "Christian women under terror grip in Pakistan."
578 Ibid.

— are common in Pakistan."[579] A lawyer, Sardar Mushtaq Gill, said: "Such cases are frequent: abuse against women and girls by Muslim men are examples of how the minorities in Pakistan live under constant fear of persecution. We believe that many cases of violence go unreported."[580]

Sometimes authorities try to make sure that these crimes go unreported. In Lahore in October 2024, a Muslim security guard at a primary school raped a six-year-old Christian girl. According to International Christian Concern, "when the girl returned home from school that day in late October, her family noticed blood stains on her clothes and bruises on her body. The girl shared what had happened and identified the school's security guard, Husnain, as the attacker. She said that he had covered her mouth to silence her during the assault."[581]

The girl's "family and members of the local Christian community said the staff member, named Husnain, sexually assaulted her because of her family's Christian faith."[582] However, when the victim's parents "met with the school's principal, who initially told them the girl had fallen. When the parents shared what their daughter had told them, the principal threatened them, saying they would face problems if they took any action."[583]

A Pakistani Christian remarked: "It is shameful. Such incidents occur frequently. Christian girls are considered goods to be damaged at leisure. Abusing them is a right. According

---

579 Ibid.

580 "ASIA/PAKISTAN – A 7-year-old Christian Girl raped on Easter Sunday."

581 "Muslim Man Rapes 6-Year-Old Christian Girl at School," International Christian Concern, November 15, 2024, https://www.persecution.org/2024/11/15/muslim-man-rapes-6-year-old-christian-girl-at-school/. Accessed March 14, 2025.

582 Ibid.

583 Ibid.

to the community's mentality it is not even a crime. Muslims regard them as spoils of war."[584]

Spoils of war? Where did they get that idea? This was a Qur'anic idea that was related to the Islamic obligation to wage jihad warfare against non-Muslims and subjugate them under the hegemony of Islamic law. And so in Pakistan as well as in the United Kingdom and elsewhere in the West, the widespread practice of abducting and raping non-Muslim women came back to its practitioners' Islamic beliefs and assumptions. Yet the religious aspect of this sadly recurring phenomenon was the one part of it that non-Muslim authorities were unwilling to explore, whether out of fear or of hoping to keep community tensions to a minimum.

584 "ASIA/PAKISTAN – A 7-year-old Christian Girl raped on Easter Sunday."

CHAPTER EIGHTEEN

THE SAME PHENOMENON?

INDIA, TOO

It was a story that could have come from Rotherham or Telford, but instead, it all happened in Vijay Nagar, a town in the Indian state of Rajasthan. A group of minor girls had been sexually abused, and once again, the victims and the perpetrators were from different religious backgrounds. *The New Indian Express* reported in February 2025 that "a group of miscreants trapped and blackmailed girls from a private school, subjecting them to rape and allegedly even tried to force them into conversion."[585]

Police arrested seven young men and detained two others who, like the victims, were underage. The criminal gang "targeted a girl by assaulting and blackmailing her and coerced her

585 Rajesh Asnani, "Police arrest seven as minors blackmailed, sexually exploited in Rajasthan's Beawar," *New Indian Express*, February 18, 2025, https://www.newindianexpress.com/nation/2025/Feb/18/police-arrest-seven-as-minors-blackmailed-sexually-exploited-in-rajasthans-beawar. Accessed March 14, 2025.

into befriending other schoolgirls and systematically entrapping multiple victims."[586] The girls were "lured through gifts of Chinese mobile phones and were even forced to make their underage friends chat with the offenders who would sexually exploit them."[587] The attackers also "had taken obscene photos and videos of the girls and were blackmailing them."[588]

Amid all this, the suspects, who were named as Rihan Mohammad, Sohail Mansuri, Shoaib, Arman Pathan, and Sahil Qureshi, kept up the religious pressure on their Hindu victims: "The victims have also alleged that the criminals were even pressurising them to recite Kalma, keep Rozas or fasts, and adopt Islam."[589] A kalma is an Islamic statement of faith.

EGYPT, TOO

The Christian Emergency Alliance describes itself as "an evangelical ministry dedicated to helping Christians stand, wherever they are," including "helping them endure persecution and hardships today."[590] On March 3, 2025, it posted on X about a young Coptic Christian woman in Egypt, Marina Khalaf Bekhit, who had gone missing a week before. Christian Emergency Alliance accused a Muslim named Ayman Mohammed of kidnapping and raping Marina, and forcibly converting her to Islam. It added that "there are reports that two police officers are also complicit in the disgusting crime."[591]

---

586 Ibid.

587 Ibid.

588 Ibid.

589 Ibid.

590 "Who We Are," Christian Emergency Alliance, https://www.christianemergency.com/about-us. Accessed March 4, 2025.

591 Christian Emergency Alliance, X, March 3, 2025, https://x.com/ChristianEmerg1/status/1896570952667824388. Accessed March 4, 2025.

The stories followed a dispiritingly similar pattern. The American Center for Law and Justice (ACLJ) reported that "on January 22, 2024, a 21-year-old Christian woman, Irene Ibrahim Shehata, was abducted and later forced to convert to Islam in Egypt. We're demanding an investigation from the U.N. and that Egypt find and free her."[592] No such investigation was forthcoming.

The ACLJ explained that Irene, "a second-year medical student, suddenly disappeared during midterm exams. Weeks later, she stole her captor's phone and tearfully pleaded for her life in a desperate call to her brother."[593] At that point, however, her captor discovered what she was doing and snatched the phone away from her, telling her brother, "Okay, you heard her voice and know she's okay, right? Now go to hell!"[594] The ACLJ added that "Irene's family immediately contacted the police. But the police refused to act and threatened to arrest her family if they attempted to rescue her."[595]

As in Pakistan, this sort of thing had been going on for many years in Egypt. In July 2011, Father Filopateer Gamil of St. Mary's Church in Giza remarked: "More than two to three girls disappear every day in Giza alone. The cases that are brought to public attention are few compared to what the

---

592 Robert Spencer, "Egypt: Muslim abducts Christian woman, forces her to convert to Islam," Jihad Watch, August 3, 2024, https://jihadwatch.org/2024/08/egypt-muslim-abducts-christian-woman-forces-her-to-convert-to-islam. Accessed March 4, 2025.

593 Ibid.

594 Ibid.

595 Ibid.

numbers actually are."[596] One of these was a seventeen-year-old girl named Jackline Ibrahim Fakhry, who, according to the Assyrian International News Agency (AINA), "disappeared from a town on the outskirts of Cairo, prompting her parents to stage a sit-in until her appearance. They accused 31-year-old Muslim Shokry Abdel-Fatah, who used to take lessons with her mother (a teacher) of kidnapping her. After she returned, Shokry said in a television interview that he has loved her since she was nine years old. He brought her to Alexandria where she met many sheikhs to convert, but she refused."[597]

Then there were two cousins, Nancy Fathy, who was fourteen years old, and Christine Fathy, who was sixteen. They "disappeared from their town in Upper Egypt. Their parents staged a sit-in in Minya until their children surfaced and accused two Muslim brothers, in their late twenties, of being behind their disappearance. The two teens appeared in Cairo, wearing burkas and claiming they had converted to Islam, which is illegal before the age of 18. Instead of being handed over to their parents, they are now in a state care home pending investigations and until they and their parents have reconciled. The two men accused of their abduction have been discharged by the court."[598]

As far back as 1976, the Coptic Pope Shenouda III warned: "There is a practice to convert Coptic girls to embrace Islam and marry them under terror to Muslim husbands."[599] AINA noted

---

596 Mary Abdelmassih, "Egyptian Muslim Ring Uses Sexual Coercion to Convert Christian Girls: Report," Assyrian International News Agency (AINA), July 13, 2011, http://www.aina.org/news/20110712201559.htm. Accessed March 4, 2025.

597 Ibid.

598 Ibid.

599 Ibid.

that "Christian parents say their girls are underage children who disappear either due to emotional ties or to blackmail, and they do not get any assistance from the police in locating them, not even after they have been coerced into converting to Islam, which is illegal before the age of 18. Muslims claim the girls, of whatever age, flee their homes and convert to Islam of their own free will."[600] In one notorious incident, "an Alexandrian priest reported that a ten-year old Coptic girl was sexually abused by a 20-year-old Muslim university student."[601]

Egypt4Christ, an organization that "monitors the abduction and forced Islamization of Christian minors," published a report charging that prominent officials including a Salafist leader, Sheikh Osama Borhammi, were involved in the forced abduction and conversion of Christian girls. Egypt4Christ carried out a secret investigation that "exposed a highly organized Muslim ring centered in the Fatah Mosque in Alexandria. The investigation also uncovered a systematic 'religious call' plan, where young Muslim males in high school and university are urged to approach Coptic girls in the 9-15 age group and manipulate them through sexual exploitation and blackmail. The plan, called 'operation soaking lupin beans' (small dried beans, soaked until they grow in size and are then eaten raw), aims at sexually compromising Christian girls, defiling them and humiliating them in front of their parents, thereby forcing them to flee their homes, and use conversion to Islam as a 'solution' for their problems."[602]

Rasha Nour of Egypt4Christ charged that "the architect of this idea, who diligently promotes it among the Muslim youth,

---

600 Ibid.

601 Ibid.

602 Ibid.

is Salafi Muslim Sheikh Osama Borhammi, in collaboration with other Sheikhs."[603] Others involved in this activity include "co-operating department heads and officers of the Alexandria headquarters of State Security."[604]

With that powerful backing, the forces involved in seizing Christian girls were able to act with impunity, and they did. Between 2011 and 2014, Muslims kidnapped over 550 Coptic Christian schoolgirls and forced them to convert to Islam and marry the men who had abducted them. Christian Post reported that "40 percent of the girls and women that are abducted ages 14 to 40 are raped and subsequently forced to marry their captors after their conversion to Islam. The victimization often begins with coercion by young Muslims, who first gain trust, then force the girls and women to convert and marry, according to the organization."[605] One defender of the Christian girls stated: "Some maintain there are Islamic cells dedicated exclusively to the abduction of Coptic Christian girls and young women."[606] Indeed.

A STAPLE OF ISLAMIC WARFARE

The abduction and rape of the enemy's women meanwhile remained a staple of Islamic warfare, even in the twenty-first century. When civil war began in Sudan early in 2023, the Arabs of Sudan's Rapid Support Forces (RSF) and their allies

---

603 Ibid.

604 Ibid.

605 Alex Murashko, "More Than 550 Coptic Christian Schoolgirls in Egypt Kidnapped Since 2011," Christian Post, June 18, 2014, https://www.christianpost.com/news/more-than-550-coptic-christian-schoolgirls-in-egypt-kidnapped-since-2011-121724/. Accessed March 4, 2025.

606 Ibid.

began engaging in mass sexual abuse of their non-Arab foes, committing numerous rapes and forcing captive women into sex slavery.

A UN fact-finding mission found that the victims ranged from eight years old to seventy-five years old; the Associated Press reported that most of the sexual assaults and rapes were "committed by the RSF and allied Arab militia in an attempt to terrorize and punish people for perceived links to enemies."[607]

Mohamed Chande Othman, the chair of the UN mission, interviewed victims and their families, as well as eyewitnesses to the RSF's actions, and stated: "The sheer scale of sexual violence we have documented in Sudan is staggering."[608] One woman from West Darfur "was held captive for over eight months by RSF guards and impregnated by her main captor during repeated rapes, it added."[609]

A rapist told his victim: "We will make you, the Masalit girls, give birth to Arab children," recalling how so many Pakistani rapists in Britain had disparaged their victims as "white sluts."[610]

#BRINGBACKOUR GIRLS

On April 15, 2014, the Nigerian jihad group Jama'atu Ahlis Sunna Lidda'awati wal-Jihad, that is, The Group Committed to the Propagation of the Prophet's Teachings and Jihad,

---

607 Associated Press, "Sudan's RSF, allies sexually abused victims from 8-75 years, UN mission says," Voice of America, October 29, 2024, https://www.voanews.com/a/sudan-s-rsf-and-allies-sexually-abused-victims-from-8-75-years-un-mission-says-/7843151.html. Accessed March 14, 2025.

608 Ibid.

609 Ibid.

610 Ibid.

popularly known as Boko Haram ("Books Forbidden," or Western Education is Sinful), abducted at least one hundred schoolgirls in predawn raids. Ultimately they abducted over two hundred girls, with some estimates ranging much higher. Their intentions were unmistakable, as was reflected in a *New York Post* headline at the time: "Islamists kidnap 100 schoolgirls who face living hell as sex slaves."[611]

Even the Council on Foreign Relations, which generally shied away from recognizing the Islamic motivations of jihad activity and actions related to it, acknowledged why Boko Haram had done this, although it implied that the practice was antiquated and rejected in modern Islam: "Invoking 7th century Islamic practice as its justification, Boko Haram claims that the wives and daughters of 'infidels' or 'pagans' are legitimate 'booty,' and thus they can be sold into slavery."[612]

Boko Haram's seizure of these girls drew an unusual amount of international attention. This was in large part due to Michelle Obama, the wife of US President Barack Obama. On May 7, 2014, the first lady posted a message on Twitter: "Our prayers are with the missing Nigerian girls and their families. It's time to #BringBackOurGirls. -mo."[613] Accompanying these words was a photo of Michelle Obama looking solemnly into the camera and holding up a piece of paper on which was written "#BringBackOurGirls."

---

611 "Islamists kidnap 100 schoolgirls who face living hell as sex slaves," *New York Post*, April 15, 2014, https://nypost.com/2014/04/15/extremists-abduct-100-girls-from-nigerian-school-after-killing-guards/. Accessed March 20, 2025.

612 John Campbell, "Boko Haram's Sex Slaves?" Council on Foreign Relations, May 7, 2015, https://www.cfr.org/blog/boko-harams-sex-slaves. Accessed March 20, 2025.

613 Michelle Obama, Twitter, May 7, 2014, https://x.com/FLOTUS44/status/464148654354628608. Accessed March 20, 2025.

The hashtag campaign was widely popular and brought a great deal of attention to what Boko Haram had done. Little or no attention was given, however, to the Islamic justification for what the group had done, except to deny it.

Boko Haram did not bring back our girls. And no one called for an end to the Islamically sanctioned sexual abuse of girls anywhere else.

"THE FIGHTERS FREQUENTLY PHYSICALLY AND SEXUALLY ABUSED US"

The same scenario played out elsewhere without the benefit of a hashtag campaign. In December 2017, a woman who had managed to escape from the Somali jihad group al-Shabaab said, according to Kenya's *The Standard*, that "she and other captives were repeatedly raped by at least six men at a time for the five years she was in the terror group's captivity."[614]

The escapee said: "The women in the camp had to cook, wash clothes for the militants and undertake other household duties. The fighters frequently physically and sexually abused us. Some militants would beat us if they did not like something we cooked, which was often for me as I was not familiar with cooking Somali injera (bread) that was preferred by the militants."[615] She added that the captive women "were forced to use contraceptives or procure abortions when they got pregnant."[616]

---

614 Dominic Wabala, "Al-Shabaab returnee's horrid tales of sex slavery," *The Standard*, December 10, 2017, https://www.standardmedia.co.ke/article/2001262655/al-shabaab-returnee-s-horrid-tales-of-sex-slavery. Accessed March 20, 2025.

615 Ibid.

616 Ibid.

The situation got even worse for the women when the jihadis returned from battles with the Somali military or the forces of the African Union Mission to Somalia: "The sexual and physical violence was worse when the militants came from engaging with the AMISOM forces. They would drink and take drugs all day and night, whether celebrating the killing of Somalia National Army or AMISOM soldiers or mourning their own, and that's when the gang rapes would happen."[617]

The woman said that she had "lost count of the number of times she was raped and forced to use contraceptives but adds that female captives married to commanders were allowed to have children. There were about 15 such children in the Boni Forest camp."[618] The wives were the fortunate ones: "If you were lucky, a commander would take you as a wife and that would stop other militants from raping you. But those who were made wives were only native Somalis."[619]

NOODLES IN MOZAMBIQUE

The Guardian reported in April 2021 that "insurgents" (that is, Islamic jihadists, but neither *The Guardian* nor other establishment media outlets were ever willing to call them honestly what they were), "in Mozambique have abducted hundreds of women and girls, forcing many into sexual relations with fighters and possibly trafficking others elsewhere in Africa, interviews with some who have escaped the extremists reveal. Most of the abducted women are under 18, with the youngest about 12 years old. They are being held in a series of camps

617 Ibid.

618 Ibid.

619 Ibid.

and bases across insurgent-controlled territory in north-eastern Mozambique. Many are chosen by young fighters as 'wives' and forced into sexual relations."[620]

Researcher João Feijó, who wrote a report based on interviews with some women who escaped, estimated that the jihadis in Mozambique had taken over a thousand girls and women as sex slaves. "These kinds of numbers," he said, "would be a major logistic problem for the insurgents, and I believe that some girls have been trafficked. We have reports of women being selected to study English in neighbouring Tanzania, which sounds like a euphemism for being trafficked."[621]

The escapees said that the jihadis abducted only "young and attractive girls," to whom they referred as "noodles," a rare delicacy in Mozambique, rather than "sorghum," which was commonplace food.[622] One escapee noted that "adolescent girls are the most favourite victims; other ages are spared."[623]

The Guardian reported that "captive women are forced to attend 'education' sessions of Qur'anic instruction."[624] Feijó added that "efforts are made to integrate them as 'wives'. But this is not a choice."[625]

---

620 Jason Burke, "Escaped girls tell of insurgents' mass abductions in Mozambique," *Guardian*, April 17, 2021, https://www.theguardian.com/world/2021/apr/17/escaped-girls-tell-of-insurgents-mass-abductions-in-mozambique. Accessed March 20, 2025.

621 Ibid.

622 Ibid.

623 Ibid.

624 Ibid.

625 Ibid.

THE SAME PHENOMENON AS IN BRITAIN AND CONTINENTAL EUROPE?

The mistreatment of non-Muslim girls in Britain and elsewhere in the West on the one hand and Pakistan, Egypt, and in other regions in Africa on the other may appear to be fundamentally different. Both involve Muslims abusing non-Muslims, principally Christians, but in Pakistan and Egypt, the most common scenario involves kidnapping, forced conversion to Islam, and forced marriage, while in Australia and Britain, there were few kidnappings, and vanishingly few, if any, forced conversions and forced marriages. Instead, non-Muslim girls and women were simply raped and often forced into prostitution.

So can the two phenomena really be seen as the same, or even similar? Certainly. Both emanate from the Islamic imperative to humiliate non-Muslims and to work toward the day that they are subjugated as inferiors under the hegemony of Islamic rule. The Qur'an tells Muslims: "Fight against those do not believe in Allah or the last day, and do not forbid what Allah and his messenger have forbidden, and do not follow the religion of truth, even if they are among the people of the book, until they pay the jizya with willing submission and feel themselves subdued." (9:29)

The most effective way to ensure that "willing submission" is to demonstrate the overwhelming power of the Muslims, and what more effective way to do that could there be than seizing the women of the non-Muslim communities with impunity and using them sexually, whether the women are then discarded or incorporated into the Muslim community by forced conversion and marriage? In all cases, the seizure and violation of infidel women is a declaration of Muslim power over the non-Muslims, and a demand that they meekly accept the situation, which, of course, British authorities in particular were all too eager to do.

One of the principal ways in which they showed that eagerness was in steadfastly and repeatedly denying that this deeply rooted Islamic practice had anything to do with Islam at all.

IN AMERICA AS WELL?

Was the religiously sanctioned Muslim rape of non-Muslims happening in the United States as well? In light of the fact that this issue simply did not exist for law enforcement officials or the establishment media, it was impossible to know for sure, but there were a few stories that showed telling signs of being part of the larger pattern.

In October 2024, Ahmed Yaqoob traveled from the hamlet of Greece, New York, to another town, North Collins. Once there, according to Buffalo's WIVB, "he picked up a 12-year-old female and a 14-year-old female," and was duly arrested.[626] Yaqoob was charged with "predatory sexual assault against a child less than 13 first-degree rape: forcible compulsion, two counts second-degree rape."[627]

There are, of course, rapists who profess to adhere to all creeds and belief systems. And there is no country on earth in which rape does not take place. It could be that this case was simply a matter of statutory rape, similar to thousands of such cases all across the country, and that Ahmed Yaqoob's Muslim identity had nothing to do with his actions. It was also possible

---

626 Katie Skoog, "Greece man arrested for alleged sexual assault of 2 minors," WIVB, November 18, 2024, https://www.wivb.com/news/crime/greece-man-arrested-for-alleged-sexual-assault-of-2-minors/. Accessed March 14, 2025.

627 Ibid.

that animating Yaqoob were the same beliefs about infidel women that animated so many Muslim rapists in Britain and elsewhere.

The same could be said of the strange case of Dr. Oumair Aejaz of Rochester Hills, Michigan, an Indian citizen in the US on a visa, who was arrested in August 2024. Oakland County, Michigan, Sheriff Michael Bouchard explained that Aejaz was suspected of situating hidden cameras "in places like hospital rooms, changing rooms, bathrooms and bedrooms to record women and children."[628] He also was charged with recording himself "sexually assaulting unconscious hospital patients."[629] According to the *Detroit Free Press*, Bouchard "said there could be potentially hundreds of victims and investigators are working to identify people who may have been victimized."[630]

Bouchard also declared that "this individual potentially is one of the worst I've ever seen because there's no particular category. It's not just children. It's not just women. It's not just men. It goes from a 2-year-old to a grown woman. And so, the victimization is so broad and the perversion so great, that we're just beginning to wrap our arms around it."[631]

Aejaz was charged with "one count of child sexually abusive activity, four counts of capturing an image of an unclothed person and five counts of using a computer to commit a crime."[632] Later, as more information about his activities came to light,

---

628 Gina Kaufman, "Sheriff says charges against doctor for recording women, children the 'tip of the iceberg,'" *Detroit Free Press*, August 20, 2024, https://www.freep.com/story/news/local/2024/08/20/investigators-suspect-dr-oumair-aejaz-recorded-explicit-videos-for-years/74875345007/. Accessed March 14, 2025.

629 Ibid.

630 Ibid.

631 Ibid.

632 Ibid.

he received more felony charges. At Goldfish Swim School in Rochester, Aejaz was accused of having "filmed two women and two children, ages 2 and 4, in a changing area," according to Oakland County Prosecutor Karen McDonald.[633]

Investigators said that they had "sifted through really jarring, alarming images" that Aejaz had in his possession.[634] McDonald said: "We fully expect and actually know that there are thousands and thousands of images and videos that we will have to work, law enforcement in partnership with others, to identify who those victims are and those are all being investigated."[635] One of Aejaz's external hard drives contained thirteen thousand videos, and Bouchard said Aejaz's activities had been going on for six years. Of what had been found in the initial stages of the investigation, Bouchard said: "This is, and I can't stress this enough, so much the tip of the iceberg."

The *Free Press* also reported that Aejaz was accused a "series of assaults on a 6-year-old child in Novi spanning six different dates in 2023 and 2024. Prosecutors allege Aejaz touched the child sexually and recorded himself doing so. The charges include two counts of first-degree criminal sexual conduct, which are the most serious in this case and carry a maximum sentence of life in prison if convicted and a mandatory minimum of 25 years in prison. Aejaz also is charged with three counts of second-degree criminal sexual conduct, three counts of aggravated child sexually abusive activity, three counts of capturing an image of a nude person and six counts of using a

---

633 Ibid.

634 Ibid.

635 Ibid.

computer to commit a crime."[636] Bouchard emphasized: "Due to the lengthy time that he's been involved in this activity and the large amounts of storage that we have in our possession, we believe there's obviously a lot more to be uncovered."[637]

Once again, this could simply have been a story of monstrous perversion, of which there are unfortunately so many. No one in Michigan was even asking if Aejaz had regarded his victims as fair game for such behavior because they were non-Muslim. That would have been "Islamophobic." But the idea that this possibility could really be ruled out without any consideration at all was, at best, unproven.

---

636 Tresa Baldas and Gina Kaufman, "Jailed Rochester Hills doctor now charged with taping himself molesting 6-year-old," *Detroit Free Press*, October 11, 2024, https://www.freep.com/story/news/local/michigan/oakland/2024/10/11/rochester-hills-dr-oumair-aejaz-now-charged-with-molesting-6-year-old/75617571007/. Accessed March 14, 2025.

637 Ibid.

CHAPTER NINETEEN
DENIAL

"SET UP TO SMEAR THE IMAGE OF ISLAM"

After Boko Haram's mass abduction of Nigerian schoolgirls became the target of Michelle Obama's hashtag campaign, there was a rush to deny that the group had anything to do with Islam. *Time* magazine, renowned everywhere as a guide to what is authentic Islam and what is not, declared that the Boko Haram jihadis thought they were Muslims but were deceiving themselves: "The members of Boko Haram certainly consider themselves Muslims but their actions make them traitors to their faith. We should start referring to them as a criminal group rather than an Islamist group."[638]

The Iranian Parliament Speaker's Adviser for International Affairs, Hossein Sheikholeslam, said:

---

[638] Carla Power, "5 Reasons Boko Haram is Un-Islamic," *Time*, May 15, 2014, https://time.com/99929/boko-haram-is-un-islamic/. Accessed March 20, 2025.

"The behavior of this group is very horrible and has not been witnessed even in the Medieval ages and I clearly state that such behavior isn't related to Islam at all."[639]

Two Muslim congressmen, Keith Ellison (D-MN) and André Carson (D-IN), were the lead signers of an open letter to Boko Haram leader Abubakar Shekau that many other Muslim leaders also signed, saying: "Your justification for stealing these children – that education for girls goes against Islam – has no basis whatsoever in our faith. The Prophet Muhammad (Peace Be Upon Him) wisely emphasized that every Muslim man and woman has a duty to seek education. You have truly strayed from Islam when your actions betray its first command: 'Iqra!' [Read!]"[640] Yet Boko Haram had not seized the girls in order to prevent them from getting an education. The open letter also did not address, or even mention, the Islamic justifications for the sexual enslavement of infidel women.

The US State Department agreed. At a hearing of the Senate Foreign Relations Subcommittee on African Affairs in May 2014, Ambassador Robert Jackson, principal deputy assistant secretary of state for African affairs, stated that "the fact of the matter is that Boko Haram is trying to portray its philosophy as being a Muslim philosophy, and that's just not

---

639 "Parliament Advisor: Boko Haram's Behavior Not Related to Islam," Fars News Agency, May 18, 2014, in Robert Spencer, "Iranian Parliament Adviser: Boko Haram's behavior not related to Islam," Jihad Watch, May 18, 2014, https://jihadwatch.org/2014/05/iranian-parliament-adviser-boko-harams-behavior-not-related-to-islam. Accessed March 20, 2025.

640 Yasmine Hafiz, "Muslim Leaders Condemn Boko Haram In Letter Led By Representatives Ellison And Carson," Huffington Post, May 21, 2014, https://www.huffpost.com/entry/muslim-leaders-condemn-boko-haram_n_5367486?1400709252=&ncid=tweetlnkushpmg00000067. Accessed March 20, 2025.

accurate."[641] Florida Senator Marco Rubio, who was questioning Jackson, agreed, assuring the State Department official and the world that he was "not claiming that this is somehow driven by legitimate teachings of Islam."[642]

Numerous Muslim authorities and spokesmen said the same thing. The grand mufti of Saudi Arabia, Sheikh Abdulaziz Al al-Sheikh, asserted that Boko Haram was "set up to smear the image of Islam."[643] The secretary-general of the Organization of Islamic Cooperation, said that by their actions, the Boko Haram jihadis "not only disavow their Islam, but their humanity."[644]

Faheem Younus, Baltimore president of the Ahmadiyya Muslim Community USA and a senior fellow at the Hoffberger Center for Professional Ethics at the University of Baltimore, complained peevishly in the Huffington Post: "That nothing in Islam, today or 1,400 years ago, justifies the abduction of any human being, let alone innocent girls, is a fact I have explained ad nauseam. Man, at times, I feel exhausted."[645] Yet he did not explain, or even mention, the justifications in the Qur'an and Islamic tradition for taking female "captives of the right hand" and having sexual relations with them.

Islamic apologist and politician Qasim Rashid likewise claimed for Fox News that "Boko Haram's claim that Islam motivates their kidnappings is no different than Adolf Hitler's

---

641 Bridget Johnson, "State Dept. Official: 'Just Not Accurate' to Characterize Boko Haram as Muslim," PJ Media, May 15, 2014, https://pjmedia.com/bridget-johnson/2014/05/15/state-dept-official-just-not-accurate-to-characterize-boko-haram-as-muslim-n191731. Accessed March 20, 2025.

642 Ibid.

643 Power, "5 Reasons Boko Haram is Un-Islamic."

644 Ibid.

645 Faheem Younus, "Don't Blame Islam for Boko Haram," Huffington Post, May 10, 2014, https://www.huffpost.com/entry/dont-blame-islam-for-boko-haram_b_5292964. Accessed March 20, 2025.

claim that Christianity motivated his genocide. This terrorist organization acts in direct violation of every Islamic teaching regarding women."[646] He quoted several Qur'an verses that he claimed forbade the practice of taking women as sex slaves, but like Faheem Younus, Rashid did not even mention, much less bother to explain, the Qur'an passages that Muslims have used throughout history to justify this practice.

Another Islamic apologist, Arsalan Iftikhar, addressed the Nigerian jihadis for CNN: "Hey Boko Haram, have you read the Quran lately? Most of the 1.6 billion Muslims in the world have, and we're utterly certain that it condemns kidnapping young girls and selling them into slavery – no matter what you say 'Allah' tells you."[647] Iftikhar, too, did not make any reference to the Qur'an's justifications for sex slavery.

"THE ABSOLUTE ABSENCE OF RELIGION"

This kind of denial was the world's default mode. On New Year's Eve, December 31, 2024, in Milan's Piazza del Duomo, forty Muslim migrants engaged in a frenzy of mass sexual assault of young women in the crowd to ring in the new year. Just under three weeks later, one of the victims, a nineteen-year-old woman from Britain, told a reporter about how horrified she was: not by the sexual assaults, but by those who were using

---

646 Qasim Rashid, "What Prophet Muhammad would say to Boko Haram," Fox News, May 8, 2014, https://www.foxnews.com/opinion/what-prophet-muhammad-would-say-to-boko-haram. Accessed March 20, 2025.

647 Arsalan Iftikhar, "Hey Boko Haram, pick up a Quran and bring back our girls," CNN, May 6, 2014, in Robert Spencer, "US Muslim prof says Boko Haram violates Qur'an — but omits sex-slavery verses," Jihad Watch, May 6, 2014, https://jihadwatch.org/2014/05/us-muslim-prof-says-boko-haram-violates-quran-but-omits-sex-slavery-verse. Accessed March 20, 2025.

them to push a "political agenda."[648] This young woman was determined to set the record straight. In attempting to do so, she only confused the issue further.

The *Daily Mail* reported that an "organized" group had assaulted her, but instead of speaking out against sexual assault, the victim wanted to "dispel some of the disinformation being shared online and ensure our story is heard."[649] The men had been reported as being migrants, but she claimed that some of the reporting about the incident had been false: "It is a total, blatant lie, to claim that our group were attacked by men holding Palestinian flags."[650]

Full of righteous indignation, the victim, whom the *Daily Mail*'s James Reynolds called Imogen, continued: "I think it is disgusting that people would use our traumatic story to push a political agenda and I want people to understand that many of the descriptions I have read are wholly untrue. I will not allow my sexual attack to become an opportunity to divide people – it is a moment to unite women, and the people of Italy, in outrage that this was allowed to happen during a joyful celebration."[651]

Imogen was especially angry that some reports had suggested that the attacks had to do with Islam: "I am so upset after reading many articles that claim it was a matter of religion, indirectly blaming Islam, whilst claiming our attack was

---

648 James Reynolds, "EXCLUSIVE: British teen's 30-man rape hell which will horrify every parent: How a young woman's trip to Italy turned into a fight for survival against mob 'who grew more excited' the more terrified she became," *Daily Mail*, January 19, 2025, https://www.dailymail.co.uk/news/article-14296287/british-sexual-assault-rape-victim-italy-milan-new-years-eve.html. Accessed March 11, 2025.

649 Ibid.

650 Ibid.

651 Ibid.

'Taharrush Gamea.'"[652] That is a term referring to mass sexual assault that is considered acceptable in Islam, as it involves the seizing of infidel women.

The Milan victim, however, was adamant: "The evil we experienced that night was the absolute absence of religion. Those men had no motive but to take advantage of innocent women, knowing they would escape without suffering the consequences. It was not in the name of religion, it was not in the name of political activism, it was an act of vocalized disrespect towards the Italian people and their principles."[653]

Imogen also insisted that she had done nothing to "provoke" the perpetrators: "I dress modestly. I am tall, strong and did not encourage my attackers. Sexual assault is random. We are not to blame and I could never have expected our attack."[654] She said that "this is also not a reflection of all Bangladeshi people, or people non-native to Italy."[655]

Imogen was reflecting what she has been taught in Britain throughout her nineteen years, but it is unlikely to have been reflected in any of the mob's behavior that night. It is doubtful that anyone paused and told her, "We're not doing this because of Islam, you know." Nor was it likely that Imogen knows the first foggiest thing about Islam, or actually has an informed opinion about the motives of her attackers. It is testimony to the power of leftist indoctrination that after all she suffered, she thinks it necessary to speak out in order to exonerate Islam.

The *Daily Mail* was only too happy to give Imogen space to do this, but if, on the other hand, she had said: "My

---

652 Ibid.
653 Ibid.
654 Ibid.
655 Ibid.

attackers were motivated by Islam," the *Mail* would have suddenly lost interest.

"THIS EPISODE HAS NOTHING TO DO WITH MIGRANTS, WE GET ALONG VERY WELL WITH THEM"

Imogen was not alone. In October 2024, a Muslim asylum seeker from Bangladesh was accused of raping and impregnating a ten-year-old girl at the Hotel Il Cacciatore in the hamlet of San Colombano di Collio in Brescia, Italy. The hotel was being used as a center for migrants.

This revolting incident took place nearly a decade after locals in San Colombano di Collio had protested against the Hotel Il Cacciatore being used to house migrants. All the unrest, however, was a thing of the past, according to Don Battista Dassa, the local parish priest. Dassa insisted that today there is a "climate of peaceful coexistence."[656] Of the rape case, he said: "This episode has nothing to do with migrants, we get along very well with them."[657]

And so that was that. But was it?

"THEY FEEL SUPERIOR BECAUSE THEY ARE MUSLIMS"

In sharp contrast to Imogen, the president of the Association of Arab Women in Italy, Dounia Ettaib readily avowed that the New Year's Eve sexual assaults in Milan had to do with Islam. Ettaib, who moved to Italy from Morocco, explained that

---

656 Miriam Kuepper, "Asylum seeker, 28, 'rapes 10-year-old girl and gets her pregnant' in controversial migrant centre in Italy," *Daily Mail*, October 13, 2024, https://www.dailymail.co.uk/news/article-13954855/Asylum-seeker-rapes-10-year-old-girl-pregnant-Italy.html. Accessed March 14, 2025.

657 Ibid.

Muslims "feel superior because they are Muslims, so they target women of other religions. And it is no coincidence that such violence occurs on New Year's Eve, as if to say, 'You celebrated, but we prove that we are stronger.'"[658]

Ettaib explained the mindset of the attackers, which most European authorities were determined to ignore: "It's more than just gang violence. In the case of gang violence, the surrounding of victims reflects the perpetrators' belonging to the same community, which is none other than the Muslim community."[659] She recommended that if the migrants were "not studying or working, they should be immediately returned to their countries of origin."[660]

This was sound advice, but it was certain to be denounced as "racist."

"RISING ANTI-MUSLIM HATE"

And of course, Imogen, the Italian woman who stoutly denied that Islam had anything to do with the motives of those who sexually assaulted her, was not alone. In March 2018, the *Independent* published a lengthy article by a survivor of a Muslim rape gang in Rotherham. She was writing under a pseudonym, evidently at least partly out of fear of those who had used her in such a terrible manner. "Ella Hill," however, was also clearly afraid of those who were supposedly spreading what she referred to as a "rising anti-Muslim hate," as she

658 "Muslims feel superior, target women of other religions, says head of Association of Arab Women," Remix News, January 13, 2025, https://rmx.news/article/muslims-feel-superior-target-women-of-other-religions-says-head-of-association-of-arab-women/. Accessed March 14, 2025.

659 Ibid.

660 Ibid.

expressed concern that her account would add grist to their mill.[661] "If anything," she declared, "rising anti-Muslim hate will probably make groomers stronger in their convictions, and drive ordinary young Muslim men towards fundamentalism, grooming gangs and terrorism."[662]

So if non-Muslims grew to dislike Islam because of the role that it played in her victimization, Ella Hill was arguing that this would only lead more Muslims to join rape gangs. Thus apparently she thought that non-Muslims had to steadfastly ignore the evidence that she herself was presenting about how Islam had played such a pivotal role in the core assumptions and motivations of those who had destroyed her life, or other girls would suffer the same fate when they otherwise might have been spared.

This was a most peculiar form of emotional blackmail and manipulation, as Ella Hill's own account was unsparing in detailing the Islamic aspects of her rapists' outlook. One would think that it would be good to know these details, not in order to engage in "anti-Muslim hate," but in order to understand fully what happened, so as to prevent it from happening again.

Whatever sentiments it should or should not have aroused in readers, Ella Hill's account was harrowing. "As a teenager," she wrote, "I was taken to various houses and flats above take-aways in the north of England, to be beaten, tortured and raped over 100 times. I was called a 'white slag' and 'white c***' as they beat me. They made it clear that because I was a non-Muslim, and not a virgin, and because I didn't dress 'modestly', that they believed I deserved to be 'punished'. They said I had to

---

661 Ella Hill, "As a Rotherham grooming gang survivor."

662 Ibid.

'obey' or be beaten."[663] She said of the rapists: "Like terrorists, they firmly believe that the crimes they carry out are justified by their religious beliefs."[664]

The rapes were not simply "justified by their religious beliefs"; those beliefs helped the rape gangs actually recruit new members: "Religious indoctrination is a big part of the process of getting young men involved in grooming gang crime. Religious ideas about purity, virginity, modesty and obedience are taken to the extreme until horrific abuse becomes the norm. It was taught to me as a concept of 'othering.'"[665]

Ella Hill stated that the rapists compared her unfavorably to Muslim girls, who, they said, were modest while she was not, and thus she deserved what was coming to her. She described the rapists as saying to her:

> Muslim girls are good and pure because they dress modestly, covering down to their ankles and wrists, and covering their crotch area. They stay virgins until marriage. They are *our* girls.
>
> White girls and non-Muslim girls are bad because you dress like slags. You show the curves of your bodies (showing the gap between your thighs means you're asking for it) and therefore you're immoral. White girls sleep with hundreds of men. You are the *other* girls. You are worthless and you deserve to be gang-raped.[666]

---

663 Ibid.
664 Ibid.
665 Ibid.
666 Ibid.

She even noted that "my main perpetrator quoted scriptures from the Quran to me as he beat me," but she characterized this as "hateful religious hypocrisy" and offered a moral equivalence exoneration of Islam: "But it's far from unique.... almost identical scriptures (about the stoning to death of virgins who don't scream when they are raped) can also be found in the Bible.... All the major world religions, including Hinduism and Buddhism, have also at some time been associated with extreme human rights abuses against men, women and children."[667]

"The problem," Ella Hill claimed, "isn't the text itself; it's how it's fundamentally interpreted. In fact, there are many cases of Bible quotes being used to justify terrible human injustices, like the enslavement of people from Africa, antisemitism and violence towards LGBT+ people."[668]

And so while Ella Hill "experienced horrific, religiously sanctioned sexual violence and torture," and believed "that we need to be aware of religious extremism as something potentially harmful, so that we can protect people from it," she also thought that it was inexcusable to single out Islam for criticism on this score: "But for Tommy Robinson and his followers to focus on an entire religion, based on the cruel interpretations of *some* scriptures by *some* people, is unhelpful, to say the least. Many of his religious theories and conjecture are not anything that I can relate to in my real life experiences. Most grooming gang survivors I know absolutely condemn anti-Islamic hate, and we're uncomfortable with English Defence League protests. We certainly don't want random attacks on 'all Muslims'. You can't cure harm with more harm. Free-thinking men from

---

667 Ibid.
668 Ibid.

Pakistani Muslim backgrounds, like Nazir Afzal, agree, and many deal with all of this incredibly graciously."[669]

This was a straw man. No one, including activist Tommy Robinson and the English Defence League, who for many years were virtually alone in calling attention to the rape gang activity and calling it out for what it really was, ever called for "random attacks on 'all Muslims.'" They weren't trying to incite "anti-Muslim hate"; they were simply speaking honestly and accurately about the motivations of the rape gangs, which Ella Hill demonstrated that she herself knew quite well. Ella Hill's article appeared in the far-left *Independent* because it aided that publication's agenda of portraying all those who spoke of the Islamic character of the rape gang as racists and bigots.

It was actually an audacious attack on such people for the *Independent* to publish, since Ella Hill had provided so much information about how her rapists viewed with her contempt because she was not a Muslim. Her strong denunciation of "anti-Muslim hate" was designed to disarm those who pointed out the Islamic aspects of rape gang by admitting that such aspects existed while simultaneously discounting them as something that all religions had, while warning that too much attention to such matters would only make a bad situation worse.

Meanwhile, while Ella Hill insisted that all religions had teachings that were similar to the Islamic tenets that animated the Muslim rape gangs, there was no record of any rapists quoting the Bible or Hindu or Buddhist texts while brutalizing their victims.

---

[669] Ibid.

INVESTIGATED FOR TELLING THE TRUTH

In the British political and media establishment, lies about the Muslim rape gangs were the norm. Those who dared to tell the whole truth about what motivated the gangs would feel the full weight of the power of that establishment. Yet in Sweden, the situation was even worse.

Kristina Sundquist, a professor at Lund University in Sweden, several years ago began research into the type of people who were guilty of sexual crimes in that country. Remix News explained in April 2022 that "the research was not aimed at racially profiling the offenders, as the scientists themselves put it, but they nevertheless have discovered some facts about the ethnic profile of rapists by accident."[670] And that was where their troubles began.

Because her findings ventured into areas that the Swedish authorities did not wish to explore, Sundquist was placed under investigation "for publishing an unauthorized research report, and may face prosecution for coming to the conclusion that the vast majority of rapes are committed by immigrants to the country."[671]

Yet this was simply the facts of the matter: data showed that "immigrants are not only disproportionately over-represented in rape cases, but despite being a minority in Sweden, they commit the vast majority of sexual violence. This is despite the fact that the study only analyzed cases between the period of

---

670 "Swedish scientists prosecuted for finding that most rapes are committed by immigrants," Remix News, April 26, 2022, https://rmx.news/article/swedish-scientists-prosecuted-for-finding-that-most-rapes-are-committed-by-immigrants/. Accessed March 18, 2025.

671 Ibid.

2000 and 2015 — that is, before the enormous 2015 influx of migrants from the Middle East and Africa."[672]

Sundquist emphasized that verifying this had not been the purpose of the research: "Immigrants were just a variable, and it turned out to be quite a remarkable discovery as there were many immigrants and foreign-born people in this group."[673]

Sundquist and her coauthor, Professor Ardavan Khoshnood, submitted their report to the Board of Appeal, which reports to the Swedish Ministry of Education. Now they faced investigation over whether they had an "ethical license" to deal with "sensitive data."[674] They also came under fire for failing to show how their findings would "reduce exclusion and improve integration."[675]

Said Khoshnood: "It's a shame" that they had been accused of "conducting and publishing illegal research."[676] He explained: "The purpose of the study was not to find out what immigration is like. Surprisingly, this variable turned out to be quite important, and we didn't know in advance what the study would show. We wanted to create a profile of the perpetrator, to know who the typical perpetrator is."[677]

The board disputed the idea that the academics needed some special permission to conduct research in this area: "I don't see anywhere that ethical permission is sought to test the hypothesis if immigrants are over-represented in statistics on convicted rapists."[678] Indeed. They were being investigated

---

[672] Ibid.
[673] Ibid.
[674] Ibid.
[675] Ibid.
[676] Ibid.
[677] Ibid.
[678] Ibid.

solely because of Swedish authorities' anxiety that unwelcome truths might be told too loudly and reveal how disastrous their mass migration policies had really been for their country.

"NOT A SERIOUS CRIME"

Just a few months later, on September 10, 2022, a thirteen-year-old girl in the Stockholm suburb of Märsta was raped twice. The first rapist was a Muslim migrant named Abbas, who was called "Abbe" in Sweden. Abbas was born, according to conflicting records, either in Afghanistan or Iran, and came to Sweden as an "unaccompanied refugee child."[679] He later became a Swedish citizen. The other rapist was another Afghan Muslim migrant who remained unnamed in the official documents on the case.

The Swedish publication Fria Tider reported that "during police questioning, the girl said that she met a friend at around 3-4pm during the day. The girls met Abbas, another man called Mohammad and a third unknown man at a preschool. At the preschool, Abbas performed oral and vaginal intercourse with the girl. A while later, the same girl was raped again, this time by the unknown man in a wooded area by Östregårds väg."[680]

Abbas was arrested. As police investigated the case, they found that in 2018, he "was suspected of attempted rape of children. This by having tried to force a girl to have intercourse by pulling down her pants. The girl had just turned 15 at the time of reporting. However, the investigation was dropped due

---

679 "Abbas och okänd man våldtog flicka vid förskola – hovrätten: 'Inte grovt brott,'" Fria Tider, May 23, 2023, https://www.friatider.se/abbas-och-okand-man-valdtog-flicka-vid-forskola-hovratten-inte-grovt-brott. Accessed March 18, 2025.

680 Ibid.

to evidence problems."[681] Also, "between 2017 and 2021, Abbas was guilty of shoplifting, illegal driving, weapons offenses, drug offenses, unlawful threats, driving bans, minor drug offenses and attempted robbery."[682]

The verdict came on February 27, 2023. Abbas was "convicted of child rape, three counts of drug offenses and drunk driving." He was sentenced to three years in prison and also ordered to pay 225,000 Swedish kronor to the girl for the rape and 30,000 kronor for her mental and physical anguish; that amounted to roughly $25,000. Mohammad "was sentenced for sexual molestation of children then allegedly hit the girl on the bottom at the time the rape was committed. The penalty was a suspended sentence and SEK 8,800 in daily fines. He was also sentenced to pay SEK 10,000 in damages to the girl." That's around $1,800.

The victim and the prosecutor thought Abbas had gotten off too lightly, and asked the Swedish Court of Appeal to give him a longer prison term. The court, however did not oblige, stating: "Like the district court, the court of appeal finds that it has not been shown that Abbas has had sexual intercourse together and in agreement with another unknown perpetrator. The court of appeal shares the district court's assessment that the act should not be classified as a serious crime."[683] Mohammad, meanwhile, was acquitted altogether.

Sweden had made its choice. Its girls and women would suffer many other non-serious crimes of this kind.

---

681 Ibid.
682 Ibid.
683 Ibid.

TORONTO'S SCHOOL BOARD BANS A BOOK

Canada's largest school board, the Toronto District School Board (TDSB), made its choice as well. From 2017 to 2021, the TDSB participated in a partnership with Tanya Lee, whom *The Globe and Mail* described as a "Toronto mother and entrepreneur."[684] Lee ran "a book club for teenaged girls called A Room Of Your Own, which is rooted in her conviction that reading and open conversation can empower young women, as it did for her. Ms. Lee makes a point of targeting the club to schools in high-priority neighbourhoods, and emphasizes its inclusive, positive atmosphere."[685]

With her initiative popular and growing, Lee would choose books for the girls to read, and even bring in authors to speak to the groups. The TDSB, meanwhile, "supported Ms. Lee's club by distributing books to participating students, discussing them in class and allowing club members to take a day off school to attend (back when in-person meetings were still possible)."[686] In October 2021, however, the Toronto District School Board ended its support for A Room Of Your Own. TDSB superintendent Helen Fisher told Lee that the board would not promote two of the books Lee had chosen for the girls to read.

One of the unloved books was *The Last Girl: My Story of Captivity, and My Fight Against the Islamic State* by Nadia Murad. Nadia Murad is a Yazidi woman whom the Islamic

---

684 Naomi Buck, "Curiosity is at the core of education. Canada's largest school board has showed a stunning lack of it," *Globe and Mail*, November 17, 2021, https://www.theglobeandmail.com/opinion/article-curiosity-is-at-the-core-of-education-canadas-largest-school-board-has/. Accessed March 19, 2025.

685 Ibid.

686 Ibid.

State abducted in 2014 and held as a sex slave for three months. She managed to escape, and in her book, speaks frankly about how her captors tortured, abused, and frequently raped her. *The Globe and Mail* reported that Fisher told Lee "that Ms. Murad's book could foster Islamophobia."[687]

That was the Toronto District School Board's concern: that someone might come away from reading Nadia Murad's book thinking ill of Islam. The girls and women who suffered were of no importance. Only Islam's image was.

687 Ibid.

CHAPTER TWENTY

THE TOXIC THEOLOGY THAT DOESN'T EXIST

DEFENDING EVEN ISIS

The general denial of the reality of Islamic sex slavery led the establishment media to deny its existence even when evidence for it was right in front of their noses. On October 4, 2024, Israeli authorities rescued a Yazidi woman, Fawzi Amin Sido, who was being held captive in Gaza. The Islamic State (ISIS) had abducted her in Iraq in 2014, when she was eleven years old; ultimately, she was sold as a sex slave into the Gaza Strip.

CBS News, however, opted not to tell the truth about why she was in Gaza in the first place. The Indian news outlet OpIndia reported that "while Sido could regain freedom after a decade of sexual abuse, torture and other unspeakable atrocities, US media outlet CBS News blatantly attempted to downplay ISIS sex crimes. The CBS News article and relevant X post suggested that the Yazidi woman was 'stranded' in Gaza, even though she was trafficked from Iraq into Gaza by ISIS terrorists and held in captivity by Hamas terrorists there, forcefully married and turned into a sex slave of the Islamic terrorist."[688]

ADDRESSING THE TOXIC THEOLOGY THAT DOESN'T EXIST

The founder of the Oxford Institute for British Islam, Dr. Taj Hargey, said forthrightly in January 2025 that "every Friday when the congregational prayers end, up and down the country the imam says we should condemn the disbelievers and the non-believers and all those who are not Muslim, and only Muslims are going to heaven."[689]

This supremacist mindset, he said, fed directly into the Muslim rape gang activity: "So when you have that idea of superiority, of supremacy, of segregationist mentality, then yes, these people then go out and then do bad things to these young, vulnerable teenage girls who most of them are in care, they abused them and used them as chewing gum."[690]

Hargey added: "It's an astonishing thing to hear. They believe that they are alone, going to heaven. For example, I met a Muslim man here in Oxford. He said that the Muslim rapists

---

688 Shraddha Pandey, "American media house CBS downplays ISIS crimes after Israeli forces rescue a Yazidi woman trafficked to Gaza and held as a sex slave for 10 years," by OpIndia, October 4, 2024, https://www.opindia.com/2024/10/american-media-house-cbs-downplays-isis-crimes-after-israeli-forces-rescue-a-yazidi-woman-trafficked-to-gaza/. Accessed March 14, 2025.

689 Gabrielle Wilde, "'Astonishing!' Islam leader staggeringly claims he was told 'Muslim rapists will go to heaven' as he DEMANDS rooting out of core issue," GB News, January 8, 2025, https://www.gbnews.com/news/islam-leader-muslim-rapists-go-heaven-grooming-ganngs. Accessed March 11, 2025.

690 Ibid.

would go to heaven before a Christian person. Now imagine that. I mean, I was totally astounded that you could do this."[691]

This was not actually astonishing at all; what was most astonishing about it was that Hargey, who was setting himself up as an Islamic authority, professed to be astonished about it. The Qur'an states that "Allah does not forgive that a partner be ascribed to him. He forgives all except that, of whom he wills. Whoever ascribes partners to Allah has indeed invented a tremendous sin." (4:48)

If Allah forgives everything except ascribing a partner to him, then idolatry or polytheism are the worst sins in Islam, far worse than rape. Yet the Qur'an charges Christians with both, in that they are supposedly deifying a man and worshiping him along with Allah (5:116). Thus it is not at all surprising that a Muslim would consider a Muslim rapist more likely to enter paradise than a religious Christian, and Hargey should have been aware of this.

Nonetheless, Hargey was correct when he said: "Rape and evil crime is a wicked thing, especially when you do this to young children. I think we shouldn't give them a free pass. I think what's important is, yes, we should investigate the criminality of sexual grooming, rape gangs. But we should also look at the interlinkage between religion and criminality as far as Muslims are concerned. Unless we do address the toxic theology coming from the mosque and from the elders of the Muslim community, nothing much will change."[692]

Curiously, however, Hargey also denied the existence of this "toxic theology." He said that imams were perpetuating the beliefs and attitudes that gave rise to the rape gangs, saying:

---

691 Ibid.

692 Ibid.

"The theology from the Mosque and the elders is to perpetuate this idea of 'them and us.'"[693] He denied, however, that this idea had any actual basis in Islam: "The criminality is fuelled by the ideology of the Islamic fundamentalism which has no basis in the Qu'ran [*sic*]."[694]

Hargey's statements are odd on a number of levels. He claims that "Islamic fundamentalism" has "no basis in the Qur'an." This is a completely incoherent claim. "Fundamentalism" is a Protestant Christian idea that actually corresponds to nothing in Islam. It refers to taking the text seriously and literally, and the vast majority of Muslims worldwide do that. Even if one takes the term simply to refer to those of any faith who interpret their sacred texts literally, that would mean that Hargey is claiming that there is no basis in the Qur'an for taking the Qur'an literally. Actually a literal reading is the paramount understanding of the Qur'an throughout Islamic history. And even if it weren't, the idea that taking the text seriously has no basis in the text just makes no sense.

Hargey continued: "These fundamentalist Muslims believe 'If the Prophet Muhammad can sleep with a nine-year-old, what's wrong with me sleeping with a 12-year-old?', even though the story is not true."[695]

Yet in reality, the idea that Muhammad had sex with a nine-year-old is based on traditions that are contained in Sahih Bukhari, the hadith collection that Islamic scholars consider the most reliable, as well as in other respected hadith collections. In

693 Ben Chapman, "Imams 'PROMOTE grooming rings', says Muslim leader 11 years after first raising concerns about white girls being seen as 'easy meat,'" GB News, January 8, 2025, https://www.gbnews.com/news/imam-grooming-gangs-promoting-rings-muslim-leader. Accessed March 11, 2025.

694 Ibid.

695 Ibid.

one hadith Bukhari records, Aisha is depicted as saying "that the Prophet married her when she was six years old and he consummated his marriage when she was nine years old. Hisham said: I have been informed that Aisha remained with the Prophet for nine years (i.e. till his death)."[696]

Bukhari also says that others attested to this as well: "Narrated Urwa: The Prophet wrote the (marriage contract) with Aisha while she was six years old and consummated his marriage with her while she was nine years old and she remained with him for nine years (i.e. till his death)."[697] And: "Narrated Hisham's father: Khadija died three years before the Prophet departed to Medina. He stayed there for two years or so and then he married Aisha when she was a girl of six years of age, and he consummated that marriage when she was nine years old."[698]

Undaunted, or perhaps secure in the knowledge that most or even all of his hearers would take what he said without questioning it, Hargey continued: "The idea is, when you can delegitimise these youngsters as being less than human and being less than equal and for you to do whatever you please, that is the basis for these men to act like that. There is this ideology, this interpretation of Islam which makes this possible. Why is virtually every single person in these grooming gangs Muslim? It seems like 95 per cent of them are. We need to look at the interconnection between Islam, promoted by the clergy and the

---

696 Sahih Bukhari, vol. 7, bk. 67, no. 5134, https://sunnah.com/bukhari:5134. Accessed March 20, 2025. See also Sahih Bukhari, vol. 7, bk. 67, no. 5133, https://sunnah.com/bukhari:5133. Accessed March 20, 2025.

697 Sahih Bukhari, vol. 7, bk. 67, no. 5158, https://sunnah.com/bukhari:5158. Accessed March 20, 2025.

698 Sahih Bukhari, vol. 5, bk. 63, no. 3896, https://sunnah.com/bukhari:3896. Accessed March 20, 2025.

establishment in the UK, because Islam is not promoting this reprehensible behaviour."[699]

Hargey was refusing to acknowledge that the impetus for seeing unbelievers as less than human came from the Qur'an itself, which likens them to "animals" (8:55) and calls them "the most vile of created beings." (98:6) Nevertheless, he was raising good and important points regarding the interconnection between what Muslim clerics taught and rape gang activity, but by insisting that Islam actually had nothing to do with this behavior, Hargey was simply not being honest, and was, in fact, being actively misleading.

"THE WEIGHT OF TRADITION"

Amid the prevailing denial, a lawyer in one trial in France revealed that she knew very well that the rape of captive infidel women was perfectly acceptable in Islam. The defendant, El Bachir Rahmouni, was on trial for the rape of a teenage girl. "On November 7, 2021," according to the French newspaper *La Provence*, Rahmouni "allegedly gained the trust of Neïla, a 17-year-old runaway, and took her to a sordid squat in Aubagne, where, according to the young girl's statements, he raped her with great brutality. She was found by the police the next day, and immediately reported a traumatic scene, corroborated by the medical examinations carried out on her."[700] Rahmouni

---

699 Ben Chapman, "Imams 'PROMOTE grooming rings.'"

700 Marguerite Dégez, "10 à 12 ans de réclusion criminelle requis pour le viol d'une adolescente dans un squat à Aubagne," *La Provence*, January 14, 2025, https://www.laprovence.com/article/region/2460733218138915/10-a-12-ans-de-reclusion-criminelle-requis-pour-le-viol-d-une-adolescente-dans-un-squat-a-aubagne. Accessed March 14, 2025.

initially denied that he had sexual relations with the girl, and then claimed that she had wanted it.

The attorney general of the departmental criminal court, Sylvaine Schumacher, called Rahmouni "a predator," and spoke of the rape of Neïla as the "very opportunistic act of someone who managed to target a victim who was somewhat vulnerable because of her situation and personality and who will allow himself to act without taking into account what she may want and feel," a characterization that was strongly reminiscent of so many victims of the Muslim rape gangs in Britain.[701] Rahmouni's lawyer, however, argued for his acquittal, saying that the young man was acting in accord with "the weight of tradition."[702]

Indeed he was. But it was a tradition that few in the West wanted to admit even existed.

THE "MUSLIM MARTIN LUTHER" CONVICTED OF RAPE

One of those who seemed all too aware of this tradition was Tariq Ramadan, a Muslim intellectual who had been one of the foremost exponents of Islamic reform, at least to non-Muslims in Europe and North America. In September 2024, Ramadan was convicted of rape.

It is impossible to overstate how shocking this was for those who had praised Ramadan to the skies for so very long. For many years, Tariq Ramadan was the darling of the Western intelligentsia. In 2002, Salon hailed him as "the Muslim Martin

701 Ibid.
702 Ibid.

Luther."[703] In 2004, *Time* magazine listed him as one of the one hundred most influential people in the world today.[704] In 2012, *Foreign Policy* included him on its list of the top one hundred global thinkers "for telling us that Islam and democracy can go together — just when it matters."[705]

Now those accolades, and the many others that Ramadan received, stand as mute witness to the left's tendency to shower with honors those who tell it what it wants to hear. Agence France-Presse (AFP) reported that Ramadan was "convicted on appeal of rape and sexual coercion by a Geneva court."[706] This had been a long time coming, as Ramadan had faced numerous accusations in recent years of "masking violence and radicalism behind a mild facade."[707]

For years, Ramadan had dismissed such allegations as "racism" and "Islamophobia." In a December 2019 video, he claimed that the accusations against him were all an attempt to discredit

---

703 Paul Donnelly, "Tariq Ramadan: The Muslim Martin Luther?" Salon, February 15, 2002, https://web.archive.org/web/20051212031635/http:/www.salon.com/people/feature/2002/02/15/ramadan/index_np.html. Accessed March 14, 2025.

704 "The 2004 TIME 100," *Time*, https://content.time.com/time/specials/packages/completelist/0,29569,1970858,00.html. Accessed March 14, 2025.

705 Alicia P.Q. Wittmeyer, "The FP Top 100 Global Thinkers," *Foreign Policy*, November 26, 2012, https://foreignpolicy.com/2012/11/26/the-fp-top-100-global-thinkers-2/. Accessed March 14, 2025.

706 "Tariq Ramadan, disgraced former star of European Islam," AFP, September 10, 2024, https://www.france24.com/en/live-news/20240910-tariq-ramadan-disgraced-former-star-of-european-islam. Accessed March 14, 2025.

707 Ibid.

him and thereby "neutralize the Muslims."[708] He added: "We have to be clear that there is discrimination, stigmatization, racism that is at stake in the whole issue. And I was a symbol. To destroy me meant, let the people understand: If you want to be vocal you have to face the reality. It happened to Tariq Ramadan now, it could happen to anyone in the future."[709]

Even worse, Radio France Internationale reported in 2020, after two more women accused him of rape, that "supporters of Ramadan, who is a professor of contemporary Islamic studies at Oxford's St. Anthony's College, have called the accusations against him part of a 'international Zionist plot' to blacken his name."[710] Of course!

It couldn't have been that a cosseted Muslim academic, hailed and feted all over Europe and the United States despite the abject vacuity and sinister disingenuousness of his thought, began to indulge his worst impulses, could it?[711] He couldn't

708 "Islamic Scholar Tariq Ramadan, after Serving Time for Rape Charges: The French Judicial System Imprisoned Me as Part of a Political Plot to Destroy My Reputation; This Can Happen to Any Vocal Muslim," Middle East Media Research Institute (MEMRI), December 20, 2019, https://www.memri.org/tv/oxford-professor-tariq-ramadan-rape-allegations-french-prisons-political-plot-silence-vocal-muslims-west. Accessed March 14, 2025.

709 Ibid.

710 "Tariq Ramadan formally charged with two more counts of rape," Radio France Internationale, February 13, 2020, https://www.rfi.fr/en/france/20200213-Rape-accused-scholar-Tariq-Ramadan-back-court. Accessed March 14, 2025.

711 For abject vacuity, see Robert Spencer, "Deep Thoughts from Tariq Ramadan," Jihad Watch, October 20, 2017, https://jihadwatch.org/2017/10/deep-thoughts-from-tariq-ramadan. Accessed March 14, 2025. For sinister disingenuousness, see Robert Spencer, "Journalist who wrote book about Tariq Ramadan says he has other sexual assault victims," Jihad Watch, October 27, 2017, https://jihadwatch.org/2017/10/journalist-who-wrote-book-about-tariq-ramadan-says-he-has-other-sexual-assault-victims. Accessed March 14, 2025.

have been tempted to do so when it became clear that, in light of his value to Western authorities as a "moderate Muslim" who seemed to prop up their fantasies about the jihad threat, he would be allowed to get away with virtually anything—could he?

"Virtually anything" was actually an understatement. One of his accusers said he subjected her to "blows to the face and body, forced sodomy, rape with an object and various humiliations, including being dragged by the hair to the bathtub and urinated on."[712] His sadism appears to have been, if one allegation is true, closely intertwined with his celebrated Islamic piety: another one of his accusers said he told her he was raping her because she didn't wear a hijab.[713] In a similar vein, as more and more women began to accuse him of rape, one of those accusers was beaten and threatened.[714]

Ramadan's public persona was shot through with duplicity. French journalist Caroline Fourest's illuminating book *Brother Tariq: The Doublespeak of Tariq Ramadan* states that this much-lionized putative "Muslim Martin Luther" was actually anything but a reformer: in reality, Ramadan was "remaining scrupulously faithful to the strategy mapped out by his grandfather, a strategy of advance stage by stage" toward the imposition

---

712 Hugh Fitzgerald, "Tariq Ramadan: One More Accusation with 'Aggravating Circumstances,'" Jihad Watch, April 15, 2018, https://jihadwatch.org/2018/04/tariq-ramadan-one-more-accusation-with-aggravating-circumstances. Accessed March 14, 2025.

713 Hugh Fitzgerald, "Tariq Ramadan rape accuser says he told her he was raping her 'because you don't wear a hijab,'" Jihad Watch, April 23, 2018, https://jihadwatch.org/2018/04/tariq-ramadan-race-accuser-says-he-told-her-he-was-raping-her-because-you-dont-wear-a-hijab. Accessed March 14, 2025.

714 Hugh Fitzgerald, "Accuser of Tariq Ramadan Beaten and Threatened: 'Next Time It Will Be Gasoline,'" Jihad Watch, April 6, 2018, https://jihadwatch.org/2018/04/accuser-of-tariq-ramadan-beaten-and-threatened-next-time-it-will-be-gasoline. Accessed March 14, 2025.

of Islamic law in the West. Ramadan is the grandson of Hasan al-Banna, founder of the Muslim Brotherhood.[715]

Fourest was the first to reveal, back in 2017, that Ramadan had at least four other victims besides the first woman who came forward, Henda Ayari. "A request for religious advice turned into a compulsive sexual relationship, sometimes consented to, often violent and very humiliating, before ending in threats."[716]

Fourest had evidence. "I presented it to a judge. But Tariq Ramadan scared him too much.... I am well-placed to know the violence of the networks of the Muslim Brotherhood when one stands up to 'brother Tariq.'"[717]

"It was a plot," Ramadan insisted. "It was a political set up. And this could happen to anyone."[718] The worst part of this duplicitous whining was that even after Ramadan was convicted, there were hordes of deluded leftists who would fall for it. Amid all the controversy surrounding Ramadan, however, no one at all even suggested the possibility that Ramadan's actions were not a violation of his deep Islamic faith, but a manifestation of that faith. The question never came up even despite the fact that one of his victims said he had chosen to brutalize her because she did not wear hijab—as the Qur'an says that women "draw their veils close around them" so that they not be molested (33:59). Those who do not do so, then, are fair game.

---

715 Caroline Fourest, *Brother Tariq: The Doublespeak of Tariq Ramadan*, trans. Ioana Wieder and John Atherton, (New York: Encounter Books, 2008), 268.

716 Caroline Fourest, "La double vie de Tariq Ramadan," *Marianne*, October 27, 2017, https://www.marianne.net/agora/les-signatures-de-marianne/la-double-vie-de-tariq-ramadan. Accessed March 14, 2025.

717 Ibid.

718 "Islamic Scholar Tariq Ramadan," MEMRI.

But in Tariq Ramadan's case as in so many others, such questions were too "Islamophobic" even to consider.

CHAPTER TWENTY-ONE
THE REAL VICTIMS

THE LEFT'S SPIN

Over the years, there were ongoing efforts to give the public the impression that the real victims of the Muslim rape gang scandal were Muslims themselves.

On December 7, 2024, *The Spectator* reviewed a new play called *Expendable*, which was running at London's venerable West End theater, The Royal Court. According to *The Spectator*, *Expendable* was "an urgent bulletin from the front line of the grooming gang scandal in the north of England."[719] The Royal Court website was no less effusive, saying: "Playwright Emteaz Hussain's *Expendable* spotlights the often-overlooked voices of

[719] Lloyd Evans, "This Muslim playwright believes Yorkshire is headed for civil war," *The Spectator*, December 7, 2024, https://www.spectator.co.uk/article/this-muslim-playwright-believes-yorkshire-is-headed-for-civil-war/. Accessed February 25, 2025.

Pakistani women, delving into the shortcomings of law enforcement, politicians, and the media."[720]

The prospect of a play about the rape gang scandal was astounding in itself. To some, it might have seemed for a fleeting moment as if Britain was actually coming to its senses. Shedding some light on the seldom-heard voices of Pakistani women also sounded like a capital idea, particularly in this context. Those women could have informed the London audience, and the world, about how the Qur'an directs men to beat women from whom they "fear disobedience" (4:34). They could have told us about how it devalues a woman's testimony (2:282) and inheritance rights (4:11), and allows for the marriage, and even the divorce, of prepubescent girls (65:4). They could have told us about honor killings, the jailing of rape victims, and more.

Yet that was not what *Expendable* was about at all. "The setting," *The Spectator* noted, was "a kitchen in Yorkshire where Zara is trying to keep her family together after her son, Raheel, was outed as a rape suspect by a national newspaper."[721] It wasn't just the shame of the charge; it was the attendant harassment from racist Englishmen: "White thugs dump parcels of excrement on their porch and Zara cowers under the kitchen table, too scared to answer the door. The racists have mounted a mass demonstration, supported by the cops, which causes local bus services to be cancelled."[722]

This was essentially a 100 percent inversion of the reality in Britain. There weren't any "white thugs" who were menacing poor, huddled groups of fearful Muslims under the approving

---

720 "Expendable by Emteaz Hussain," RoyalCourtTheatre.com, https://royalcourttheatre.com/whats-on/expendable/. Accessed February 25, 2025.

721 Evans, "This Muslim playwright."

722 Ibid.

eye of the police. Instead, Starmer has earned the nickname "Two-Tier Keir" for cracking down harshly on the mildest of protests against mass migration and the Islamization of Britain. Starmer oversaw the imprisonment of people who posted rude statements on social media or chanted slogans that the government found offensive.[723] Meanwhile, police notoriously turned a blind eye to Muslims who were genuinely violent.

Having started off badly, *Expendable* just got worse: "Every Muslim in town is terrified of a white vigilante gang who recently targeted a blameless Yemeni pensioner and kicked him to death. It gets worse. Zara and her daughter, Sofia, join a peaceful counter-demonstration, but the heavy-handed cops arrest ten innocent Muslims and charge them with violent disorder. Meanwhile, the white thugs are free to scrawl 'Rape capital of the UK' across the side of the local mosque."[724]

This was the kind of thing that made for a hit play in this age of absurdity, but it was nothing like what was really happening. The British police did not single out Muslims and ignore "white" violence. Instead, they demonstrated their pro-Muslim bias on numerous occasions, even telling some English counter-protesters to take down a lone Israeli flag while pro-Hamas demonstrators waved Palestine flags everywhere.[725]

Then there were the "whites" in *Expendable* who scrawled "rape capital of the UK" on the mosque. Here again, this was

---

723 Daniel Greenfield, "British Man Jailed for Blaspheming 'Allah,'" Jihad Watch, August 14, 2024, https://jihadwatch.org/2024/08/british-man-jailed-for-blaspheming-allah. Accessed February 25, 2025.

724 Evans, "This Muslim playwright."

725 Robert Spencer, "UK: London cop tells protesters to take down Israeli flag after repeatedly allowing Palestinian flag to be flown," Jihad Watch, December 14, 2023, https://jihadwatch.org/2023/12/uk-london-cop-tells-protesters-to-take-down-israeli-flag-after-repeatedly-allowing-palestinian-flag-to-be-flown. Accessed February 25, 2025.

an inversion of reality. Britain has seen numerous churches daubed with Islamic graffiti.[726] Mosques, however, were not being targeted. And as for the linking of a mosque with rape, one needed only to recall that the rape gang members were almost all Muslims. As journalist Uzay Bulut noted, "August 26 [2024] marked ten years since the publication of the *Jay Report*, an independent inquiry into child sexual exploitation in the British town of Rotherham. The 2014 report found that at least 1,400 underage girls were abused predominantly by Muslim men of Pakistani heritage between 1997 and 2013 in this South Yorkshire town."[727] Yet aside from a few prosecutions, all that had been done in the decade since the *Jay Report* appeared was more denial, more obfuscation, more excuse-making.

As shattered, staggering, dhimmi Britain entered its final period as a free society, its leftist intelligentsia were indulging their fantasies about how much poor Muslims are persecuted in what was once the land of Churchill. To dramatize this farce properly would take not the author of *Expendable*, but no one less capable than William Shakespeare. The Bard, however, would not have recognized his old homeland. In his day, someone would have dared to get to the heart of the problem.

Instead, the British government denied that it existed at all.

---

[726] Jenny Loweth, "Teen admits his part in 'mindless vandalism' at church," *Telegraph & Argus*, September 10, 2019, https://www.thetelegraphandargus.co.uk/news/17893352.teen-admits-part-39-mindless-vandalism-39-church/. Accessed February 25, 2025.

[727] Uzay Bulut, "Pakistani Grooming Gangs in the UK: An Islamic Problem," FrontPageMag.com, October 18, 2024, https://www.frontpagemag.com/pakistani-grooming-gangs-in-the-uk-an-islamic-problem/. Accessed February 25, 2025.

THE EPIDEMIC OF WHITE, NON-MUSLIM BRITISH GANG RAPISTS

In a January 2025 recap of the controversy over the Muslim rape gangs that Elon Musk had revived once again in Britain, *The New York Times* claimed that Musk was "using his social media platform X to attack and spread misinformation about Prime Minister Keir Starmer and other members of the Labour government."[728] The *Times* also noted that the situation in Rotherham was "highly combustible because of the racial contrast between the victims, who in the Rotherham case were mostly white, and the perpetrators. Prosecutions in Oxford and the northern towns of Oldham and Rochdale in 2012 for the abuse of dozens of girls included men of Pakistani, Bangladeshi and Afghan heritage who received long prison terms."[729]

Starmer and his government, however, might have accused the *Times* itself of spreading "misinformation," for the *Times* report stated matter-of-factly that "most of the perpetrators were of British Pakistani heritage."[730] The British government under both Conservative and Labour governments denied this, and the *Times* itself appeared to contradict its own statements on the ethnicity of the perpetrators. It stated that "identification data on the ethnicity of child sexual abuse victims and suspects was released by the Labour government in November," and that the data showed that "83 percent of suspects in 2023

---

728 Megan Specia, "What Is the U.K. 'Grooming Gang' Scandal Seized On by Elon Musk?" *New York Times*, January 7, 2025, https://www.nytimes.com/2025/01/07/world/europe/uk-grooming-gangs-elon-musk.html. Accessed March 13, 2025.

729 Ibid.

730 Ibid.

were recorded as white and 7 percent were recorded as Asian, broadly in line with the country's overall demographics."[731]

In the course of all this, the *Times* explained that "in official U.K. statistics, 'Asian' is a very broad term that can refer to people with Indian, Pakistani, Bangladeshi or Chinese heritage, or from other parts of South Asia," but this was more "misinformation," as in virtually every case regarding the rape gangs, at least, the term is used to refer to Pakistani Muslims.[732]

Even as it skewered Musk for spreading supposedly false claims, the *Times* report was riddled with inaccuracies. Whatever the term "Asian" meant, however, the claim that 83 percent of the perpetrators were "white" and only seven percent were "Asian" seemed to contradict the *Times*' own assertion that "most of the perpetrators were of British Pakistani heritage."

The *Times* also falsely claimed that the November 2024 report was the "first of its kind published by any British government."[733] In October 2020, the UK Home Office under the Conservative government of Prime Minister Boris Johnson published a report entitled "Characteristics of group-based child sexual exploitation in the community: literature review (accessible version)."[734] How this report differed from an apparently inaccessible version, that is, one that was not available to the public, was not explained.

---

731 Ibid.

732 Ibid.

733 Ibid.

734 "Characteristics of group-based child sexual exploitation in the community: literature review (accessible version)," Gov.uk, https://www.gov.uk/government/publications/group-based-child-sexual-exploitation-characteristics-of-offending/characteristics-of-group-based-child-sexual-exploitation-in-the-community-literature-review-accessible-version. Accessed March 13, 2025.

The 2020 report gave an overview of the ethnicity of the gang rapists that was generally similar to the claims of Labour's 2024 report:

> The CSA [Child Sexual Abuse] Centre compared the ethnicity of convicted defendants with the proportions of different ethnic groups in the population and found that whilst 14% of the population of England and Wales were from a Black, Asian and Minority Ethnic (BAME) background according to the 2011 Census, only 8.4% of convicted defendants were from BAME backgrounds, where ethnicity was known (Parke and Karsna, 2019). Whilst they did not look specifically at certain ethnic minority groups, this would appear to suggest that those from an ethnic minority background more generally are not over-represented in CSA offending.[735]

In noting this, it chastised the media for misleading the public about this question:

> However, the media has given much attention to the model of offending involving an Asian perpetrator and White victim (The Children's Society, 2018; Cockbain and Tufail, 2020) and it is important to examine the evidence underlying such perceptions.... Coverage of these cases tends to suggest that a disproportionate number of Asian, Muslim and

[735] Ibid.

> Pakistani-heritage men are generally involved in the organised grooming and abuse of White British girls (Cockbain and Tufail, 2020), and pays less attention to the other forms of CSE [Child Sexual Exploitation] that occur (Eaton and Holmes, 2017).[736]

This skewed media coverage had resulted in such a widespread misapprehension of the problem that the real perpetrators were being ignored:

> Indeed, it has been noted that over the past decade, the 'Muslim grooming gangs' narrative has become entrenched in public discourse (Cockbain and Tufail, 2020). It has been suggested that this can result in a stereotyping of what this type of abuse looks like, which can be harmful as offenders and victims who do not fit the image drawn out in the media may be under-identified or dismissed (Eaton and Holmes, 2017) and attention may not be paid to tackling the diverse forms of offending. For example, the Drew review reported one police superintendent describing the challenge in his local area as being characterised by 'White European males, in their mid-40s, making extensive use of the internet for initial grooming, often of boys, and not operating as gangs at all' (Drew, 2016), which is a drastically

736 Ibid.

> different picture to that commonly portrayed in the media.[737]

So there wasn't really a Muslim rape gang problem at all. There was a problem of white British gang rapists, along with a few Pakistani Muslim rapists, that a sensationalistic media and ambitious "far right" agitators distorted in order to target a vulnerable and marginalized immigrant community in Britain.

Yet these two reports were themselves distorted, as they both assumed that the salient details regarding both perpetrators and victims had to do with race. There was some sound basis for this, for so many of the rapists had referring to their victims contemptuously as white. If, however, the Islamic faith of at least some of the perpetrators played a role in their action, studies of the race and ethnicity of the offenders would provide only a partial and potentially misleading picture, as there was no curiosity whatsoever on the part of official Britain as to whether any of the rapists were white British converts to Islam, and if so, how many.

Meanwhile, others in Britain rushed to correct Musk's "misinformation." The UK's Press Association reported in January 2025 that "The vast majority of grooming gang offences are carried out by white men, the National Police Chiefs' Council (NPCC) has said. New figures from the police database show that, where ethnicity data was available, 85% of 'group-based' child abusers were white in the first three quarters of 2024.

[737] Ibid.

The same data for the whole of 2023 showed 83% of offenders were white."[738]

Richard Fewkes, the director of the NPCC's Hydrant program, the stated goal of which was to combat child sexual abuse, said that the data reflected "what you would expect to see across the country in terms of ethnicity. Offences where grooming gangs are involved are predominantly white. There is not a significant issue here with any particular ethnicity or setting."[739]

This reflected what "anti-racist" campaigners had been saying for years. In April 2023, Home Secretary Suella Braverman observed that "the perpetrators are groups of men, almost all British-Pakistani."[740] In another interview, she said that the rapists were "overwhelmingly" made up of Pakistani men.[741] In response, leftist critics accused Braverman of sounding a "dog whistle" and trafficking in "discredited stereotypes."[742] The BBC cited the 2020 Home Office report stating that it was "likely that no one community or culture is uniquely predisposed to offending."[743] It also mentioned a 2015 report that "found that of 1,231 perpetrators of 'group and gang-based child sexual exploitation', 42% were white, 14% were defined as Asian or Asian British and 17% black."[744]

---

738 George Lithgow, "Most grooming gang offences carried out by white men, police chiefs say," Yahoo News, January 10, 2025, https://uk.news.yahoo.com/most-grooming-gang-offences-carried-184750758.html. Accessed March 13, 2025.

739 Ibid.

740 Tom Symonds, "Grooming gangs and ethnicity: What does the evidence say?" BBC, April 4, 2023, https://www.bbc.com/news/uk-65174096. Accessed March 13, 2025.

741 Ibid.

742 Ibid.

743 Ibid.

744 Ibid.

Back in 2017, the MP Naz Shah, who had so famously retweeted the statement that the rape gang victims needed to "shut their mouths" for "the good of diversity," stated: "Yes Pakistani men are disproportionately involved in grooming gangs and this particular model of abuse. And no that is not a racist statement. Neither is it racist to say that when it comes to wider child abuse nearly 90 per cent of those convicted and on the sex offenders register are white men."[745]

Yet these findings were not necessarily accurate. A fact-checking organization pointed out in 2017 that the ethnicity of the perpetrators was not reported in a large number of cases: "Of the 6,200 or so defendants in these prosecutions, 67% were white, 4% were Asian, 3% were black, 1% were mixed race and 1% were other. For 24% of defendant's there was no information on their ethnicity. Of all these prosecutions, around three quarters resulted in a conviction. The information on defendant's ethnicity came from information given by the defendants to police, the CPS [Crown Prosecution Service] told us that 'It follows that there may be errors or omissions at local levels.'"[746]

In an atmosphere in which those who noted that many members of rape gangs were Pakistani Muslims were excoriated as "racists" and "Islamophobes" and faced professional and possibly even personal ruin, was it possible that many of the cases in which the ethnicity of the perpetrators was not recorded had to do with the fear of this outcome? Might some officials have omitted all mention of the perpetrators' ethnicity in some cases

---

[745] "What do we know about the ethnicity of people involved in sexual offences against children?" Full Fact, September 6, 2017, https://fullfact.org/crime/what-do-we-know-about-ethnicity-people-involved-sexual-offences-against-children/. Accessed March 13, 2025.

[746] Ibid.

because recording it would have exposed those officials to harm from ever-vigilant "anti-racism" crusaders?

There could be no doubt about this, and there were other problems as well with the official dismissal of the idea that there was any Muslim rape gang problem at all. These studies variously found that the percentage of "white," that is, British and presumably non-Muslim offenders, was 42% and 83%, and that the proportion of "Asian," that is, likely Pakistani Muslim, offenders was seven percent, 8.4 percent, and fourteen percent. This is a significant variation, and suggests that all this data should be taken with extreme caution.

There were other problems with the official narrative as well. In 2014, the *Jay Report* had found that "in Rotherham, the majority of known perpetrators were of Pakistani heritage including the five men convicted in 2010. The file reading carried out by the Inquiry also confirmed that the ethnic origin of many perpetrators was 'Asian.'"[747] Alexis Jay was not a "far right" polemicist or "racist Islamophobe." She was a respected researcher who reported her findings honestly. If the vast majority of the members of rape gangs were white non-Muslim Britons, why wasn't this reflected in her findings?

The same questions could be asked regarding the Quilliam Foundation, a self-proclaimed moderate Muslim organization in Britain. In 2017, Quilliam undertook large-scale research on the rape gang phenomenon. *The Times* of London reported that Quilliam "looked at 58 cases of grooming gangs identified in the UK between 2005 and 2017, which led to 264 convictions

---

[747] Alexis Jay OBE, "Independent Inquiry," 92.

for grooming. Of the 264 offenders, 84% were of Asian heritage, mostly Pakistani; 8% were black and 7% were white."[748]

This is exactly the opposite of the government's findings. Yet Quilliam was not an organization of "racists" or "far-right" polemicists. When its report was announced, its chief executive, Haras Rafiq, said: "There has been a lot of coverage of grooming gangs recently, ranging from the politically correct, who don't want to talk about it, and the bigots who want to use it for hate. Not talking about it doesn't make the problem go away, and letting bigots hijack the debate creates further division in society. We as a society need to tackle this head on."[749]

Indeed. Smearing people who pointed out the Islamic aspects of these crimes as "bigots" was not helpful, either, but it made it clear that Rafiq and Quilliam were not trying to portray the Muslim community in Britain in a negative light. Quilliam was simply presenting its own findings, which sharply contradicted those of the British government. What accounted for this difference?

Also, why were there so many documented cases of Pakistani Muslims preying upon non-Muslim British girls, and comparatively few about British rape gangs? Was this really just a matter of newspapers stirring up hysteria and race hatred in order to sell papers? Was it really a matter of venal public figures vilifying the Muslim community on false pretenses out of a deeply ingrained "Islamophobia"?

---

748 Iram Ramzan, "Asians make up 80% of convicted child-grooming gang members – study," *The Times*, December 10, 2017, https://www.thetimes.com/uk/society/article/asians-make-up-80-of-convicted-child-grooming-gang-members-study-fvk6k30zx?ref=quillette.com®ion=global. Accessed March 14, 2025.

749 Ibid.

A 2017 Channel 4 summary of the rape gang controversy reflected the popular perception of what had been going on: "In recent years, there have been a number of high-profile cases in which groups of predominantly Asian men have been found exploiting girls and/or young women for sex. In 2012, nine men were jailed for running an exploitation ring in Rochdale, abusing girls as young as 13. Eight of those men were of Pakistani origin; the remaining one was from Afghanistan. Earlier this year, six men were convicted of abusing two girls in Rotherham between 1999 and 2001. All of the men convicted were British-Pakistani."[750]

Was this conjured out of thin air? Was Channel 4 really ignoring other cases of a similar nature, simply because the perpetrators were native and non-Muslim Britons? Or was that a narrative that the British government very much wanted its citizens to accept, in line with its years-long habit of turning a blind eye to Muslim rape gang activity?

The anomalies were so obvious, and the questions so numerous, that many simply ignored the British government reports. In a January 2025 recap of the Musk controversy, Dominic Green stated that "the grooming and serial rape of thousands of English girls by men of mostly Pakistani Muslim background over several decades is the biggest peacetime crime in the history of modern Europe."[751]

Green observed that in general, "the media showed no interest," explaining that this was "because this was the wrong kind of racially motivated crime, committed by the wrong kind

750 Georgina Lee, "What do we know about the ethnicity of sexual abuse gangs?" Channel 4 News, August 18, 2017, https://www.channel4.com/news/factcheck/what-do-we-know-about-the-ethnicity-of-sexual-abuse-gangs. Accessed March 13, 2025.

751 Green, "The Biggest Peacetime Crime."

of criminal."[752] He added that "the majority of the victims were white, plus some Sikhs. The majority of their abusers were of Pakistani and Bangladeshi Muslim extraction."[753] This was a problem with the left as well: "The majority of their crimes were committed in cities with a Labour Party–controlled council and a Labour Party MP who needed Muslim votes. This led to institutional racism of the inverted kind, and that enabled the perpetrators to do as they liked."[754]

The left's unwillingness to deal with the matter may have led to an artificial suppression of cases in which the perpetrators were Pakistani Muslims: "In multiple cases, local Labour politicians of Pakistani background interfered with police inquiries. In Telford in 2016, 10 members of the Labour council wrote to the Home Secretary, the Conservatives' Amber Rudd, claiming that allegations of abuse were 'sensationalized' and that there was no need for action. Two years later, an investigation by the *Sunday Mirror* newspaper counted some 1,000 victims. The superintendent of the West Mercia regional police 'significantly disputed' the figures and said the *Mirror* had 'sensationalized' the issue."[755]

Maybe it had. Or maybe there were people in power who were intent on protecting the perpetrators.

---

752 Ibid.
753 Ibid.
754 Ibid.
755 Ibid.

CHAPTER TWENTY-TWO

TO THIS DAY

"NOT CONFINED TO THE PAST"

The *Jay Report* had said in 2014 that "this abuse is not confined to the past but continues to this day."[756]

Eleven years later, Dr. Taj Hargey, for all his denial and evasion about the Islamic theological justification for the rape gang activity, said much the same thing. In 2013, he had said that the rape gang activity was "bound up with religion and race," as Muslim men "deliberately targeted vulnerable white girls, whom they appeared to regard as 'easy meat', to use one of their revealing, racist phrases."[757] In late 2024, when asked if imams in Britain were still teaching this perspective, Hargey responded: "Absolutely. There's a perpetuation of 'them and us.'"[758]

Having such an assumption might tend to make one freer with his actions than one might be in the company of fellow

---

756 Alexis Jay OBE, "Independent Inquiry," 1.

757 Chapman, "Imams 'PROMOTE grooming rings.'"

758 Ibid.

human beings. In February 2024, a Muslim from Egypt who was seeking asylum in Britain, Hamada Salah, began showing pornography to two women in separate instances while riding on the TransPennine Express from Leeds to Middlesbrough. Salah approached a twenty-year-old woman and told her that she was "the perfect age for sex."[759] He began touching the woman's legs, but apparently something made him decide that it was time to move on; he later began fondling himself in front of a sixty-seven-year-old woman on the train. The women recounted that they felt "objectified" and "unnerved."[760]

Judge Carolyn Scott, according to the *Daily Mail*, let Salah off easy: gave him a suspended prison sentence "and also gave him a sexual harm prevention order which prohibits him from communicating with any unknown female on public transport unless it is a member of staff in relation to her duties."[761] He was also "ordered to sign the sex offenders register and abide by the sexual harm prevention order for ten years."[762] Why, that will fix everything.

Salah was able to avoid prison, the Mail reported, because Judge Scott was told that he "has no friends in the UK."[763]

In February 2025, three Muslim brothers, Shaha Amran Miah, Shaha Alman Miah, and Shaha Joman Miah were given

---

759 Dan Woodland, "Asylum seeker sex pest targeted two women on the train in 'terrifying ordeal' before sexually assaulting one – but is SPARED jail after judge is told he 'has no friends in the UK,'" *Daily Mail*, November 29, 2024, https://www.dailymail.co.uk/news/article-14140803/Asylum-seeker-sex-pest-targeted-two-women-train-terrifying-ordeal-sexually-assaulting-one-SPARED-jail-judge-told-no-friends-UK.html. Accessed March 14, 2025.

760 Ibid.

761 Ibid.

762 Ibid.

763 Ibid.

prison sentences for raping and sexually abusing five girls who ranged in age from six to fifteen. Judge Ian Stephen Unsworth scolded the brothers from the bench, saying: "I am satisfied each of you acted in a predatory and paedophilic manner. You saw your victims as vehicles to be used and abused at will. You treated them with utter contempt. You were each aware at different times of each other's sexual proclivities and conduct. The bonds that tie you three together are strong and it would appear, unbreakable. There was an omerta. What you were all doing was taking away childhoods."[764]

Unsworth also noted with dismay that the Miah brothers abused the girls "in plain sight."[765] And why not? What conceivably could have caused them to pause and conclude that such behavior might not be a good idea? After the way the entire rape gang scandal had been handled in Britain over the course of decades, it was easy to see why these brothers thought they could act with absolute impunity.

"ANY INTERACTION WAS ONLY BRIEF AND WAS INITIATED BY THE COMPLAINANT"

The stories continued to be reported regularly, and bore a numbing similarity to so many stories that had been reported in the past. In February 2025, Ziad Khawla, a Palestinian Arab asylum seeker in Northern Ireland was charged with rape for

---

764 Pat Hurst, "Brothers who acted 'in plain sight' jailed for grooming girls," Yahoo News, February 21, 2025, https://uk.news.yahoo.com/brothers-acted-plain-sight-jailed-203038060.html. Accessed March 13, 2025.

765 Ibid.

a "chance encounter" he had with a fifteen-year-old boy at a Belfast nightclub.[766]

The UK's *News Letter* reported that Khawla was "charged with rape and two counts of sexual assault over the incident on March 2 last year." Khawla, however, denied all of the charges against him, "insisting," as so many other Muslim rapists had done, that "any interaction was only brief and was initiated by the complainant."[767] Khawla did not speak English, so the court supplied an Arabic interpreter for him, but it hardly needed to have bothered, as Khawla "declined to give evidence or call any witnesses at this stage in proceedings."[768]

"MAKE SURE THAT YOU ARE KEEPING WELL AWAY FROM INFLAMING ANY KIND OF DISCRIMINATION"

Maybe he would be more cooperative later, but it was clear that many Muslim rapists had complete contempt for Western justice, and had the idea that they would likely get away with anything. Fueling that impunity was the fact that even after it became widely known that the rape gangs had been able to continue for so many years because authorities were afraid of appearing "racist" or "Islamophobic," nothing changed. Authorities remained desperately afraid of being charged with these ultimate sins of the woke catechism, and continued to shy away from any behavior that might run them afoul of the left's

766 Alan Erwin, "Asylum seeker to stand trial on charges of raping teenage boy at derelict Belfast nightclub," *News Letter*, February 14, 2025, https://www.newsletter.co.uk/news/courts/asylum-seeker-to-stand-trial-on-charges-of-raping-teenage-boy-at-derelict-belfast-nightclub-4991854. Accessed March 18, 2025.

767 Ibid.

768 Ibid.

arbiters of acceptable behavior. Any who did not do this were quickly brought back into line.

In January 2025, Darren Millar, the leader of the Conservative Party in the Senedd Cymru, the Welsh Parliament, joined the calls for a new national inquiry into what were still universally known as the "grooming gangs." As Millar described what had happened to one victim, however, the Llywydd of the Senedd, that is, the presiding officer, Elin Jones, interrupted him to say: "You are being overly descriptive, and I think verging on not being totally respectful of the victim at this point. So, can you tone down the rhetoric slightly?"[769]

It quickly became clear, however, that Jones was less concerned about being respectful to the victim than she was about being respectful to the perpetrators. She warned Millar that "the use of language in this place needs to make sure that you are keeping well away from inflaming any kind of discrimination or inciting any kind of discrimination."[770] It is noteworthy that in two BBC stories on this incident in the Senedd, there is no mention of the word "Asian," much less of the word "Muslim," or, indeed, any information at all about who the gang rapists were. With this one warning about inciting discrimination, however, Jones made it clear: Darren Millar was talking about Muslim rape gangs, and that kind of talk was still not acceptable in Britain, even after hundreds of thousands of British girls had fallen victim to these gangs.

---

769 Daniel Davies, "Tone down grooming gangs rhetoric, top Tory told," BBC, January 15, 2025, https://www.bbc.com/news/articles/cjex9w227j3o. Accessed March 16, 2025.

770 Cemlyn Davies, "Grooming gang victim's story 'downplayed' in Senedd," BBC, January 19, 2025, https://www.bbc.com/news/articles/cly44xrvgdyo. Accessed March 16, 2025.

Millar later recounted that he was in the course of describing one case of this rape gang activity "before being interrupted, I thought inappropriately, by the presiding officer."[771] The BBC noted, however, that nothing was going to be done: "Tory sources said they would not take the matter up with the presiding officer."[772]

Nevertheless, one of the rape gang victims was unhappy with Elin Jones: "It was quite hard to watch. It felt like she was downplaying my experience and other victims' as well."[773] Referring to Millar recounting what she had experienced, she said of Jones: "She obviously thought I would not want him to say anything like that, but he was saying the right things because it's got to be talked about."[774]

This young woman began to be the victim of sexual abuse when she was fourteen, and was raped repeatedly as she was taken to various places in Wales, as well as to Telford and Blackpool, in order to be used as a sex slave. The rapes were constant, she said: "It was almost every single day. People think with sexual exploitation that you're taken to a place, and you're raped once. You're not. People think sexual exploitation is just rape. It's not. You're being tortured, you're being bitten, you're beaten."[775]

She said that the rape gangs had learned how to stay ahead of the British police, even when those police were inclined to brave the possibility of racism charges by going after them: "Perpetrators are so advanced — they're cleverer than the police. They're smarter than a lot of people think they are, and things

---

771 Daniel Davies, "Tone down grooming gangs rhetoric."
772 Ibid.
773 Cemlyn Davies, "Grooming gang victim's story."
774 Ibid.
775 Ibid.

are changing all the time. The public need to be aware of it. The public need to be involved in it."[776]

That, however, might be seen as "inciting discrimination" against Muslims, and so it was not to be. The Muslim rape gangs would continue victimizing British girls. Activist Jayne Senior observed in February 2025: "Of course it's still going on — I think it's going on across every town, every city in the U.K."[777] The gang rapists had taken the measure of British authorities and found them wanting. They knew they could act with impunity.

---

776 Ibid.
777 Pheby, "'Life's ruined' in U.K. town broken."

CHAPTER TWENTY-THREE
WHAT IS TO BE DONE

STOP BEING AFRAID

Like so many other issues related to Islamic jihad, as well as Islamic jihad itself, discussion of Islam's abuse of women and its sanction of rape and sex slavery is shrouded in confusion. Many Westerners will note that their Muslim neighbors are gentle souls who would never dream of raping someone or taking a sex slave, and for them, that will be the end of the matter. Among the many effects of the decline in Western education has been the large-scale loss of the ability to distinguish between the teachings of Islam, which are based on the Qur'an and Sunnah and not on the behavior of any individual Muslim, and the practice of those Muslim individuals, who may or may not be following Islamic teachings.

Others, meanwhile, no matter what evidence is adduced from Islamic theology, history, or present-day practice, will dismiss any concern about this issue, and even the issue itself, as an example of the "Islamophobia" that they believe to be the real problem. This is another byproduct of contemporary education: a generation or more of college and university students have been taught that the primary result of the September 11, 2001, jihad attacks that killed nearly three thousand people in New York City, Washington, and rural Pennsylvania was that there was a sharp rise in the unjust and unjustifiable suspicion of innocent Muslims.

The chief lesson of 9/11 has become that Americans must shun "Islamophobia" at all costs, and anyone who continues to talk about Islamic jihad, much less Muslim rape gangs, at this late date is an example of exactly the kind of "Islamophobe" that right-thinking students have been taught to regard with disgust and treat with contempt.

And yet while the fear of charges of "Islamophobia" will effectively put an end to any chance of a mature public debate of these issues, the abuse of women will continue. As Muslim populations rise in Western countries, rates of rape and sexual abuse will rise as well. The wisdom of continuing to remain silent about this for fear of appearing "racist" or "Islamophobic" is shown in the example of Britain. Authorities can and will choose that course of action, and in doing so, they will be consigning unknowable numbers of girls and women to lives of pain and misery.

Britain appears to have chosen national suicide rather than confronting these difficult issues. Other countries in the West seem poised to follow suit. But does it really have to be this way? Is it simply a settled matter that the modern, technologically advanced, secular West must tolerate the presence of people who believe that their god has given them a mandate to seized and rape females who do not believe in that god?

The leftist Westerner will reply, No, of course not. And just as with all other rapists, the rapist who believes he has theological justification is chased after, apprehended, tried, and duly punished. To expel or forbid entry to the overwhelming majority of Muslims who do not engage in such behavior and never will is to indulge in the worst impulses of human nature, the tendency to see someone who is outside of one's own group as "the other," a hostile, alien being who must be shunned, avoided, and meanwhile vilified, demonized, and excoriated.

That may be the last word on the matter. It certainly is at this point. But would it be too much to ask Muslim communities in the West to teach against, in mosques and Islamic schools, the theological justifications for rape and sex slavery? It would, in fact, for those teachings are embedded within the Qur'an and the actions of Muhammad, whom the Qur'an calls, without any qualification or caveat, the "excellent example" (33:21). For Muslims to reject the Qur'an and Muhammad would mean that they were no longer Muslim, and so that is not likely to happen on any large scale.

A QUESTION OF SURVIVAL

Yet the West has a choice. It can continue to allow the proliferation of this ideology that will result in the victimization of more of its women, or it can take action against it. Yet through the years, the focus remained largely on the political ramifications of the scandal, rather than on the protection of Britain's young girls. Even in February 2025, CNN was worrying that Elon Musk's calling attention to the Muslim rape gangs in Britain would only empower the ever-present bogeyman of the political and media establishment, the "far right."

"Many," said CNN, without naming who exactly they were, "worry Musk's words have given new momentum to far-right figures bent on using the historic abuse, which was primarily carried out by groups of men of mainly Pakistani heritage, to stir racial hatred.... Far-right figures capitalized on the firestorm kicked up by the billionaire, with Musk also posting support for the imprisoned, anti-Islam far-right figurehead Tommy Robinson, who is currently serving an 18-months sentence for repeating false accusations about a Syrian refugee and who argues multiculturalism in the UK has failed."[778]

Yet in reality, this is not now and has never been a question of "racism" or "Islamophobia." It's a question of survival. If a culture allows what happened in Britain to continue, and stigmatizes action against it, that culture is not long for this world, and that's why Britain's demise is at hand.

If other free or by now semi-free societies in the West wish to survive and preserve some semblance of equality of rights for women, they will have to make hard choices: They will have to require that the Muslims in their midst abide by the law of the land. They will have to demand that Muslims not teach doctrines or beliefs that contradict the law of the land even if those teachings are in their holy book or taught by their revered prophet. They will have to back up such a demand, and other related demands, with the threat of the deportation of non-citizens and the long-term incarceration of citizens. Naturalized citizens must be made to face the prospect of the loss of their citizenship, followed by deportation.

---

[778] Nic Robertson, Florence Davey-Attlee, and Niamh Kennedy, "Musk's posts on UK child sex abuse gangs cast a spotlight on survivors. But he also stoked the fire of the far-right," CNN, February 6, 2025, https://www.cnn.com/2025/02/06/uk/musk-uk-child-sex-abuse-gbr-intl-cmd/index.html. Accessed March 16, 2025.

HARD CHOICES

These are hard policies. The alternative, as Britain illustrates in abundance, is national suicide. Nigel Farage, the architect of Brexit (Britain's withdrawal from the European Union) and great hope of British patriots, illustrated how advanced the rot is in Britain today when he upbraided and suspended a member of his party, Rupert Lowe, for his remarks about what should be done about the Muslim rape gangs, as well as for his criticism of Farage's leadership.

Lowe charged in a long post on X on March 12, 2025, that Farage had ordered him not to recommend the deportation of the family members of Muslim gang rapists who were involved in aiding the rapists' actions: "There have been repeated attempts from within Reform, including senior leadership, to silence me on the Pakistani rape gangs. At a speech in Essex, I was instructed by Farage's team, sanctioned by him, to remove a call to deport all complicit foreign national family members. I ignored them."[779] Lowe further charged: "My repeated pleadings for Reform to follow up on its promise to deliver a national inquiry into the rape gangs were ignored. There was a belief from senior Reform figures that my language on the rape gangs was too strong, too robust, too tough. Why pander? Why appease? Why dilute? To appeal to the 'middle ground'? I do not care. We must do what's right, and we must be honest."[780]

Farage, however, charged Lowe with trying to "pretend that he's the only person who wants to deal with the Pakistani

---

779 Rupert Lowe, X, March 12, 2025, https://x.com/RupertLowe10/status/1899716465667842425. Accessed March 16, 2025.

780 Ibid.

rape gangs."[781] The Reform UK leader added defensively: "My record on this goes back to 2013. I in fact did an exclusive with *The Telegraph* at the time in 2014 about a couple in Rotherham who had been taken off the foster list for being Ukip members at the same time as all these things were going on. I've campaigned strongly on this for years and it's a completely false assertion."[782]

Farage was likewise dismissive of Lowe's recommendation for the mass deportation of the complicit: "The idea you can deport whole communities who have British passports is just not possible under British law and never was."[783] Very well, then. But weren't there numerous families that did not hold British passports and were complicit in rape gang activity? Indeed. Those were the people to whom Lowe had been referring, not to British citizens, as he had made it clear in his lengthy X post.

Farage was disingenuous in the extreme to have misrepresented Lowe's position on this. Lowe had said: "My view is clear. Anyone with any knowledge of these crimes, and who failed to act, is as guilty as the rapists themselves. We must deport foreign nationals who knew. If that means entire communities go, then that is what must happen. Get them out of our country, and back in Pakistan. They can rot in prison there. I won't be silenced on that, by anyone."[784]

What, moreover, did Farage recommend as an alternative solution to the problem? During his controversy with Lowe, he

---

781 Dominic Penna, "Farage: No way back for Lowe after rape gangs claims," *Telegraph*, March 12, 2025, https://www.telegraph.co.uk/politics/2025/03/12/farage-no-way-back-for-lowe-after-rape-gangs-claims/. Accessed March 16, 2025.

782 Ibid.

783 Ibid.

784 Lowe, X, March 12, 2025.

didn't offer one, contenting himself instead with charging that Lowe's language was "dark and dangerous, without remarking about what a dark and dangerous world British girls had been living in for so many years: "Furthermore, his speech in Essex that he talks about, what I stopped him from using was the word 'repatriation'. I told him not to use the word 'repatriation' as well as 'mass deportations', because I thought it was a very grave, dark and dangerous use of language. This is all an attempt not just to damage Reform, but to get Elon Musk thinking that he's the good guy."[785]

Elon Musk's self-image was not really what was at stake. The future of Britain was. Farage was clearly still afraid of the usual charges. Western nations are going to have to decide that it is simply not important to them that the leftist intelligentsia brands them as "racist" and "Islamophobic." Authorities must be ready and willing to brush aside such charges and no longer allow themselves to be cowed by them. They must make it clear that the women of their countries are neither "white sluts" for the taking or potential sex slaves, the spoils of war.

The alternative is simple: The women will be taken. And the nation as such will then have no future, but only a period of decline before its demise.

This is the choice Europe faces. This is the choice Canada faces. This is the choice the United States faces. Either make it clear that Islam's abuse of women is intolerable and unacceptable, or acquiesce to it and surrender.

Which one will they choose?

---

785 Penna, "Farage: No way back."

ACKNOWLEDGMENTS

This is a book about cowardice, and so it is altogether fitting and proper that in closing, I thank once again David S. Bernstein of Bombardier Books, the indefatigable publisher who knows very well what the defenders of Islam can do to those who speak truths that they would prefer remain concealed. Yet despite that knowledge, and his experience of it in numerous contexts in the past, he was enthusiastic and encouraging about this book. And so now the truth will be told, in large part thanks to him, and let the chips fall where they may. Or more fittingly, in light of the name of his imprint, let the bombs fall where they may. The truth bombs, that is.

Aleigha Koss, the ever-patient, ever-upbeat production manager, also deserves one more tip of the hat for shepherding this thing through the process of editing, typesetting, the choosing of the cover, and no doubt a thousand other duties that don't even cross my mind. All I have to do is write it, and then, like magic, it appears sometime later, as if by magic, but in actual fact due to the long hours of work of Aleigha and others at Bombardier Books. You're all invited over to my place next weekend for a barbecue!

Meanwhile, other duties have impinged, as they always do, and so thanks as always to the perceptive, witty, and ever-surprising Hugh Fitzgerald, as well as to the steady, reliable, and thorough Christine Douglass-Williams, who have kept the embers aglow at JihadWatch.org, where we chronicle this madness every day, while I gave even more of my attention than usual to this particular examination of the dark side.

Thanks likewise to Michael Finch at the David Horowitz Freedom Center, a man with a tremendous reservoir of good will, optimism, patience, and perseverance. Mike, long may you wave; I am honored to have stood so long with you on these particular front lines. Jamie Glazov at FrontPage Magazine has also been a fellow warrior for lo these many years, and an endlessly amusing and frequently quite insightful one at that. I am obliged to the good folks over at PJ Media for being one of the few outlets remaining that have the courage to publish the truth about this and numerous other related issues.

For details on those, see my other books. I've been deeply blessed to be able to spend the bulk of my life as a scribbler of thoughts; I am duly thankful and also pray that these and other scribblings of mine may end up doing someone some good.

ABOUT THE AUTHOR

Author Photo by Glenn Marzano

Robert Spencer is director of Jihad Watch and a Shillman Fellow at the David Horowitz Freedom Center. He is the author of thirty-one books, including the bestsellers *The Politically Incorrect Guide to Islam (and the Crusades)*; *The Truth About Muhammad*; *The History of Jihad: From Muhammad to ISIS*; and *The Critical Qur'an*. Spencer has led seminars on Islam and jihad for the FBI, the United States Central Command, United States Army Command and General Staff College, the U.S. Army's Asymmetric Warfare Group, the Joint Terrorism Task Force (JTTF), the Justice Department's Anti-Terrorism Advisory Council, and the U.S. intelligence community. He has discussed jihad, Islam, and terrorism at a workshop sponsored by the U.S. State Department and the German Foreign Ministry.

He is a senior fellow with the Center for Security Policy and is a regular columnist for *PJ Media* and *FrontPage Magazine*. His works have been translated into numerous languages.